In 1953, Jimmy Edwards published his autobiography, *Take It from Me*, an event celebrated on episode 161 of his hit show, *Take It from Here*, broadcast by the BBC on April 6, 1953, and, so popular was the program, that it was rebroadcast on April 9, 12, 19, 21, 24, and 25, 1953:

> WALLAS EATON: Look at those highly successful films, *Goodbye, Mr. Chips*, *The Good Earth*, and *Limelight*. Each one is a *biography* — of a schoolmaster, an ignorant farmer and a tatty music-hall comedian.
>
> ANNOUNCER: So one film producer thought he must be on a cert if he filmed the autobiography of somebody who has been *all* these things. Strangely enough, there *is* such an autobiography.
>
> JIMMY EDWARDS: And I am prepared to sign copies at a very nominal charge.
>
> WALLAS EATON: Yes, Jimmy Edwards, schoolmaster, ignorant farmer and tatty music-hall comedian — all rolled, rather untidily, into one.
>
> ANNOUNCER: Ladies and gentlemen, we present the Edwards biography, *From Non-Stop Nudes to the BBC* or *The Naked and the Dead*.

This book is my somewhat eccentric and opinionated tribute to that same Professor Jimmy Edwards, a great and sadly forgotten British comedian.

WAKE UP AT THE BACK THERE!

It's JIMMY EDWARDS

ANTHONY SLIDE

Published in the USA by:
BearManor Media
PO Box 71426
Albany, Georgia 31708
www.bearmanormedia.com

Hardcover: ISBN 978-1-62933-321-2
Paperback: ISBN 978-1-62933-320-5

Printed in the United States of America.
Book design by Brian Pearce | Red Jacket Press.

Table of Contents

Acknowledgements 9

Introduction 11

Chapter One: The Early Years 25

Chapter Two: The War Years 37

Chapter Three: The Windmill and the Road to Fame 47

Chapter Four: The Handlebar Club 57

Chapter Five: *Take It from Here* 63

Chapter Six: *Bottoms Up!* 83

Chapter Seven: The Stage 111

Chapter Eight: The Screen 129

Chapter Nine: Sex and the Comedian 145

Chapter Ten: The Perfect English Gentleman 163

Epilogue 191

Bibliography 193

Index 199

About the Author 205

Acknowledgements

In writing this book, I have been helped and encouraged by H.R.H. The Duke of Edinburgh, Gyles Brandreth, Geoff Brown, David Buckley, Barry Burnett, Sharry Clark, Ned Comstock and Steve Hanson (Library of the Cinematic Arts, University of Southern California), Pat Coward, Barry Cryer, Tom Cutler (Handlebar Club), Sir Ken Dodd (you are the greatest!), Samantha Eggar, Tony Fletcher, Ron Grant and Martin Humphries (the Cinema Museum, London), Melvyn Hayes, Janice Healey, His Majesty's Theatre Museum of Performing Arts (Perth), Matt Hood (Equity), Keith Nichols, Jeffrey Richards, the Royal Western Australia Historical Society, John Scott, Geoff Stovoid (Old Surrey, Burstow & West Kent Hunt), Keith Turley, David Webb, Barbara Windsor, and Mark Wynter.

I would like to thank various residents of two Sussex villages, closely associated with Jimmy Edwards. In Fittleworth, West Sussex, I am grateful to Mike Elliott and Tony Poole. In Fletching, East Sussex, I thank Liz Bennett of the Fletching Parish Council, Jim Bradford, and, most of all, Barry Dickens, Andrew Hudson and David Hollings, current owner of Atheralls Farm, all of whom were incredibly kind and helpful. David Hollings was a delightful host on my visit to Fletching and provided me with a first-rate tour of Atheralls Farm.

I can write with all sincerity that this book could not have been written without the support, encouragement, enthusiasm, and knowledge of Glenn Mitchell and Michael Pointon. I owe these two gentlemen so much, and I can never adequately repay them. I am honored that Britain's Queen of Comedy, June Whitfield, found the time to answer some of my questions. Major institutional help was provided by Sarah Currant at the British Film Institute Digital Library, Trisha Hayes at the BBC Written Archives, and William Edwards of the National Archives of Australia.

Initially, I had assumed that I would receive little help or support from Jimmy Edwards' family. His nephew, Rolly Wilkinson, responded simply that "I don't really know how I can help you over this matter," and failed to reply to later e-mails. Then, I was fortunate enough to discover another nephew, Roy Pennington, whose mother was Jimmy's older sister, Margaret (born 1918); he not only took the time to talk with me, but also introduced me to his cousin, Anne Gravett, whose father was Alan Edwards. Thanks to Annie, I was able to understand the family's response to Jimmy's homosexuality and also have a better understanding of the relationship between Jimmy and his domestic partner, Philip Aylemore.

Thanks to Roy Pennington, I met his delightful wife Kathy, and I made contact with his brother Jim, who not only had some interesting observations to make, but also gave me access to many of Jimmy Edwards' papers that he had preserved.

I am most grateful to Robert Gitt for scanning the photographs for me, and I am also grateful to Barry Dickens, David Hollings, Jim Pennington, and the Old Surrey, Burstow & West Kent Hunt, who augmented my own collection of Jimmy Edward photographs.

In the process of publication of my books published by BearManor Media, I have had the honor and privilege of working with Brian Pearce, who is undoubtedly the best production editor in the business. Again, Brian has been my partner on this book, and I wish again to acknowledge my thanks to him.

It was Ben Ohmart, who suggested I tackle the subject of Jimmy Edwards, and I am grateful for his support and enthusiasm. Obviously, any complaints that readers might have concerning the book should be addressed to Ben.

Introduction

Comedians in 20th Century Britain might well be divided into two categories: those who gained international fame, particularly in the United States, and those whose comedic style was so resolutely British, so insular that recognition beyond the shores of their native land was as incomprehensible as some, or perhaps much, of their humor. In the former category are those whose fame in the United States far out-reached anything that might have been accomplished in the United Kingdom — with the obvious examples being Charlie Chaplin and Stan Laurel, as well, and to a lesser extent, the likes of Terry-Thomas and Norman Wisdom. The resolutely British brigade includes brilliant stand-up comedian Ken Dodd, screwed-up magician Tommy Cooper, the stars of the "Carry On" films, Bud Flanagan, Chesney Allen and the other members of the "Crazy Gang," and those who made an easy transition from British music hall, in its dying days, to radio and/or television, including Tony Hancock, Eric Morecambe and Ernie Wise, Harry Worth, Hylda Baker, Bruce Forsyth, Ted Ray, and, of course, the "star" of this volume, Jimmy Edwards.

Why did some comedians enjoy international fame while others did not? There is no easy answer. Perhaps it was a matter of taking a chance on America while still in the early stages of their careers. In acknowl-edging Chaplin and Laurel, one tends to forget other Britishers who came to Hollywood in the 1920s — a decade later than that most famous pair — and enjoyed brief careers there, men such as Dick Henderson, Sr. (appearing on screen alongside his son, Dickie Henderson), or even Dougie Wakefield, so closely associated with the Manchester-based Mancunian Films in the 1930s, but who had been under contract to Hal Roach a decade earlier. Some veterans of the British Music Hall, such as Billy Bennett, Jimmy James and Robb Wilton, were simply too paro-chial to have a following outside of their native land. It mattered not that Jimmy James was known as "the comedian's comedian" for, in reality, he was the English comedian's comedian. Like Dougie Wakefield, George Formby's persona and accent confirm and emphasize his North of England background, and yet, at the end of his career in the 1940s, he was placed under contract to Columbia Pictures and his films were seen in the United States, albethey in limited release.

Watching George Formby on screen in one of his American-produced and released films, one wonders why the Production Code Administration (Hollywood's self-censoring body) did not get the covert meaning behind his singing of "My Little Stick of Blackpool Rock" with its obvious (at least to British audiences) substitution for/reference to the male sex organ. Perhaps just as Formby's risqué humor was lost on Americans, so was the often outrageous low comedy of Max Miller, the "Cheeky Chappie." Possibly America's attitude towards risqué humor changed with the passing years in that Max Wall, a brilliant comedian, was a big enough draw in New York in *Earl Carroll's Vanities* to enjoy a year's engagement in 1932-1933, an event he was unlikely to repeat in the 1970s as his act had him both as a comedian who savored the comedy of language, facial eccentricity and an obscurest, perhaps influenced by his appearing in a British production of *Waiting for Godot*.[1]

In an odd way, there could be something surreal about aspects of British comedy, be it the trio of Wilson, Keppel and Betty performing a sand dance dressed as Egyptian slaves or Arthur Lucan dressed as Irish washerwoman, Old Mother Riley, playing opposite his wife, Kitty McShane, in the character of his daughter Bridget and later Kitty. It is impossible to describe the impact on an audience even today of Michael Barrymore, a comedian who was later to be identified as gay, singing "Will You Still Love Me Tomorrow" to a military drill team comprised of members of Her Majesty the Queen's Armed Forces in the 1980s. Or that national treasure, Sir Ken Dodd, who as late as 2017 could perform a brilliant stand-up comedy routine lasting in excess of five hours.

Today on British television, and not I think destined for transfer to any American network, we have Irish writer/comedian Brendan O'Carroll as the filthy-mouthed, middle-aged Mrs. Brown, to whom four-letter words are a (substantial) part of life. Trying to come up with the word, foreskin, she asks her neighbor, "What is that useless thing on the end of a dick?" "A man" is the response. In a tradition dating back to Old Mother Riley, there is little attempt at verisimilitude. When Mrs. Brown asks one of the actors what he is doing there, sitting in a chair and saying nothing, he replies, "It's in the script." There is no fourth wall, as evidenced by the cast's being seen taking bows in front of the studio audience at the show's conclusion.[2]

Equally surreal, if not positively perverse — and I do use that word rather than "perverted," as might some commentators — is the television series for which Jimmy Edwards is best remembered. The BBC broadcast *Whack-O!* from 1956 through 1960, with Edwards playing a drunken, loud-mouthed, dishonest headmaster, whose favorite prop was the cane, which was always ready for immediate application to the upturned bottoms of the young boys at the school. He was unloved by all, with the exception of his long-suffering assistant headmaster, Mr. Pettigrew (brilliantly played by Arthur Howard). Jimmy will often call him "Petters," but there is no obvious fondness in the nickname.

It might be considered relatively innocuous by the standards of the day — the bottoms receiving punishment, after all, are not shown in close-up and always hidden within trousers — except for the reality that Jimmy Edwards was a closeted homosexual male, and Arthur Howard had been arrested for importuning in a public toilet in the seaside resort of Brighton. That both men were presented to television audiences as individuals who should be allowed in close proximity to under-age boys is decidedly odd — even for the BBC which permitted the scandal of Jimmy Savile's hosting a number of popular shows from the 1960s through the 1990s while indulging in sexual abuse to such an extent that after his death he was labeled perhaps the most prolific, predatory sex offender of the 20th Century.[3]

One sequence in the 1960 film *Bottoms Up!* that certainly must raise an eyebrow or two is the scene in which Jimmy Edwards escorts the younger brother of one of the boys, Price, from his dormitory. As the young boy, "Half Price," leaves, his pajama trousers come down revealing a naked bottom. In that the boy is perhaps only about eight years old, it is more than merely unfortunate, and simply not funny.[4]

But, of course, Jimmy Edwards and Arthur Howard were never the subjects of a whiff of scandal as far as young boys were concerned. Their interests lay in older men, and both were married. As writer Frank Muir points out, "Arthur's particular homosexual inclination had no connection whatsoever with corrupting young boys."[5] They were not pedophiles, I hasten to note, and the presence of those boys in that series adds a note of farce to the whole episode rather than a shudder of horror. It is, in a word, surreal, nothing more and nothing less.

While quite obviously Jimmy Edwards' homosexuality is worthy of discussion along with its implications, particularly in regard to his obvious alcoholism, it should not and cannot detract from his importance as a leading British comedian on stage, screen, radio, and television. As Ken Dodd pointed out to me so succinctly, "Jimmy Edwards was a *Great British Entertainer.*"[6]

Jimmy Edwards was a star in all fields of entertainment, comfortable and adept no matter the medium. He was a standup comic who made an effortless transfer from one medium to another. As did Victor Borge, Jack Benny, on the international stage, Jimmy Wheeler (with his catchphrase, "Aye, Aye, That's Your Lot"), Vic Oliver (who married Winston Churchill's daughter much to the politician's displeasure, in large part perhaps because he was Jewish), and others in the U.K., Jimmy Edwards used his musical gifts — he was particularly adept on the trombone and had a good singing voice — as part of the act. Jimmy's use of the trombone, a somewhat aggressive instrument, is indicative of his approach to his audience. He was not a gentle, concilia-tory comedian, but rather one

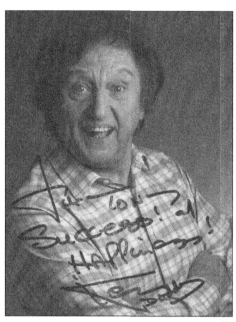

Ken Dodd.

who could bully a crowd into accepting him and laughing at his humor. Jimmy could bring an intellectual style to a comedic description of music:

"Music is divided into two distinct categories: loud and soft. In soft, we have piano, mezzo-piano, not-so-piano, pianissimo, and, of course, pianola. In loud, we have mezzo-forte, forte, fortissimo and eighty — which is double forte!"[7]

Another delightful musical anecdote concerns the origin of the term "cadenza," described by Jimmy as "a sort of gap-filling noise on the harp or piano." It came about as the result of a romance between a young conduc-tor, Sir Allen Cad, and a pianist and page-turner named Miss Louise Enza. The two married and produced a number of musical babies, "a cadenza."

There were a number of catchphrases associated with Jimmy that were to enter the British vocabulary of the 1940s and 1950s, although most, sad to report, are pretty much unused and forgotten today. "What a ghastly name," he would proclaim, with the emphasis on "ghastly." "Gently Bentley," spoken to radio colleague Dick Bentley, soon because used by Britishers to urge restraint from others. "Clot," meaning stupid or fool, and generally used in an endearing fashion, had primarily been spoken by members of the armed forces, one to another, until Jimmy introduced it to a wider audience in the mid-1940s. On September 16, 1951, he appeared on BBC television in a fifteen-minute program titled *The Cream — As Seen by a Clot*,[8] in which he recreated routines he had performed while in the R.A.F. "Clot" had become a household word. Later, in 1952, Jimmy gave the name of "The Clot" to a donkey he was training to run in the 100 Guineas Licensed Victuallers' Stakes.[9] "Wake up in the back there" was an order given to members of the audience at the Windmill Theatre in the 1940s, at the start of Jimmy's professional career, and later to the boys in the *Whack-O!* television series. About to play his trombone, the audience would be told to "Pin back your lugholes."

Unlike many of his contemporaries, Jimmy Edwards was well-educated, came from a different, solidly intellectual culture, and had a stable, middle-class background. Unlike other comedians of the 1940s, he had not learned his craft on the variety and music hall stages. The story is told that once while traveling on a train with Bud Flanagan[10] and other members of the Crazy Gang, he sat reading *The Times* while they exchanged gags and played tricks on each other. At one point, an exasperated Flanagan tapped him on the knee and said, "The trouble with you, Jimmy is — you think you're doing the business a favor!"[11]

In a similar vein, BBC radio writer Michael Pointon recalls walking down a crowded London street, one night after a recording. Jimmy turned to him and remarked, "Why does the human race have to be so blasted ugly?"[12]

In fact, Jimmy Edwards was very much his own man, totally unconcerned although not necessarily oblivious to the opinions of others. He was proud to be a participant in such barbaric sports as fox hunting and stag hunting, defending them if necessary. He had no problem entertaining in white-run Rhodesia, and seemed almost to delight in the outrage from members of his own union, Equity. He was a Conservative both politically and ethically, unperturbed that probably a large number of his audience comprised working class, Labor-leaning voters.

In the early 1950s, the publishing house of T. Werner Laurie, which in its early years had published the likes of Joseph Conrad, Upton Sinclair and W.B. Yeats, realized that the radio-listening public might well be willing to purchase and read autobiographies from its favorite stars, including Wilfred Pickles (*Personal Choice*, 1950), Donald Peers (*Pathway*, 1951), Ted Ray (*Raising the Laughs*, 1952), and Jimmy Edwards. Unlike other celebrities involved, Jimmy actually wrote his own autobiography, *Take It from Me*. That placed his book significantly above the other T. Werner Laurie celebrity autobiographies, all of which were "ghosted" by Gail Pedrick [13] who worked in the BBC's Variety Department.

The comedian was never vulgar in the way that, say, "Mrs. Brown" routinely uses four letter words. In private life, his speech might be peppered with such expressions, but not on stage. With one exception; in Melbourne Australia, while appearing at the Chevron Hotel on April 10, 1970, he was arrested by the Vice Squad, and he was actually brought to court for using four letter words while inebriated on stage. Jimmy promised that he would not be guilty of a repeat offense. As *The Guardian* (November 7, 1988) noted, here, far removed from the restraints of English society and English decorum, "the ratio of funny to filthy got rather out of hand." "I followed three prostitutes and two drunk-in-charge cases. It was the worst bill I ever topped," he told the *Daily Mirror* (February 6, 1973). [14]

There is a photograph of him in 1963, leaning against a van with the sign, "Jas. Edwards Purveyor of Family Humour." It is obviously intended as sarcastic, but, in reality, it is close to the truth — at least in an age in which political correctness was not an issue. Jimmy was featured in two popular children's weekly comic books, *Radio Fun* and *TV Fun*, and in the later comic book with which they merged, *Buster*. In *TV Fun*, the comic strip is titled "Whack-O! Jimmy Edwards The Pride of St. Capers," and aside from the weekly edition of *Radio Fun*, he is also featured on the cover of the 1959 *Radio Fun Annual*, with a goat between his legs. [15] Few may perhaps be aware of Jimmy's theme song, but it was the childlike and simplistic, "I'm Forever Blowing Bubbles." To most of his fans, the obvious theme song, and one that he would often perform on the trombone, was "The Acrobat" by J.A. Greenwood (1876-1953), which requires the slide of the instrument out to its fullest extent.

Jimmy Edwards has a forceful, commanding, fruity voice that demands attention and obedience, in equal number. There is no hint of the working class or of the servant class in his voice or in his demeanor. He is a Conservative, both with a large and a small "c", in the nice, British way — not like the offensive American who glorifies in that identification — and it is should be no surprise that he actually ran for Parliament as a Conservative candidate. He lost, of course, for winning would have been too much of a joke.

He was obviously a bit of a snob, both on stage and off. In December 1960, at the annual dinner of the Concert Artistes' Association, at the Park Lane Hotel, London, he arrogantly proclaimed, "Television is the greatest single mistake humanity has invented since gun-powder. Far too many people watch it instead of doing other things."[16] It bothered him, he neither knew nor cared, that his future career basically lay in television.

Jimmy Edwards Trombonist.

Thanks to his size and his bluster, and the note of exasperation found so often in his conversations — "Jim does the funnies," he would yell at a live audience, just as in *Bottoms Up!*, he exclaims in more scholarly terms, "Jim does the oratory" — he would have been ideal to play, on stage or screen, Shakespeare's creation of Sir John Falstaff, the fat and boastful knight with a surprisingly deep understanding of the human condition, a companion to the future Henry V. Sadly, Jimmy's only opportunity to play the role came on April 23, 1962, when he acted opposite Beryl Reid as Mistress Quickly in a BBC Home Service[17] radio presentation of *The Merry Wives of Windsor*.[18]

As a teenager, he had been taken to the St. James Theatre to see the great comedian George Robey play Falstaff; it was as he wrote an "instructive" performance[19] and perhaps stayed in his memory as a result of Robey's later sending him an autographed photograph. Plans were twice announced for Jimmy to star as Falstaff in a musical version of *The Merry Wives of Windsor*, first in 1962 and again in 1965; the latter was to be a modernized version of the play produced by Bernard Delfont. Like Falstaff, Jimmy Edwards was a true eccentric, and while the former lived his life on the printed page in approximately the right century, Jimmy and much of his boisterous activities belong to a different era. Perhaps he would have been most at home in Regency England. He would doubtless have been dismissive of the American Colonies, and urged George III to dispose of them. Jimmy and the Prince Regent would have been firm friends, enjoying excess and self-indulgence.

The moustache bristles with anger and irritation, inferring belligerence and a disagreeable personality. And yet above the moustache are the eyes, which sparkle with kindness and good humor. It is an unusual combination, suggesting the complexity of the individual concerned.

It is obvious that, as writer Denis Norden once noted, *Take It from Here*, arguably the most prominent British radio show of all time, was "completely post-war in its attitudes and it recognized the literacy of the listener."[20] And it is equally apparent that a show such as *Take It from Here* needed an anchor, a principal player, who was literate and intelligent, even if some of the characters that he portrayed might not always suggest that same adequacy of knowledge and education. Such a man was Jimmy Edwards.

Yes, Jimmy Edwards was obviously a complex man if judged by the secrecy of his private life, so much at odds with his public persona. At the same time, he was a brave and courageous man, as his war service illustrates. He was a genuinely funny man although not always ready to give a performance offstage, as history records. He was "a charismatic person," writes June Whitfield, "when he walked into a room all eyes turned towards him. He wasn't particularly funny in private, indeed he described himself as a grumpy man, but he had tremendous energy and a wide range of interests which he pursued with great enthusiasm."[21] To Melvyn Hayes, who worked with him on *Whack-O!*, *The Seven Faces of Jim*, *Sir Yellow*, and *Bottoms Up!*, "Behind that great big moustache was a big softy."[22]

Melvyn Hayes.

Similarly, Edwin Apps, who worked with Jimmy in *Whack-O!*, astutely notes that he would look at one "over that immense moustache with an unexpectedly gentle expression."[23] Jimmy's friend from later years, Michael Pointon, writes that "In the final analysis, I feel that Jim was a sensitive person and I got the impression that he sometimes felt trapped within the image of the personality so many people expected of him."[24]

Whatever else one might say about Jimmy Edwards, he was neither bitter nor depressed away from the stage. As one writer has noted, "Almost alone among the top names of his day, he did not give a damn. If that audience didn't take to him, that was their fault."

Despite being very quiet and thoughtful in private, Jimmy Edwards was a man who swore a lot. He could be extremely rude to people, which perhaps arouse from his own insecurity. Comedy writer/performer Barry Cryer, whom younger comedians call "Uncle Baz," was a close friend of Jimmy's. They actually shared the same birthday, and once on their joint birthday, the two were on a train bound for Leeds and a luncheon engagement. "Champagne for breakfast," demanded Jimmy, and the restaurant car steward was happy to oblige. "Champagne whenever you want it, Mr. Wheeler," he replied. The waiter had mistaken Jimmy for the raucous comedian Jimmy Wheeler, and Jimmy Edwards was not amused. "You've just ruined our fucking birthday," he told the man.

Upon arrival in Leeds, Jimmy and Barry went to their hotel, signed in, and Jimmy went off to the nearest pub. He arrived back in time for the luncheon in mellow form, only to discover that a sycophantic vicar was seated at his table. When Jimmy got up to speak, his first words were, "God, we've got a fucking vicar at our table."[25]

LEFT: *Jimmy Wheeler.* RIGHT: *Tony Hancock.*

With the exception of Eric Sykes, with whom Jimmy co-starred in later years, he had few close friends among the comedy fraternity. He made no effort to gain their affection. While appearing in the West End with Tony Hancock, taking on his first major role, Jimmy was sitting with a friend in his dressing room and turned off the tannoy so he did not have to listen to Hancock's act. When Hancock came rushing into the dressing room after his performance, he asked how he was, to which Edwards replied, "Bloody awful." Hancock was about to burst into tears when he realized the tannoy was turned off.

"You weren't listening," he exclaimed. "You never heard a word of the act!"

"Better things to do," Jimmy said. "But I'll still bet you were bloody awful."[26]

One should never under-estimate the comedian's intelligence, often hidden in an alcoholic blur. Throughout his later life, Jimmy came up with many, unrealized ideas for radio or television programs. For the latter, he conceived of a series titled *PC 444: The Lonely Copper or I Then Became Suspicious*. It was to be filmed without dialogue but with subtitles with the stories told in the manner of a police constable giving evidence.

Who else back in the 1950s could have conceived of an unrehearsed radio program in which a panel of resident celebrities, with both humor and discernment, answered questions from a studio audience? *Does the Team Think?* began airing in October 1957, with Edwards, David Tomlinson, David Nixon (a popular magician of the day), and Jimmy Wheeler, chaired by Peter Haigh, and was last heard in July 1976. The almost twenty-year run of the program reminds one of just how successful were Jimmy's other two, major series, *Take It from Here* and *Whack-O!*, evidential also of how the comedian's popularity did not wane with the passing decades.

Despite his background, Jimmy was always ebullient, with the high spirits generally aided by a good amount of alcohol. He was instantly recognizable, thanks to the handlebar moustache and bright red cheeks (again thanks to alcoholic intake). He was the subject of immediate attention whenever he appeared in public. Once, while walking down Piccadilly, he was approached by a working class chap who asked him to say something funny. "Why don't you fuck off?" was Jimmy's response, sufficient in its non-existent humor to leave his accoster convulsed in laughter.

The in-your-face approach to his audience might suggest that Jimmy Edwards relied on unsubdued anger and animosity to fuel his performances. Yet, as Michael Deacon has written in the *Daily Telegraph*, there is an element of pathos beneath the façade. While pathos is generally associated with the likes of Charlie Chaplin or Norman Wisdom (who never got it quite right), it is there within the characterizations of most British comedy actors:

"Take *Dad's Army*. Captain Mainwaring is a pompous fool, but that's not all he is. He has a quality shared by all the great British sitcom heroes. Pathos. Mainwaring, Tony Hancock, Basil Fawlty, Alan Partridge, David Brent: these men with dreams, big dreams, which we know they're doomed never to realise, because they're trapped — whether by the class system, by bad luck, by their own inadequacies, or by all three. None of them is an unassuming sort of chap who just wants a quiet life. All have a profound yearning for recognition. All are desperate to succeed in some role to which they're nakedly unsuited. That's what makes them funny, and makes them sad. The pathos is key."[27]

As early as 1953, a reviewer in *The Spectator*, writing of Jimmy Edwards, noted, "Behind the hearty exterior, there are glimpses of a sensitive mind and that keen musicality which is so often found in the great clowns, and which goes far to explain their acute sense of timing."[28]

Professor James Edwards in *Whack-O!* is such a chap. Behind the strut and the swagger, the loud voice compensating for a failure to communicate is a man who is lost and alone. As his brother Alan once pointed out, the bombast was all a veneer, covering up the sensitive person that he was.[29]

It was on radio that Jimmy got his big break, co-starring for some ten years, from 1948-1959 in *Take It from Here*,[30] and on which he is best remembered for the character of Mr. or Pa Glum (not actually introduced on the program until 1953). Jimmy Edwards played Mr. Glum on television in a briefly resurrected television version in 1978 and 1979, but he is, of course, best known in that medium for the aforementioned *Whack-O!*, playing the cane-happy headmaster of a very sordid boys' school. One fan magazine summed up why the show and Jimmy Edward was so successful on television, noting he had "the essential knack of coming right into your lounge and doing a personal appearance for you."[31]

Thanks to YouTube, one can access a clip from circa 1966 of Edwards' appearing live on stage, playing the trombone and joking with the orchestra. He kicks his music stand over, ad libs outrageously. "When the right things go wrong I'll be happy." And the dialogue is brilliant and original: "The name's Edwards not Vladimir Kuts [the Soviet long-distance runner]. That dates me. He was shot about twelve years ago." And, of course, he manages to draw beer from a xylophone. "You go down there and join your friends," he says as he begins to empty his glass down to his throat. "Let's drink a toast to the Iron Curtain. May it rust in peace." Here is Jimmy Edwards as he must have appeared to British audiences when they first saw him on stage or television, and with an act almost identical to that he introduced on stage to Australian audiences around the same period. He is beyond brilliant; he transports the viewer to a world of comedic nirvana.

Whack-O! was brought to the screen in 1960 under the title of *Bottoms Up!*, which despite some limitations as to its humor, is surprisingly funny and entertaining and, best of all, captures Jimmy Edwards headmaster character for posterity. He had been on screen intermittently since 1948, but *Bottoms Up!* and *Three Men in a Boat*, released four years earlier, are the only features worthy of recognition. However, it was a 1967 short comedy,

The Plank, and friendship with fellow comedian Eric Sykes, that led to Jimmy's last major contribution to British humor — not on radio, television or film, but on the stage (where he had appeared frequently since the 1940s), with the comedy *Big Bad Mouse.*

1. Michael Pointer writes (e-mail dated April 9, 2017), "I recall an enjoyable lunch at the East India Club when our mutual friend David Mills, who was visiting London from Bahrain, invited Jim and myself. Since he knew of my longtime friendship with Max Wall, he decided he'd invite Max, too, but without telling him in advance. I knew that, as a comic of a later generation, Jim respected Max's work but when I'd mentioned to Max I'd been working with Jim I got the impression he'd taken against his bombastic persona. Perhaps this also had something to do with the fact that Jim had been an officer in the R.A.F. but Max's short wartime service only culminated in his becoming a corporal. So I was somewhat apprehensive. Regardless, the long lunch proved to be a great success with Max and Jim's contrasting personalities really hitting it off. I think Max was pleasantly surprised at how much the offstage Jim differed from his public image."

2. The final shot of the cast and audience in *Mrs. Brown's Boys* shows that it is photographed with a similar layout to that used in the recording of *Whack-O!*, with sets side-by-side facing the audience.

3. The scandal of Jimmy Savile (1926-2011) is widely covered in the British press, but less so in the United States. In all, hiding in plain sight, he is believed to have abused some 500 boys and girls, mostly between the ages of thirteen and fifteen, as well as an untold number of adults, both male and female. Savile was never accused during his lifetime because of, as noted by the *Washington Post* (June 27, 2014), "the pervasive and intimidating power of celebrity. He was so well-known that even when his behavior struck some as strange or lewd, he was allowed to carry on because he was Jimmy Savile."

4. A 1930 British film, *The Black Hand Gang* contains three scenes in which a boy no older than six is seen without his trouser and with his buttocks on display. The leading child in the film is played by a thirty-six-year-old midget, Wee Georgie Wood. Extraordinary!

5. Frank Muir, *A Kentish Lad*, p. 247.

6. Ken Dodd to Anthony Slide, November 25, 2016.

7. Quoted in Harold Watson, "Raising the Wind," p. 1.

8. The title is a pun based on the popular, highly rich clotted cream, usually paired with strawberry jam and scones.

9. Victualler is an antiquated term used to identify the owner or proprietor of a public house or pub.

10. In October 1953, Bud Flanagan deputized for Jimmy Edwards on stage in *London Laughs* while the comedian was on vacation in the South of France.

11. George Greenfield, *A Smattering of Monsters: A Kind of Memoir*, p. 93.

12. Michael Pointon to Anthony Slide, e-mail dated April 25, 2017.

13. Frank Gail Pedrick Harvey (1906-1970) was also a scriptwriter, whose work included the first thirty-five episodes of the British version of *This Is Your Life*.

14. Jimmy Edwards had last appeared in court on April 24, 1952, when he was fined one pound for leaving his car for 110 minutes in a no parking zone near London's Covent Garden.

15. *Radio Fun* was published from 1938-1961, and *TV Fun* was published from 1953-1959.

16. *The Stage*, December 5, 1960, p. 6.

17. The BBC Home Service provided regional radio service, beginning in 1939 with the outbreak of World War Two, and continuing through 1967, when it was renamed BBC Radio 4.

18. Cedric Messina produced this play and also co-produced, with Val Gielgud, *Twelfth Night*, starring Reid and Edwards (as Sir Toby Belch), broadcast on the BBC Home Service on January 6, 1962 (and rebroadcast in 1964).

19. Jimmy Edwards, *Take It from Me*, p. 24.

20. "Charles Maxwell," p. 35.

21. June Whitfield, *...And June Whitfield*, p. 142.

22. Melvyn Hayes to Anthony Slide, e-mail dated July 27, 2016.

23. Edwin Apps, *Pursued by Bishops*, p. 278.

24. Michael Pointer to Anthony Slide, e-mail dated April 9, 2017.

25. Anthony Slide interview with Barry Cryer, February 6, 2017.

26. Jimmy Edwards, *Take It from Me*, p. 94.

27. *The Week*, November 5, 2016, p. 10.

28. *http://archive.spectator.co.uk/article/10th-april-1953/take-it-from-me-by-jimmy-edwards* (accessed March 2016).

29. Ronni Davis, producer, and Nigel Farrell, presenter, *Wake Up at the Back: The Life of Jimmy Edwards*.

30. The BBC had broadcast an earlier radio show titled *Take It from Here* from 1943-1944, with no connection to the later program, and starring Richard Haydn, whose character work in Hollywood is fairly well known.

31. Dick Richards, "A Whack-O Bang-On Type," p. 13.

CHAPTER ONE

The Early Years

James Keith O'Neill Edwards came from an upper middle-class background, dissimilar to that of most of his contemporaries. Northern comedian Frank Randle was the son of an unwed mother; Frankie Howard the son of a soldier; Tommy Cooper the son of a coalminer; Ken Dodd the son of a coal merchant; and Norman Wisdom the son of a chauffeur. Only Tony Hancock fared somewhat better, with a father who ran a hotel and sent his son to private school — but ultimately the end result was far tragic than that of any of his fellow comedians. Certainly, Hancock did not enjoy the intellectual and one assumes stimulating family life enjoyed by Jimmy Edwards.

Jimmy's father, Dr. R. [Reginald] W. [Walter] K. [Kenrick] Edwards had married New Zealander Phyllis Keith Cowan on December 14, 1909. He was a mathematical lecturer at King's College, London, and had gained some fame as the author of *The Mermaid of Inish-Uig: A Tale*, published by Arnold in 1898 (and still available in reprint from the British Library). One of nine children (six male and three female), James Keith O'Neill Edwards was born on March 23, 1920. An older brother, Alan Raven, born on November 17, 1914, was the only sibling with any close involvement with Jimmy throughout his life, although certainly Jimmy never lost touch with his extended family and was "Uncle Jimmy" to a number of nephews and nieces. In later years, with a handlebar moustache, Alan resembles a slimmed-down version of brother Jimmy, and, by all accounts, was every bit as funny.

The Edwards children would put on plays, which Jimmy produced, and the entire Edwards brood was featured shortly after Jimmy's birth in an advertisement for Allenbury's "Progressive System of Infant Feeding," a series of Milk Food products manufactured by Allen & Hanburys Ltd.[1] As the youngest, Jimmy is perched on his mother's shoulders.

The birth took place at the parents' home, 17 Woodlands Road, Barnes, a South London middle-class suburb. "No 17 was my base," he wrote, "when I was on vacation from Cambridge, and my base when on leave from the RAF. And, much later on, I sallied forth from there for my audition at the Windmill Theatre."[2] He was pushed around the neighborhood in a two-seater baby carriage that he shared with his younger sister, before attending Miss Julia A. Wright's kindergarten across Barnes Common in Ranelagh. Miss Wright reported that at the age of five, Jimmy was "making very satisfactory progress. He has ability and promises well."[3] Later, from 1928 through 1935, Jimmy would take the train from Barnes Station to Waterloo, and on to St. Paul's Cathedral School. Barnes Common was later to gain a reputation as a gay cruising ground, but there is no evidence that Jimmy Edwards had an interest in it for that reason.

His form master's report on Jimmy at the age of seventeen reveals that he was "Good" in Divinity, "Very good all around" in English, "Satisfactory" in Chemistry, and "Very Satisfactory" in Gymnastics. The headmaster noted, "He has been a useful member of society during the term. He should try to conquer his nervousness."[4]

Attendance at St. Paul's Cathedral School is evidence of the affluence of the Edwards family, although in reality in return for singing in the Cathedral choir, some of the boys there were educated at a considerably reduced fee. Established in 1123 to educate youngsters chosen to sing in the choir at St. Paul's Cathedral, the school boasts a number of entertainment figures as old boys, including actor Simon Russell Beale (closely associated with the National Theatre), conductor Charles Groves, actor Julian Ovendon (familiar to Americans for his appearances on *Downton Abbey*), and comedy straight man Nicholas Parsons, as well as poet Walter de la Mare. In 2007, the School was caught up in a pedophile scandal, with one of the masters accused and convicted of indecent assault on a number of the boys there.

Considerable time each day was spent in participation in the Cathedral choir. There was Matins at ten every morning, Evensong at four in the afternoon, and on Sundays, an additional service at 7:00 P.M. Choir practice took place between 2:00 and 3:00 A.M. each weekday. For special occasions, such as a performance of Handel's *Messiah* or Bach's *Passion*, the Cathedral would hire an orchestra, and here, for the first time, Jimmy saw the instrument that was to be so crucial to his comedy performances later, a trombone.

As Jimmy recalled many decades later, he and his fellow choirboys were "quite capable of singing of the most holy and ethereal of subjects while having their minds on the nasty subjects which concern little boys and while wondering what was for tea." As choirboys, they were in a special position to make jokes about the Scriptures, most of which were highly blasphemous.[5]

Jimmy Edwards was a pupil at St. Paul's Cathedral School from the age of eight through fifteen, following in the footsteps of older brother Alan, and during that time he studied not only the typical academic subjects but additionally learned to read music. Edwards was also involved in the sporting life of the school, including football, athletics and cricket. He did not particularly enjoy the last, usually being chosen as the last in his team to bat (a position that meant if the team was doing very well and winning one would never have to defend the wicket). He was described by the *Choristers Magazine* (October 31, 1935) as "a player of considerable bonhomie but little skill." "Bonhomie" seems an appropriate term to describe Jimmy Edwards, who despite all the bluster and anger on display in his later characterizations appears as jovial and easy-going.

In 1935, Jimmy demonstrated his ability in a non-sporting field, with the writing of a comic melodrama, *The Seances*, in which a murder is committed during the course of a séance and Edwards, in the role of an elderly lady, keeps holding séance after séance in a vague attempt to identify the killer but in reality leading only to more deaths of the participants. It concluded with his committing suicide. "I wonder if any other playwright has ever achieved the effect of killing off every member of the cast!" he wrote,[6] forgetting perhaps Agatha Christie's 1939 novel, *Ten Little Niggers*, published in the U.S. and in later reprints, for obvious reasons, as *And Then There Were None*, and which was adapted both for the stage and screen.

In addition to his work as a playwright, Jimmy also founded, in competition with the official publication, a second school magazine, *The Mortarboard*, the entire contents of which were his own. More importantly, he authored a serious poem, "The Train," detailing the brief effect of a train as it roars like thunder across the countryside. "Then, with a roar like thunder, came the train./Whose steamy siren shrieked and shrieked again." It so impressed Walter de la Mare that he included it in his 1937 compilation of children's writings, co-edited with Harold Jones, *This Year; Next Year*, published by Faber and Faber.

Jimmy remained at St. Paul's Cathedral School long enough to attend the Jubilee of King George V, as Head Boy, a position he had achieved at the age of fifteen, and was awarded his first medal, the Jubilee Medal.

He enjoyed his time at St. Paul's Cathedral School and considered himself lucky to have been there during the headmastership of the Reverend R.H. Crouchman. Jimmy's position of Head Boy, he proudly noted, allowed him to bully the younger boys or "fags," as they are called in British public schools and with no gay connotation. He was also lucky in earning a scholarship which made it possible for him to continue his education at King's College School, Wimbledon.

The scholarship was important as a result of a major tragedy in the Edwards family. In 1935, Jimmy's father died. The family income was sizably reduced; brother Alan left school and at the age of eighteen he became a mounted policeman; brother Hugh or Hughie, at the age of fourteen, joined the merchant navy as an apprentice. Hugh Edwards, whom Jimmy would always refer to as "Skip," was later to gain a reputation as a cigarette, whisky and occasional people smuggler in the Mediterranean after World War Two; he recounted his adventures in the 1959 book, *Midnight Trader*.[7]

King's College School was founded by Royal Charter in 1829 for boys from the ages of seven through eighteen as a junior department of King's College, a branch of the University of London, which stands to this day on the Strand. The School moved in 1897 to Wimbledon, a Southwest suburb of London well-known as the home of the Wimbledon Tennis Championships and for the 1,000-acre Wimbledon Common. The Common is surrounded by expensive homes and also on its border is King's College School, evidence of what is financially required of its pupils. One such pupil was Roy Plomley, the host for decades of the popular BBC radio show, *Desert Island Discs*, with its "Sleepy Lagoon" theme song, on which celebrities were asked to select records with which they would wish to be shipwrecked.

Jimmy Edwards was twice on the program, on August 1, 1951 and again on February 20, 1961. "I can't imagine anything more ghastly," commented Jimmy of the circumstance on the 1951 program, in which he chose records with brass instruments or those that reminded him of sentimental moments in his career: "The Three Bears Suite" by Eric Coates, the trumpet piece from *The Carnival of Venice* with Harry James and His Orchestra, Ray Ellington's "Little Bop Beep," "Policeman's Holiday," sung by the Keynotes ("for sentimental reasons"), "Stumbling," played by Sid Phillips and His Band (whom Edwards claimed began his career in a quartet with Gilbert and Sullivan), Dennis Brain playing Richard Strauss' "Horn Concerto No. One in E," Sid Field ("the best comedian I ever saw") performing his golfing sketch with Jerry Desmonde, and "The Storm Music" from *Peter Grimes* by Benjamin Britten. Edwards selected his euphonium to take with him as a luxury item.

For his second participation on *Desert Island Discs*, Jimmy chose "Believe Me If All Those Endearing Young Charms" played by Bert

Sullivan on the euphonium as his favorite record,[8] *Lady Chatterley's Lover* as the book he wanted to take with him, and, again, the euphonium as his luxury item.

After taking care of household chores, including cleaning out the kitchen fire and bringing a scuttle filled with coal into the house, Jimmy would bicycle across the common to King's College School, where his first duty of the day was to play the harmonium in the Great Hall for morning prayers. "I may not have been a very good harmonium player, but I was the only one," he recalled.[9] Enthusiastic about music, Jimmy decided that he would take the subject for the School Certificate Examination. Initially, he was to take English as his subject for a scholarship at Cambridge, but dissuaded by his English teacher, who assured him he would fail, Edwards determined to work for a choral scholarship.

Music played an important part of his life at King's College School, where he learned to play both the bugle and the trumpet, borrowing the instrument from brother Alan, but never becoming particularly adept at playing it. Becoming proficient in the former came about as a result of his joining the O.T.C. or Officer Training Corps. As an army cadet, Jimmy didn't like the notion of having to march around and at one point actually fainted while on parade. He noticed that the bandsmen in the O.T.C. didn't have to march and did the least work, and so he became a bugler — there being one spare. It was the beginning of Jimmy Edwards' lifelong interest in brass musical instruments, which was to include his being president of the Barnes Brass Band.

In the summer of 1938, Edwards went to Cambridge, to St. John's College, and took the musical test, which involved his singing not too well "[Voice of One Crying in] The Wilderness." Much to his surprise, he was awarded the scholarship not for the perfection of his singing but because the organist conducting the examination, Robin Orr[10], thought he had a bad cold and that was the reason for the gravelly quality of his voice.

After his acceptance by St. John's College, there was a three-month break prior to start of the fall or Michaelmas term in October 1938. Short of funds, Jimmy decided to apply for employment in the teaching profession and applied to the Gabbitas & Thring's Agency for Schoolmasters.[11] He was hired by headmaster James Hitchcock at St. Clare Preparatory School in Upper Walmer, Kent, to teach English, French, Latin, Arithmetic, Geometry, History, Geography, and Scripture to the junior classes. He was also required to interest himself in the students' "repulsive" hobbies. Edwards could only believe that there had been a major shortage of candidates for the post.

As he wrote in his autobiography, he was not a good teacher, and despite *Whacko-O!*'s suggesting otherwise, he was useless at discipline. "The angrier I got the more the children laughed," he recalled.[12] Edwards was not perhaps surprised when, at half-term, he was asked to leave St. Clair, and headmaster Hitchcock explained in a letter:

"You ask, 'Am I suitable for the teaching profession?' My answer is, 'No.'

"...you cannot teach a form properly unless you have proper disciplinary control over it... Possibly during your years at Cambridge you'll have time and opportunity to see some other road on which to travel through life."[13]

After Jimmy's departure and with the outbreak of World War Two, the school was evacuated, in 1940, to Somerset and then to Gloucestershire. Enrolment fell to an all-time low of only fifteen boys, and the school closed in the summer of 1943, after eighty-six years of existence. It had one famous "old boy" in novelist Dornford Yates, whose thrillers and comedy works are long forgotten.[14]

Upon his return to Cambridge, Jimmy rented

St. John's College.

accommodation, consisting of a living room and bedroom from a Miss L. Clifton at 26 Portugal Place;[15] there was no bathroom and to wash himself the comedian-to-be had to go to his College. To augment his savings, he again took up teaching, at the choir school attached to St. John's College, and also sang in the choir, for which he was paid. While teaching at the choir school, he made his first attempt at growing a moustache, and when he appeared in the classroom with his new hirsute appearance, one of the boys asked, "Oh sir, what have you got on your face?" There was loud laughter at Jimmy tried to explain that it was a moustache. "I knew then I would never make a successful schoolmaster," he wrote.[16]

Soon after moving to Cambridge, Jimmy Edwards acquired his first trombone. The assistant organist at St. Paul's, Dr. Douglas Hopkins, who had become a friend of the Edwards family, gifted Jimmy with an old trombone that he owned. It was an American instrument made by C.G. Conn, whose trombones remain the most popular in the U.K. Jimmy took along the trombone with him to Cambridge, through the years with the R.A.F., at the Windmill Theatre, and on his first radio broadcast in 1947. Eventually, he was able to purchase a new trombone, and he dutifully returned the old one to Dr. Hopkins.

Godfrey Winn.

In his leisure time, of which he appears to have had plenty, Jimmy joined the Cambridge Union, the oldest debating society in the world, with its slogan "Defending Free Debate Since 1815." Jimmy became noted for his lengthy, comedic contributions which would often irritate both serious speakers and members of the audience. To a certain extent, he was very obviously rehearsing for his later career as a stand-up comic. On November 21, 1939, he opposed the motion, "That Women University Students Should Have the Same Rights as Men." On May 21, 1940, he opposed another motion, "That This House Welcomes the Imminent Overthrow of Western Civilization." When he did propose a motion, on May 23, 1939, "That This House Is Tired of Politics and Politicians," he lost.

Annoyed with the Union's emphasis on political debate, Jimmy and another student founded the Cambridge University Non-Party Association (CUNPA), intended as nothing more than a joke but which actually attracted a membership of between sixty and seventy students.

In his autobiography, Jimmy writes of Godfrey Winn being asked to speak to the Union. Because he was a writer, noted for a newspaper advice column for women and because he was patently gay, having been in a relationship with Somerset Maugham in the late 1920s and

romantically linked to another writer, Beverly Nichols, some members of
the Union planned to ridicule and insult him — gay bashing before the
term was known. Winn was in Cambridge just before November 5, when
Guy Fawkes night is celebrated, his image burnt in effigy, and kids with
their home-made guys roam the streets begging for money. He began his
speech, "a small boy said to me in the streets of London, 'Penny for the
guy, sir?' 'No,' I said to him, '*I* am the guy. I am being asked to Cambridge
so that they can all make fun of me.'"

From his autobiography, it is very obvious that Edwards was both
impressed and moved by Godfrey Winn. He perhaps felt empathy with
the man in that he was quietly struggling with his own homosexuality
and the fear that he might be ridiculed as was Winn. It is perhaps no
accident that many years later, in 1958, it was Godfrey Winn who was
invited to Jimmy's home to interview him for a television fan magazine,
and later still, in 1964, to report on a typical dinner party with Jimmy and
Mrs. Edwards.[17]

Student entertainment at Cambridge was dominated by the Footlights
Dramatic Club, founded in 1883, and primarily noted in more recent years
for its satirical and comedic revues. Among the best known members
of the Footlights are the Monty Python troupe, Olivia Colman, Peter
Cook, David Frost, Stephen Fry, Jack Hulbert, Eric Idle, Hugh Laurie,
John Oliver, Emma Thompson, and Jimmy Edwards. Along with Richard
Murdoch and Kenneth Horne, both of whom enjoyed distinguished
careers on BBC Radio, Jimmy Edwards was one of the first comedians to
graduate from the Footlights and to enjoy a major career in show business. Thanks to the Footlights, Jimmy realized that he could never be a
straight actor. At Cambridge, he was cast as Ajax in a student production
of *Troilus and Cressida*, but the part was taken away from him because the
director pointed out that nobody in the audience would take him seriously
and all would be asking, "Where's the trombone?"

At least one critic, Eric Midwinter, has pointed out that what made
Take It from Here such a success was that the material was bright and
sophisticated and that the performers were young and fresh. "It was like
university revue stuff without the blasé superficiality."[18]

Thanks to his handling of the trombone, Jimmy was invited to join
the Footlights' dance band. While he was never a featured player and
thus subject to scrutiny, the same cannot be said of his audition for the
Freshmen's Concert at St. John's College. Because of continued flicking of
the instrument's spit valve, a pool of saliva was forming on the floor at the
musician's feet. The saliva, along with the noises he was making with the

trombone, reduced Jimmy to hysterical laughter. The second part of the audition involved his singing "The Moon Hath Raised Her Lamp Above," with fellow student Max Homan, who was studying medicine. The duet reduced the two to laughter. "That was my last attempt to make a serious appearance on any platform," wrote Jimmy.[19]

It did result in his teaming with Max Homan in an act, in which the latter played the piano, Jimmy performed on the trombone, and the couple sang a duet, dressed as two old men. They appeared at a Smoking Concert, organized by the Footlights, and Jimmy was also asked to appear as one of the dons in a sketch titled "K.P." and, more importantly, to perform a trombone solo at The Footlights Dramatic Club All-Male Revue, held at the Arts Theatre from June 6-13, 1939. With an act culminating in his releasing a stream of water from the trombone — a routine he was to perform many times in the years ahead — Jimmy was a success, so much so that the local *Cambridge Daily News* (June 7, 1939) noted "his admirable fooling with a troublesome trombone," while the distinguished theatre critic W.A. Darlington wrote in the *Daily Telegraph* that "Jimmy Edwards' antics with his trombone are extremely funny." The critic failed to mention that Jimmy's aim was not always accurate, and members of the audience, seated in the front rows, ran the risk of being deluged.

The act, featured in Act One, was titled "I Dream I Dwelt in Marble Halls (with Apologies to Belcher)" and based on a 1936 painting by George Belcher (1875-1947), depicting a "shabby though very happy gentleman who is obviously a street musician, who has enjoyed his beer and playing the cornet."[20]

Jimmy was directed by the Dean of King's College, Cambridge, Donald Beves, a wealthy academic, who, in the 1970s, was falsely accused of being a Soviet spy, along with Kim Philby, Guy Burgess and Donald Maclean.

Max Homan might be considered important in Jimmy's life in that it was he who persuaded the comedian to have his first alcoholic drink. The alcohol of choice was beer, and much both to Homan's and Jimmy's surprise, the latter would wake the next morning without a hangover.

The outbreak of War in September 1939 signaled that the comedy duo's days were numbered. While pursuing active service in the Royal Air Force, Jimmy did continue somewhat haphazardly with his academic pursuits and he also continued to appear on stage with Max Homan. The two men determined to put on a Footlights Revue, despite the Arts Theatre being unavailable. They were, however, able to book the Houghton Hall[21] for a new revue titled *Touch and Go*. Because of the theatre's distance from the center of Cambridge and because most students had other matters on their mind, the show was not a success, resulting in a personal loss for Jimmy of thirty shillings, which in his autobiography he appears to regard as something of a major tragedy.

Jimmy was prominently featured in *Touch and Go*, appearing in five sketches: "A Day at Broadcasting House" (with Donald McWhinnie and Donald Hewlett), "Russian with Tears" (with McWhinnie and Antony Hampton), "The Pater Pays a Visit" (with Hewlett, McWhinnie and George Thomason), "Radio B.B.C." (with Hewlett), and "Tea for Two" (with Hewlett). He also presented a spot of magic, appearing solo, in "Black Magic." Only "Radio B.B.C." and "Tea for Two" were credited to him as writer.

Jimmy was sorry to leave Cambridge, noting in his diary, apropos the boys that he taught in the choir school, "Apparently, among the boys it is said that my money is low; I am noted for my hard dictations, untidy clothes and hair all over the place. They say they like me because I am human."[22]

1. The company is now owned by GlaxoSmithKline.

2. Jimmy Edwards, *Six of the Best*, p. 144.

3. Report in the possession of Jim Pennington.

4. Summer Term 1937 Report in the possession of Jim Pennington.

5. Ian Warden, "An Antidote to Saccharine," p. 17.

6. Jimmy Edwards, *Take It from Me*, p. 25.

7. Hugh Edwards' adventures were brought to the screen, in fictional form, in the 1955 film, *The Ship That Died of Shame/PT Raiders*.

8. I can recommend this recording to readers as truly beautiful. Other selected recordings were Richard Strauss' Don Juan overture, Richard Strauss' Horn Concerto No. One in E Flat, played by Dennis Brain, "Mars" from the Planet Suite by Holst, Tchaikovsky's Symphony No. 4 in F Minor, "Solving the Riddle" from Billy May's Big Flat Brass, "Jet Plane" from USAF: A Portrait in Sound, and Jimmy himself singing "I've Never Seen a Straight Banana."

9. Jimmy Edwards, *Take It from Me*, p. 27.

10. Robin Orr (1909-2006) was a distinguished figure in British musical history. He was appointed organist at St. John's College, Cambridge, in 1938 and remained there through 1941, when he joined the R.A.F. as a photographic intelligence officer. After the War, he returned to St. John's, where he remained until 1951. In 1962, he became the first chairman of Scottish Opera, and later, from 1976-1983, he was director of the Welsh National Opera. He wrote three symphonies and three operas.

11. Founded in 1873 and still around today as Gabbitas Education Consultants.

12. Ronni Davis, producer, and Nigel Farrell, presenter, *Wake Up at the Back: The Life of Jimmy Edwards.*

13. Jimmy Edwards, *Take It from Me,* p. 33.

14. Dornford Yates was the pseudonym of Cecil William Mercer (1885-1960), at the height of his popularity in the 1920s and 1930s, with the "Chandos" and "Berry" series of books.

15. Miss Clifton read Jimmy's comments on her appearance and his accommodation when his autobiography was serialized in the magazine John Bull, and she wrote him an angry letter claiming she had been ridiculed and demanding financial compensation.

16. Jimmy Edwards, *Take It from Me,* p. 34.

17. Godfrey Winn (1908-1971), known to his fellow journalists as "Winifred God," is someone worthy of a major biographical study. During World War Two, he enlisted in the Royal Navy as an ordinary seaman, and when he was invalided out of the service, he joined the Merchant Marine. Like Jimmy Edwards, he was a brave and courageous, closeted gay man, who served his country well. And, like me, he was born in Birmingham and attended the King Edward VI Grammar School.

18. Eric Midwinter, "Take It from Here," p. 2.

19. Jimmy Edwards, *Take It from Me,* p. 39.

20. The model in the painting is a former army sergeant, Thomas Jagger, who did not play a musical instrument, as evidenced in part by the sheet music in the painting being upside down.

21. Jimmy Edwards might have been pleased to discover that it later became an equestrian center.

22. Jimmy Edwards, *Take It from Me,* p. 50.

CHAPTER TWO

The War Years

Despite the injuries he was to sustain, Jimmy Edwards had a good war. It was not without a strong and valid reason that he named the second volume of his autobiography, dealing with the war years, as *Six of the Best* (not a reference to the traditional six strokes of the cane given as punishment in British schools, but the number of years he spent in the R.A.F.). As Jimmy wrote, "I served for six years, flew for four of them, never flew anything that wasn't obsolete, never dropped a bomb or fired a gun, and finished up with the DFC…And what about this? I was too young for the Battle of Britain and too old for the film."[1]

He wanted to be a pilot, and eventually he was. Jimmy enjoyed the company of men, and in the Royal Air Force there was a camaraderie, enforced with plenty of beer, in which he might participate. Thanks to the R.A.F. he learned to hold his liquor. And, perhaps most importantly, he was able to develop his trombone act at concert parties and amateur shows.

Jimmy's war service began early in 1940, a few months after the start of World War Two. He and a friend from Cambridge, Ioan Vaughan Jones, decided to enlist in the R.A.F. Vaughan Jones was welcomed for training as a pilot, but Edwards was only accepted at his second attempt, not as a pilot as he had hoped but, because of poor eyesight, as an observer. He returned to Cambridge for a while, biding his time, and eventually on July 9, 1940, he was ordered to report to Blackpool for reception and basic training in the R.A.F.

Blackpool is a North of England seaside resort famous for its illuminations, its tower (opened in 1894, and emulating and inspired by the Eiffel Tower in Paris) and the reality that when the tide is out there is almost two miles of beach to cross to reach the North Sea. A journey most certainly not worth the effort. Jimmy would return to Blackpool a number of times, performing at theatres there when a star, but he claimed always to hate the place, particularly "That Bloody Tower," which was never out of eye range. Illustrative of his hatred for Blackpool and indicative of Edwards' intellectual capabilities, written in iambic pentameter, is his poem, "Ode to Blackpool," worth quoting in its entirety:

> *Earth hath not anything to show more base*
> *Than this detestable and loathsome place*
> *Called Blackpool…There is not in all the world*
> *A town at which there can, and should be hurled*
> *More justified and yet more vile abuse.*
> *I cannot find one single good excuse*
> *(Except as a prospective bombing target*
> *Along with Southend, Brighton, Hove and Margate)*
> *For the existence of this vice-rid sink,*
> *At once a den of men and whores and drink.*
> *It stretches mile on mile and pier on pier*
> *Offending nose as much as eye and ear.*
> *And over all…the front, the cheap hotels,*
> *The hooting trams, the crowds, the sewage smells,*
> *The "pleasure-haunts," the swarming beach, the din –*
> *The Tower stands — a Monument to Sin.*[2]

As noted earlier, Jimmy Edwards was something of a snob. It might be argued that he looked down on his audience, viewing its members with some contempt. For this reason, he must have enjoyed starring in *Big Bad Mouse* in which he could harangue the audience at any time, enjoying the potential to humiliate and belittle. As a snob, and with his upper middle class background, Edwards would despise a seaside resort such as Blackpool, which resolutely catered to the working class. Its illuminations were always somewhat tawdry, and with the advent of television emphasizing such plebeian programming as the Manchester-based soap opera, *Coronation Street*, and its most famous character, Ena Sharples.

Blackpool was a city of cheap hotels and even cheaper boarding houses, whose landladies would insist that guests vacate the premises after breakfast and not return until the evening. No matter the weather — and it could often be vile — visitors to Blackpool could not shelter at the bed and breakfast establishments wherein they had booked. It was the seaside resort adored by the working poor of Lancashire, a place for two weeks respite from the cotton mills and the coalmines in which they worked the rest of the year; its popularity for such individuals has never more brilliantly been captured than in the 1934 Gracie Fields vehicle *Sing As We*

Go, and the Blackpool that is so vividly captured on film here would have changed little in the next two decades.

In more recent times, Blackpool has gained fame as the "Gay Capital of the North," a reputation it did not hold when Jimmy was a visitor there.

The comedian enjoyed flying and once he had gained both fame and fortune, he acquired a small Cessna plane, and where did he keep it? Yes,

Blackpool.

at Blackpool's Squires Gate Airport.[3] In the 1970s, he was president of Blackpool's Westair Flying Club, which had been in operation from the 1930s and continues to this day. If anything, flying was as much a part of Jimmy Edwards' public persona as his fondness for alcohol, and both were just as important in both his public and his private life. Typically, for example, in 1966, he was in Melbourne, Australia, as starter of the two-day "Moomba" Australian Air Race, in which ninety-eight planes competed. And the newsreels cameras were there to record his presence. On March 8, 1982, Jimmy was appearing on ITV's *After Noon Plus*, talking about the DC3 Dakota in recognition of its 50th anniversary.

In 1941, Jimmy was shipped off to Canada to learn to be a pilot. He enjoyed the food and the alcohol in his new environment, but failed to pass his initial exams. After much of what can only be described as finagling, and a demand that he be discharged in order to apply to join the

Fleet Air Arm (which was under the command of the Navy), Edwards was finally sent to No. 32 Elementary Flying Training School at Swift Current, Saskatchewan, where he began flight instruction using Tiger Moths. In April 1942, he received his wings and a commission, eventually returning to England some eleven months later on *The Empress of Scotland*.

Back in Britain, in June 1943, Edwards was posted to Limavady, Northern Ireland, and later to Turnberry, near Glasgow, for training in torpedo-dropping. His first "real" job was to ferry a new Wellington bomber to North Africa. Back in the United Kingdom, Jimmy was assigned to the newly-formed Transport Command in Doncaster, where he learned to fly the recently-arrived American Dakotas. By this time, as he notes in his autobiography, he had clocked up 700 hours of flying time.[4] He also had been promoted to Flight-Lieutenant and "had a whacking great moustache."[5] From Doncaster, Jimmy moved on to Down Ampney in Gloucestershire, where he trained in glider towing and paratroop dropping, and where his first mission was dropping propaganda leaflets over France. Supposedly proficient in glider towing, on June 5 1944, he towed a troop-carrying glider or horsa of the Parachute Regiment to France:

"Owing to the smoke and dust thrown up by extensive bombing, Edwards was unable to find the bridge designated to the Airborne Troops. Apologizing profusely he was forced to let the glider go and turned for home. As he brought the Dakota, 'The Pie-Eyed Piper of Barnes,' into land he realised flak had caused the loss of all hydraulic fluid, but with the aid of his Second Pilot, 'Tiger' Hunter, DFC, he managed a successful landing."[6]

On September 21, 1944, Jimmy Edwards took part in the unsuccessful "Operation Market Garden," intended to enable allied soldiers to advance deep into Germany across the Rhine, with ground troops consolidating near Arnhem. It was considered the greatest airborne operation of World War Two, and has been the subject of two films, *Theirs Is the Glory* (1946) and *A Bridge Too Far* (1977). Disaster struck on Jimmy's fourth mission to Arnhem in as many days as the following official commendation records:

"On 21 September Flight Lieutenant Edwards was detailed for a re-supply mission over the Arnhem area. This he carried out successfully in spite of considerable opposition from the ground. After making the drop he climbed rapidly to 7,000 feet and was on his reciprocal course for base when he saw fighters on his port side. Before he could identify them he was attacked from the rear and strikes were obtained on the fuselage and wings. He also saw flak bursting in front of him which may have been fired from the ground. He took suitable evasive action and was then attacked again from the port side. Taking violent evasive action he was able to avoid the cannon fire from the attack and made for the cloud cover. The clouds unfortunately were broken and too far apart. When in the open again he was then attacked from beneath the astern and more strikes were obtained. Three or four attacks were made in rapid succession, hits being obtained in each case in spite of the violent evasive action directed by the Wireless Operator from the Astro Dome.

"Flight Lieutenant Edwards now found the elevator trims unserviceable and he lost aileron [controlling lateral balance] control; his height was 6,000 feet and he gave the orders to bale out. The Co-Pilot and Navigator jumped out, but three of the Despatchers were wounded. The Wireless Operator and the fourth Despatcher remained in the aircraft to help them. At the time both engines had caught fire and both airscrews went into the fully fine [sic] and lost power.

"Flight Lieutenant Edwards put the aircraft into a dive to maintain speed and levelled off at 100 feet and gave the order 'stand-by for crash landing.' He opened the escape hatch above his head which caused the flames which had now got a good hold in and outside the fuselage to come forward to the First Pilot's position. The heat was so intense that Flight Lieutenant Edwards had to get his head and shoulders out of the escape hatch and succeeded in crash-diving the Dakota with one hand on the controls, after which it immediately went up in flames.

"Flight Lieutenant Edwards who was burnt on the face and arm then led the Wireless Operator who was unhurt, and the Despatcher who suffered from flesh wounds, to cover of some small trees as the enemy aircraft was circling and did in fact attack them again whilst they were hiding. He then led the party in a southerly direction where they made a successful evasion with the help of some civilians and language cards.

"There is no doubt that Flight Lieutenant Edwards stuck to his controls under almost unbelievably difficult conditions, although he could have bailed out, because he knew well that he had three wounded Despatchers and two of his crew still aboard the aircraft."[7]

"I couldn't believe it was happening to me," Edwards reminisced decades later. "I was the station's entertainment officer and I had a show to do that night."[8]

The comedian, who had been reported missing for some eight days, recounts the event in his autobiography with typical modesty and good humor, noting that when he was assumed to have been killed, "there was considerable gloom in Barnes and I understand that drinking was suspended for a minute or so in the 'Market Gardener' [pub], while they bemoaned my passage."[9]

Equally lightly, he writes of his recovery over a three-month period in the burns unit at the R.A.F Hospital, Ely.[10] It is often reported that Jimmy was a member of the Guinea Pig Club, whose membership consisted of those who had undergone experimental reconstructive plastic surgery during World War Two. But this is not correct in that the Guinea Pig Club's membership was limited to those who were patients of Wing Commander Archibald McIndoe, fondly called "The Butcher," at Queen Victoria Hospital, East Grinstead. McIndoe dismissed the comedian's facial injuries — "They didn't even get your eyelashes"[11] — and no plastic surgery was necessary. In that the Guinea Pig's Club was primarily a drinking club, I am sure Jimmy would have been delighted to join.[12]

Jimmy Edwards returned to Down Ampney, still a member of the squadron, but grounded until further notice — in fact for the last few months of the war in Europe his flying duties were limited to ferrying passengers and freight around Britain and to the Continent. On February 2, 1945, the *London Gazette* reported that James Keith O'Neill Edwards had been awarded the Distinguished Flying Cross (DFC). It was reportedly sewn on his uniform next to the King George V Jubilee Medal, received in 1935 when he was a chorister at St. Paul's Cathedral.

On May 11, 1989, Jimmy Edwards Distinguished Flying Cross was sold, along with his George V Jubilee Medal, by the London auction house of Spink & Son, with the proceeds going to the St. Paul's Cathedral Choir School Jubilee Bursary Fund.

While grounded, he took on a new title, Entertainments Officer. It was not the first time he had been placed in charge of entertainment rather than merely providing it, but certainly his most important appointment in that area. The ever-resourceful Edwards had not forgotten to bring along his trombone when he enlisted, and it certainly came in handy; early in his RAF service, he had been posted to Babbacombe in Devon and as an extra-curricular activity entered a talent contest, performing his trombone act, at the local concert hall. The audience was sparse, he reported, and he was far from happy when he came in second with a crooner declared the winner. Not an auspicious started to his part-time career as an entertainer in the R.A.F. In Canada, one of Jimmy's first reported performances was at Kingston, Ontario, where he appeared at a concert party wearing oversize trousers, bicycle clips, spats, and a pince-nez, given to him by a local resident. At this point, his act with the trombone was becoming somewhat more refined, although "refined" is perhaps not the best word to use for a routine which had his filling the instrument with water prior to going on stage and then at the first blow, allowing the water to cascade out. As Jimmy noted he looked the perfect seedy professor and so he billed himself as Professor Jimmy. "I used the same suit when I started at the Windmill after the war," he wrote, "and still have it, though I have given it up in favour of less comical attire."[13]

At Mount Hope, Canada, Jimmy took on the title of station entertainment officer, and with help from brother Alan,[14] who was also stationed there, produced a camp show called *RAFter Raisers*. Edwards did his trombone act and appeared in the finale, singing a patriotic song written by him and Alan:

> " *'England our Island Home'*
> *Is a song that all bands have been playing,*
> *'There'll Always Be an England'*
> *Are words that go without saying.*
> *So let's sing a song that is more apropos,*
> *The Old Country still as our theme,*
> *Our unanimous feelings will be easy to show*
> *With a song that is right on the beam.*
> *Roll on that boat*
> *'Cross the Atlantic's raging foam,*
> *Back to where sweethearts are yearning,*
> *For our returning*
> *To Home Sweet Home.*
> *Give us the blackout and English beer,*
> *Let's get afloat;*
> *Though it's five Woodbines[15] a day*
> *And English rates of pay —*
> *Roll on that chugging boat!"*

Also, in Mount Hope, in 1942, the two brothers founded a magazine, *The Mount Hope Meteor*, first edited by Jimmy and then by Alan.

Later, in Moncton, New Brunswick, he co-wrote the lyrics and book for an operetta titled *The Transit Officers' Mess*, about officers awaiting repatriation. It was his final engagement as an entertainer in Canada.

For three months, Edwards served as Entertainments Officer at Down Ampney; "I applied myself vigorously to my new job and the careful re-cultivation of my moustache"[16] (which had been shaved off while he was in hospital). At a party on base celebrating the end of the War, Edwards met Miranda Dulley, the sister of one of the other officers there. She worked for the BBC North American Service, and when Jimmy learned that sometimes she was in need of material, he wrote a script about Arnhem, titled *Treble-4 — the Glider Tug*, which the couple

Flight Lieutenant Alan Edwards.

recorded at the BBC's Oxford Street studios, and which was broadcast initially in Canada and later on the BBC Home Service. It was Jimmy's first contact with the organization. It led to his hosting a quiz show, using the name of Michael O'Neill, which was broadcast directly to Canada.

The comedian was still in the air force, but on January 1, 1946, he went for a routine physical examination, which involved his being interviewed by a psychiatrist. He answered the latter's question in routine Jimmy Edwards fashion and was grounded. Three weeks later, he left the R.A.F. and returned to civilian life. His service during World War Two obviously remained strong and affectionate in his memory. He devotes many pages to it in his first autobiography, *Take It from Me*. And in 1982, he published a second volume of autobiography devoted exclusively to the war years and titled *Six of the Best: The Spirited War Memoirs of Ex-Flight Lieutenant Edwards, J. 123886, D.F.C.* (Jimmy was paid a 5,000 pound advance, but at the time of his death he had several hundred copies of the book that he had acquired sitting in storage.)

What Jimmy Edwards does not mention in that second volume of his autobiography is perhaps the most poignant aspect of his life with the R.A.F. He had fallen in love with a fellow serviceman, of much the same breeding and type as Jimmy, and the relationship meant a great deal to both men. It was broken up by a superior officer who recognized the situation and could not allow an obvious homosexual affair to flourish. The two men were posted to different airfields and, eventually, Jimmy's love became a victim of the war. To a few friends and family members, he identified this as the greatest love of his life, and soon after his marriage confessed it to bride Valerie. The name of Jimmy's lover is unknown and a sketch that he had once made of the man is now lost.

Jimmy was always willing and available to help R.A.F.-related charitable causes. For example, in February 1960, he was top of the bill at a Show Business Tribute in aid of the Royal Air Force Benevolent Fund at London's Victoria Palace; he played the trombone and conducted the Central Band of the Royal Air Force, the highlight of a show that also included appearances by Vera Lynn, Bruce Forsyth, Dickie Henderson, and popular Trinidad-born pianist Winifred Atwell.

Jimmy was back at the Victoria Palace on March 31, 1963, conducting the Morris Motors Band, the Luton Band and the Hanwell Band in a Massed Brass Bands Concert, which ended with a performance of the 1812 Overture by Tchaikovsky.

1. Jimmy Edwards, *Six of the Best*, p. 7.

2. Ibid, p. 16.

3. One assumes that when Jerry Lewis flies in to Blackpool in the brilliant and much under-rated 1995 film *Funny Bones*, he lands at Squires Gate.

4. Jimmy Edwards, *Take It from Me*, p. 110.

5. Ibid, p. 115.

6. Hugh A. Halliday, "Arnhem and 'Jimmy' Edwards."

7. Royal Air Force Commands archive.

8. Appearance on unidentified television documentary.

9. Jimmy Edwards, *Take It from Me*, p. 135.

10. Opened in 1940, the facility was renamed the Princess of Wales Hospital (in honor of Princess Diana) in 1987. It was closed by the R.A.F. in 1992, but continues today as a National Health Service hospital.

11. Jimmy Edwards, *Six of the Best*, p. 197.

12. In his autobiography he does write of a fellow patient, Warrant-Officer "Dicky" Richardson, on whom McIndoe operated.

13. Jimmy Edwards, *Take It from Me*, p. 88.

14. Alan was an accomplished musician, proficient on the violin, double bass, horn, trumpet, trombone, tuba, and other wind instruments.

15. A well-known brand of English cigarettes particularly popular with the working classes.

16. Jimmy Edwards, *Take It from Me*, p. 138.

CHAPTER THREE

The Windmill
and the Road to Fame

In search of a professional career as a comedian, Jimmy decided to bill himself as "Professor Jimmy Edwards" for practical purposes, in that there was another comedian in Britain in the mid-1940s also with the name of Jimmy Edwards.[1] One finds an occasional reference to the "other" Jimmy Edwards in the late 1930s, and it seems pretty obvious that a Jimmy Edwards appearing in a Hastings Mann review titled *Foolish Things* at the Grand Theatre, Brighton, in September 1945 is not our Jimmy Edwards.

Most servicemen leaving the military after World War Two with hopes of entering the professional world of entertainment made an appointment with Phyllis Rounce of recently-formed International Artistes Agency. She would book them into the Nuffield Centre, a recreational institution for servicemen, which sponsored two variety shows a week. Originally situated on Wardour Street, adjacent to the Café de Paris on Regent Street, it was forced to move to a new home off the Strand when the Café de Paris was bombed. According to a news items in *The Stage*, Jimmy, Vera Lynn and Ted Ray "once appeared on the same bill" at the Nuffield Centre.[2] However, Jimmy makes no reference to this in later years, although at the time he noted in his diary that "The troops love it." He would seem to have taken a different route to a professional career in entertainment, helped along the way by a number of individuals with different claims to fame in their own right.

As he recalled while still in the R.A.F.,

"A concert party was planned for Christmas, 1945, by the station personnel at Hendon, and I was asked to do my trombone act. I came on in my usual tail coat and baggy trousers nipped in at the ankle with bicycle clips, carrying a large trombone case. When I opened the case and took out a tin whistle, the audience roared with laughter. In fact, the whole act went down very well; but then, it always had done with service audiences."[3]

After the show, Jimmy was introduced to Alan Dent, who was at that time drama critic for the *News Chronicle* and was long associated with legendary British critic James Agate. Dent praised the act and also reviewed it favorably in next day's newspaper. Later, Jimmy and Dent met up in a London pub, and while Dent was unwilling to advocate the comedian's becoming a professional, he did confirm that he liked the act.

In that James Agate was quite a notorious homosexual male — "Complacent Guardsmen went on trooping in and out" of his flat, as his biographer noted[4] — and Alan Dent remained unmarried, one assumes a common sexuality. To those who would proclaim it irrelevant, I would point out that a surprising number of gay men appear in the Jimmy Edwards story, all helping him on the road to success.

Sid Field.

Around the same time, Jimmy had taken to visiting the Prince of Wales Theatre on a regular basis to watch the act of a comedian whom he greatly admired, Sid Field (1904-1950), in a revue titled *Strike It Again*. While little remembered in his native land, and basically unknown in the United States, Sid Field was a brilliant comedian, who would generally adopt an effeminate guise, playing a photographer or a golfer, with Jerry Desmonde as his stooge. Both sketches are preserved on film in the 1945 British Technicolor extravaganza *London Town*, released in the U.S. in truncated form some eight years later as *My Heart Goes Crazy*. There is one brilliant moment in the golf sketch, which must be seen to be truly appreciated, when Field is told by Desmonde to "get behind the ball." Field walks around the ball, muttering the instructions while remaining completely confused.

Sid Field would have a drink in the theatre bar when not on stage, and here Jimmy met him for the first time, the two men got along, and the former took to meeting his idol at a local pub, "The Railway Hotel," close to where they both lived in Barnes. Jimmy was introduced to Field's agent, Len Barry. Jimmy told Barry that he was about to appear at the Stage Door Canteen in Piccadilly (next door to Simpson's, now Waterstone's Bookstore), which was operated on similar lines to the famous New York Stage Door Canteen by the NAAFI (Navy, Army and Air Force Institutes), with celebrities dropping by nightly. Len Barry sent a colleague, Jack Adams, to see Jimmy's performance, and arranged for an audition at the Windmill Theatre in front of Vivian Van Damm (1889-1960), who perhaps unfortunately went by the initials, "VD".

The legendary Windmill Theatre on Great Windmill Street, where once had actually stood a windmill, had first opened in 1909 as a cinema, the Palais De Luxe, and was acquired in 1931 by Mrs. Laura Henderson, who operated it initially as a legitimate theatre. However, it was really too small to turn a profit and so she converted it to a motion picture theatre. In 1932, Mrs. Henderson hired Vivian Van Damm as manager, and he introduced revue-type entertainment, under the general title of "Revudeville," which ran, non-stop, from early afternoon through late at night, six shows a day and six nights a week. It was Van Damm who conceived the notion of having nudes, "The Windmill Girls," as a prominent part of the show. He was able to persuade the Lord Chamberlain, who censored all theatre entertainment in London, that if the girls stood still, did not move, then their nudity was no different to the nudity to be seen in London's art galleries in the form of statues and paintings.

In between the nude presentations or tableaux vivants were typical vaudeville acts, primarily comedians, who had a difficult time getting a response from an audience that was predominantly male and was primarily there to ogle the girls. It was said that at the end of each show, there was a mad rush, with men clambering over the backs of seats, to grab the best accommodation in the front rows. Jimmy, who christened the ritual as "The Grand National," would joke, "Really, these people down here are so close that I can almost spit on them — frequently do!" Or "Last week I fell over the footlights and killed six people. Why some of them are still here!"

Audience enthusiasm for the comedians was non-existent, but as Barry Cryer, who appeared there in 1957, points out, "They never heckled; the mood was not hostile, but one of patient silence. What a school. After that, whatever the circumstances, you weren't afraid of any audience, ever again."[5]

The Windmill Theatre was proud of the claim that it never closed, remaining open throughout the war years except for twelve days in September 1939 when the government closed all places of entertainment after the start of World War Two.

Mrs. Henderson died in November 1944 at the age of eighty-two, and left the theatre to Van Damm. He continued to operate it with the same

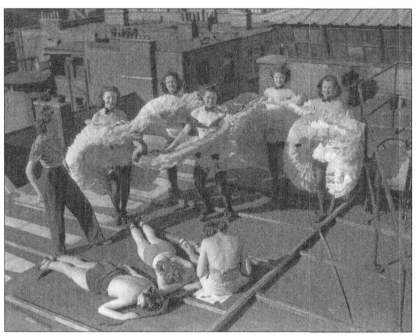

The Windmill Girls rehearsing and relaxing on the roof of the theatre.

programming, and when he died in December 1960, his daughter, Sheila Van Damm, a rally car driver, continued the tradition. It was not until October 31, 1964, when changing times forced the Windmill to close its doors. The building survives to the present.

The Windmill story has been the subject of a surprising number of films and shows, most notably *Tonight and Every Night* (1944), a Hollywood Technicolor production starring Rita Hayworth, which renames the theatre and makes no reference to nudity; *Murder at the Windmill* (1949); *Secrets of a Windmill Girl* (1966), and *Mrs. Henderson Presents* (2005). The last was adapted into a delightful 2015 musical of the same name, infinitely superior to the film, and reminiscent of the best of an old-fashioned production but with the added attraction of nudity (both female and male).

Inadvertently, the Windmill Theatre gained a reputation in later years as a training ground for some of Britain's best comedians, including Michael Bentine, Tommy Cooper, Dick Emery, Arthur English, Bruce Forsyth, Tony Hancock, Alfred Marks, Richard Murdoch, Harry Secombe, Peter Sellers — and, of course, Jimmy Edwards. Two of the Windmill Girls, Jean Kent (using the name Jean Carr)[6] and Charmian Innes, also gained

Jimmy Edwards in the 1940s.

some fame after leaving there. Vivan Van Damm's proud claim was that he had never booked a "star" name, and that, as of 1950, he had discovered thirty recognized stage, screen and radio personalities.

Vivian Van Damm, who assured Edwards that "I'm very easily entertained," gave the comedian an initial six-week contract, at twenty pounds a week, after an audition, which Jimmy claimed was the last he ever had. Some years later, Van Damm recalled,

"Jim has a perfect sense of timing. His stardom is no accident but partly the result of a painstaking precision. It is also due to his voice, and quite apart from his humor, it was his vocal delivery that first captivated me."[7]

In the intervening weeks between signing with Van Damm and his actually appearing on stage at the Windmill, Jimmy made a brief, unsuccessful appearance at the Croydon Empire. While appearing at the Windmill, he was given a six-week vacation by Van Damm, and used it to participate in a small music hall tour — Blackpool (one night), Glasgow, Birmingham, the Finsbury Park Empire (London), and Sheffield, with Geraldo and His Orchestra.

Jimmy Edwards made his debut at the Windmill on May 20, 1946. In Revudeville 194, as it was identified, he shared the bill with another ex-military man, singing guitarist Reg O'List, who had spent five years in the army. Jimmy considered his debut at the Windmill as similar to the practice of being "bloodied" after witnessing one's first kill in fox hunting.

After the Windmill, trying to make the audience laugh, he proudly proclaimed that nothing could scare him as a performer.

According to Frank Muir and others, Jimmy appeared on stage wearing gold pince-nez spectacles, a morning coat with a winged collar, and crumpled "sponge-bag" trousers. He carried a beer crate and a large euphonium case. He sat on the beer crate, and proceeded to open the euphonium case which contained a penny whistle, upon which he played. Announcing "Encore," he inserted the whistle into his nostril, and played the same tune. Finally, he placed the whistle in a top pocket of the morning suit, and explained to the audience that the second encore had been banned.

Shortly after that first appearance a reviewer from the trade paper *The Stage* (August 1, 1946) saw his act, presumably changed since the May appearance, and wrote, "Jimmy Edwards demonstrates in Revudeville 196…that his first appearance here was not a flash in the pan, but that he is a comedian to be reckoned with. He first appears as a lecturer, complete with lantern slides (but not too reminiscent of the late John Tilley), and secondly in a sketch, 'In the Bar,' in both of which his unique sense of humour is given full play. Another scene, an epic, is the 'To Be or Not to Be' sketch with Eric Woodburn[8] as Shakespeare and Stanley West as Anne Hathaway."

The Stage (July 17, 1947) was back at the Windmill a year later, and reported that Jimmy's "inconsequent patter has wit and ingenuity to enliven it." Eric Woodburn and Stanley West were still on the bill, but apparently not appearing in a sketch with Jimmy.

Show business journalist Dick Richards also saw Jimmy at the Windmill on what he described as a dismal Monday morning in May 1946:

"It was just before lunch. It was drizzling. And it was lonely in the Windmill Theatre whence I had been abducted by an exuberant press-agent to see the first professional appearance of a new comedian.

"A handlebar moustache, a red face, a portly body and a huge pair of hands clutching a trombone lumbered on to the stage supported by a nervous grin.

"A bit of patter, a few toots on the trombone and it was all over. Jim Edwards might just as well have 'gone back to the tenements' for all the impact he made on the handful of men who were waiting apathetically to see the girls.

"And yet one could sense that there was *something*…"[9]

The press representative at the Windmill, Kenneth H. Bandy, prepared a release documenting Jimmy's life to date, and sent it to the BBC in

July 1946, shortly before the comedian's return to the Windmill stage in Revudeville No. 196, commencing on July 29, 1946, which suggests the theatre had no objection to its contract comedians working elsewhere with appropriate credit to the Windmill. Certainly, concurrent with his time at the Windmill, Jimmy began to be heard of the BBC's Light Programme.

Carroll Levis (1910-1968) was a Canadian-born presenter of new talent initially on radio (beginning on Radio Luxembourg in the 1930s) and later television. Completely forgotten today, Levis was a highly popular and familiar figure on the BBC, with his blonde hair and somewhat plump features. Jimmy was featured on four episodes of *The Carroll Levis Show*, on August 4, September 29, December 25 (a special Christmas edition), 1946, and April 13, 1947. Later, he would be heard on *Variety Band Box* on November 3, 1946, and earlier he had been on a Summer Show from Butlin's Holiday Camp, Clacton-on-Sea, introduced by John Ellison as Professor Jimmy Edwards, on July 24, 1946.[10]

On all these programs — and there were others, including *Accordion Club* and *Stump the Storyteller* — Jimmy performed his musical lecture/ trombone routine, with a full orchestra. The scripts were written by Frank Muir, who would sometimes act as an on-microphone verbal stooge.

The performers and crew from the Windmill would gather for pre- and after-performance drinks at the Red Lion Pub, located at 20 Great Windmill Street and the corner of Archer Street. First licensed as a pub in 1718, it has a place in history thanks to Karl Marx, who walked over from his lodgings on Dean Street to introduce the Communist Manifesto in a room above the pub in 1847. Equally, it has a place in history for its connection to the Windmill Theatre, with the autographed photographs of patrons, such as Jimmy, Bruce Forsyth and Ted Ray, hanging on the pub walls. While the building remains, the Red Lion Pub closed in 2007.

If nothing else, his time at the Windmill Theatre taught Jimmy how to ad-lib, and to do it well. In 1954, he explained, "The way to fame in this business is to get together an act — make quite sure the material is right — and have the stamina to maintain it through thick and thin. Keep it fresh and real, especially the ad-libbings and make sparks out of what appears to be spontaneity. Prepared or premeditated spontaneity is most difficult to repeat deliberately — but it's an accomplishment worth acquiring."[11]

Jimmy's ability to ad-lib became apparent as early as September 14, 1950, when immediately after the interval in *Take It from Here* at the Winter Gardens Theatre, Blackpool, the curtain refused to ascend. Edwards entered the stage via the orchestra pit, and with the use of a ladder, ready to begin his twenty-minute routine. With no rising curtain and no show imminent, he continued for a full forty minutes, spending the time borrowing instruments from members of the orchestra and playing pieces on them. When the curtain started slowly to rise, Jimmy pretended to be lifting it, only to have it stick again. He asked the orchestra to accompany him in the post-horn gallop, and, much to his surprise, on the last note, the curtain went up.

Jimmy Edwards remained a year-and-a-half at the Windmill, and would often become moody and frustrated as to whether his career would lead anywhere. At one point, he considered immigrating to Canada. Another time, he thought he might re-join the R.A.F. In an effort to advance his career, or perhaps it is a joke, Jimmy took out a paid advertisement in the *Biggleswade Chronicle and Bedfordshire Gazette* of September 20, 1946:

> "Definitely Different"
> Broadcasting & Recording Soloist
> JIMMY EDWARDS
> ....and his MUSIC
> Available for Dances, Hunt Balls,
> House Parties, etc. Write for full
> particulars —
> 31B Nevern Place, London S.W.4
> Telephone FROBISHER 6271

Ultimately, it was not Jimmy but Van Damm who ended the Windmill association. He introduced a rule that all performers were to sign a book at the stage door thirty minutes before the first show. Jimmy thought this offensive and refused to sign, pointing out that he had never missed a performance. Van Damm was adamant. Jimmy must sign the book and as he would not, he was out as of Saturday.

In November 1948, Jimmy was appearing at the Croydon Empire, a theatre he despised because of audience indifference to his act, on a bill topped by organist Reginald Dixon. According to *The Stage* (November 11, 1948), the comedian "delivers an inconsequential lecture in droll style, and plays the tin whistle and the trombone with his customary urbanity." In February 1949, Jimmy appeared at the Apollo Ballroom, Manchester, with singer and comedienne Betty Driver, a talented individual with more than a passing resemblance to Gracie Fields, and who was to become loved in later years for her appearance on the Granada Television soap opera, *Coronation Street*. Later that year, Jimmy was at the Empire Theatre,

Leeds, and *The Stage* (August 4, 1949) wrote that he "keeps everybody in the best of moods." At the Town Hall, Gloucester, on December 29, 1949, he was topping the bill, along with Sam Costa (from the radio show *Much Binding in the March*), and the local newspaper, the *Gloucestershire Echo* (December 30, 1949) reported that "Three times he encored, and applause for his act thundered on for several minutes."

But all this was icing on the cake. The years at the Windmill Theatre had paid off well for Jimmy Edwards, and he was now embarked on a new career in radio that was to guarantee if not lasting fame, at least a modicum of fame and success for the rest of his life.

That payoff was equally obvious in a gradual rise in salary. At the Windmill, he had been paid a paltry thirteen shillings and eleven pence per performance, with a total of thirty-six performances a week. At the BBC, in 1947, he earned thirty-one pounds per episode for *The Handlebar*, and twenty-one pounds for an appearance on *Accordion Club*, a series on the BBC's Light Programme, hosted by Roy Plomley. When he began appearing on *Take It from Here*, Jimmy was paid twenty-six pounds and five shillings a show, rising in 1950 to fifty-two pounds per program.

1. [Terry] *Wogan's Radio Fun*, December 28, 1987.

2. *The Stage*, October 27, 1953, p. 3.

3. Jimmy Edwards, *Take It from Me*, p. 143.

4. James Harding, *Agate*, p. 204.

5. Barry Cryer, *The Chronicles of Hernia*, p. 14.

6. Jean Kent (1921-2013) appeared on stage at the Windmill as a showgirl from 1935-1938, wearing a pair of knickers on which was embroidered a telephone number. Around the same time, Jean Kent auditioned to be the new Betty in the act, Wilson, Keppel and Betty, but did not get the part. She first used the name of Jean Kent in the 1942 film version of *It's That Man Again*.

7. Vivian Van Damm, *Tonight and Every Night*, p. 154.

8. Eric Woodburn (1894-1981) was generally on screen and television from the 1950s onwards in minor Scottish characterizations.

9. Dick Richards, "A Whack-O Bang-On Type," p. 13.

10. Butlin's Holiday Camps were a British institution, conceived by Billy Butlin as all-inclusive holiday camps primarily for the working class, and popular from the mid-1930s through the 1960s. With the advent of cheap holidays abroad, the camps went out of fashion. The snob in Jimmy Edwards must have hated having to appear in such an ambiance.

11. James Hartley, "Blackpool's Bright Brigade," p. 5.

CHAPTER FOUR

The Handlebar Club

There are surprisingly few British comedians with specific physical characteristics present in their acts. They rely on facial expressions, body language and general demeanor to create a specific character, as evidenced, say, by Lenny Henry, Tommy Cooper or Tony Hancock. Obvious exceptions are such classic British comedians of the second half of the 20th Century, such as Ronnie Barker and Ronnie Corbett ("The Two Ronnies") or Benny Hill who utilize costumes and make-up to create sketch characters. While is it a blustering disposition with which Jimmy Edwards is closely identified, the large handlebar moustache, with its impressive bushiness, length and upwardly curved extremities is very much a part of the man if not necessarily a part of the act. It was often claimed that he sported the most famous "tash" in 20th Century show business, with its closest rival being that possessed by British comedian Harry Tate from a much earlier era, who used his moustache to emphasize a point, and who may perhaps have been influential in W.C. Fields' characterizations. Indeed, as Jimmy got older, the moustache and the sideburns became as one, obscuring much of his lower face. Jimmy knew how to twirl that moustache with a devilish look at an attractive female stooge. There are even those, including a female writer for the long-forgotten British tabloid, *Tit Bits* (May 8, 1954), who perceived a magnetism in Jimmy Edwards' moustache equal to that grown by romantic Hollywood leading man William Powell.

The moustache was a source of comedy on *Take It from Here*, with Joy Nichols discussing the beauty of a window filled with flowers, and then remarking to her co-star: "It must be lovely to lean out of the window and have a mass of sweet smelling foliage growing right under your nose, Jimmy." As the moustache grew longer, Edwards would twirl up the ends using Pomade Hongroise, which would wax up the tips creating an elegant or villainous look, depending upon one's point of view.

While the handlebar moustache is obviously Jimmy's trademark, it might also be argued that he had a second trademark. Not a physical characteristic, but rather an abbreviation of his name. Except for appearances in legitimate plays, always Jimmy Edwards played a character named "Jim" or "Jimmy."

In his autobiography, Jimmy notes that when he was promoted to Flight-Lieutenant during World War Two and at the age of twenty-four, he "had a whacking great moustache."[1] He had first attempted to grow one in 1938 while teaching at the choir school attached to St. John's College, Cambridge, but the unprepossessing effort was such that it induced laughter from his pupils. For the next few years, the moustache came and went at regular intervals. In 1966, Edwards shaved off the moustache for his appearance as John Jorrocks in the BBC adaptation of R.S. Surtee's *Mr. John Jorrocks*. "A ghastly experience," he proclaimed.[2] It is claimed that the comedian grew the moustache to hide scars from plastic surgery following his 1944 air crash in Arnhem, but, in fact, he had the moustache prior to that incident and indeed it had to be shaved off for the surgery.

He had planned to shave off the moustache once he left the Air Force, but was persuaded by Vivian Van Damm at the Windmill Theatre to retain it. "It's the only funny thing in the act!"[3] The moustache stayed, but was not always as fulsome as it was later in Jimmy's career; he was frequently photographed with it carefully trimmed.

In a 1958 interview, Jimmy explained that he was currently sporting the fourth edition of his moustache. The first he had shaved off as an experiment, "took one dekko, and swiftly grew it again." The second he was required to shave off just before D-Day when he was a pilot in the Transport Command. The third was burnt off "in the nastiest fashion" as a result of the plane crash in Arnhem.[4]

Once he had become a star, instantly recognizable on the street, Jimmy considered that shaving off the moustache might allow him anonymity. Edwin Apps recalls meeting with Jimmy at the BBC Television Centre, and was surprised when Jimmy asked him if he noticed anything different — he had shaved off his moustache.[5]

While he was appearing at the Windmill Theatre, Jimmy's moustache (supposedly at this time measuring nine inches from tip to tip) was the impetus for the founding of the Handlebar Club, membership of which is limited to those with "a hirsute appendage of the upper lip and with graspable extremities." Those with beards need not apply. Size was irrelevant with members praised for the texture, shape and color of their moustaches. The club was founded on April 1, 1947 (coincidentally

April Fool's Day) in Jimmy's dressing room by a group of ten appropriately hirsute individuals, including Jimmy, the BBC sports commentator Raymond Glendenning, whose coverage of the F.A. Cup Final on radio from 1946-1963 was legendary, and writer Frank Muir.[6] Glendenning was the first president, with Jimmy Edwards taking on the responsibility of vice-president. Accompanying the men, and outnumbering them, was a group of Windmill chorus girls. Surprisingly, neither Jimmy Edwards nor Frank Muir considered the Handlebar Club worthy of mention in their autobiographies, although in May 1947, the former considered the Club sufficiently important for him to establish branches in the provinces while on a tour with Geraldo and His Orchestra. It was also the subject of a segment on the radio program, "London Column," broadcast by the BBC to North America.

Jimmy Edwards twirls his trademark moustache.

The first, inaugural meeting took place on April 20, 1947, at the Windmill Theatre, a location which must have had some appeal to potential members, all of whom were directed to the theatre's stage door for admission.

Ironically, another comedian appearing at the Windmill Theatre at this time was Harry Secombe, whose act consisted in part of his demonstrating how different men approached the labor of shaving in different ways. "The act involved a razor and lots of lather," reported Frank Muir.[7] As BBC producer Cecil Madden recalled, "Harry Secombe was doing an act he called *Shaving*. He used to shave in public five times a day using a cut throat razor and real soap and probably destroying his skin at the same time."[8]

A report exists on the founding of the Club, which is worth reprinting in some detail as it serves as a record of the type of pompous erudition on which the comedian himself thrived:

"About a year ago Windmill comedian Jimmy Edwards became sadly aware of the 'dropping off' of large moustaches as worn by members of H.M. Forces during the war.

"Himself the proud possessor of a fine Pilose [soft, furry hair] append-age, he gradually formed an idea to promote the growth of moustaches by forming a fraternity of wearers and, as soon as he was ready to launch the scheme as a club, he was featured in the [London] *Evening News* with suitable description of his aim. Several setose [bristly] sympathizers wrote to him approving and offering to lend their hirsutage to the venture and function as Founder Members. A nucleus for the Club was thereby formed with some really beauteous shoots.

"At precisely the same time at which Jimmy Edwards was mulling over the possibilities of starting his idea, Cartoonist-Author Bill Hooper, the pictorial creator of 'P.O. Percy Prune,'[9] was exuded from the ranks of the R.A.F. with a gratuity, a suit of 'civvies' and a large moustache. He spent the first, part-wore the second and so was caused to cash in on the third. To this end he began a research into the evolution of the moustache and the history of hirsutage which resulted in a manuscript which described 'The Dawn of "Down"', 'Down through the Ages,' and an outline of Primordial Pilosity. These were included in a list of Hints to Expectant Moustaches, the advantages of wearing a large moustache and a chapter which touched lightly on 'Pest of the Pile.' Later Bill Hooper televised these in a series of lectures and invited Jerry Colonna, radio and screen star of Bob Hope's programme, to become New World Advocate and American President of the club he was about to form under the auspices of the Ancient Society of Pilositors and Guild of Hirsuters. Jerry Colonna was willing to 'play' and so the club was almost launched. When Jimmy Edwards and Bill Hooper became aware that they had got their wires, or anyway their whiskers crossed, they met and amalgamated."[10]

"Our meetings are held in a hostelry somewhere near the centre of London and take place once a month…At these meetings [held on the first Friday of the month] a small amount of business, and a slightly larger amount of malt liquor, are discussed," reads a document detailing the responsibilities of membership. However, on a more serious level, from its inception the Club sought to aid charitable causes, particularly those devoted to ex-servicemen and children. The Club has also been involved in defending those "persecuted" for the growing of a handlebar mous-tache, most notably an Indian airline steward fired in 2008 for refusing the shave his off.

The founding of the Handlebar Club almost coincided with the broad-cast of a three-part BBC sitcom, set in pub titled the Handle Bar Inn. *The Handle Bar* aired in October and November 1947, and starred Jimmy Edwards, Humphrey Lestocq and Richard Hearne, best known for his characterization of Mr. Pastry, an irritating creation always involved in infantile slapstick. The third and final episode of the series was written

Jimmy Edwards and the members of the Handlebar Club.

by Ted Willis, who was to go on and create the immensely popular BBC series, *Dixon of Dock Green*.

Cricket was the sport of choice among members. Five members of the Club, led by Raymond Glendenning, but excluding Edwards, played in a cricket match in Brighton in June 1949 to celebrate the opening of the Royal Air Force Association's Flying Services Club there. In September 1953, Jimmy Edwards captained the Handlebar Club in a match against Sheffield Park Cricket Club, held at Fletching in East Sussex.

Jimmy was not popular with all members of the Club. One individual, a former ITV cameraman, described him to me as "quite rude and belliger-ent," adding, "He seemed jealous of the size of my moustache." Obviously, penis envy also played a part in the activities of the Handlebar Club.

Initially, as *The Guardian* (September 25, 2004) noted, "In the early years the club served as a last refuge for ex-RAF officers whose extravagant moustaches were shunned by the outside world." Times have changed, but to the members, it is forever 1947. There was a well-publicized 60th anniversary meeting at the White Hart Hotel in Lewes in March 2007, with forty members from the U.K., the Netherlands, Sweden, Belgium, and the United States in attendance, all geared to compete in the World Beard and Moustache Championship that same weekend in nearby Brighton. The Handlebar Club is still active, meeting on the first Friday of each month, from 2006 at the Windsor Castle Pub in the Marylebone district of London, until its closure in 2016. The current president is Rod Littlewood.

1. Jimmy Edwards, *Take It from Me*, p. 115.

2. Jimmy Edwards, *Six of the Best*, p. 203.

3. Ibid, p. 146.

4. Godfrey Winn, "Life Is So Full, and Yet…I feel Very Lonely at Times," p.8.

5. Edwin Apps, *Pursued by Bishops*, p. 287.

6. Other founding members include Alan Edwards, George Hoffman, Baron Christian de Bere, Russ Allen, radio's Flying Officer Kite aka actor Humphrey Lestocq (whose fake moustache gained him honorary membership), Gerald Lanyon, and "Jeep" Ormsby.

7. Frank Muir, *A Kentish Lad*, p. 143.

8. Cecil Madden, *Starlight Days*, p. 257.

9. Private Officer Percy Prune was a wartime cartoon character created by Hooper and Anthony Armstrong.

10. *http://www.handlebarclub.co.uk/1947report1.htm* (accessed December 2016).

CHAPTER FIVE

Take It from Here

Jimmy Edwards gained prominence in British radio history as one of the three stars of *Take It from Here*, first broadcast by the BBC on March 12, 1948, and which was affectionately and in shortened form known as *TIFH* (pronounced "Tife").[1] He had made his radio debut early in 1946 in a program titled *They're In…Because They're Out*, produced by Gordon Crier, and intended to showcase newly-demobbed entertainers. In the presence of George Melachrino and His Orchestra, Jimmy made his one appearance on the program, featuring a trombone solo. At its conclusion, he was moved to realize the men in the orchestra were applauding, with some rapping their bows on their violins. As he left the studio, the producer pointed out at the trombone, and said, "Hang on to that, Edwards… It will earn you a lot of money."[2]

While the comedic content is different, *Take It from Here* has its origins in an earlier BBC series, *Navy Mixture*, "blended to suit the taste of the Royal Navy," and first heard on the General Forces Programme of the BBC on February 4, 1943. There were songs and a comedy routine with ventriloquist Peter Brough and his dummy, Archie Andrews. The content evolved with the years, but the most important changes came with the final series, which was first aired on July 12, 1947, with the introduction of a young Australian singer and comedy actress, Joy Nichols, and "Professor" Jimmy Edwards providing a lecture titled "You May Take Notes." In addition, another Australian, Dick Bentley, would sometimes be heard as a guest comedian. The last episode of *Navy Mixture* was heard on November 22, 1947, and broadcast from the Royal Navy Barracks in Plymouth.

Joy Nichols (1925-1992) had started her entertainment career as a child on Australian radio, and in a somewhat old-fashioned song-and-dance double act with brother, George, and the couple came to Britain in 1946. There was a vague notion that George might also perform on *Take*

It from Here, but he was not particularly suited to radio and he returned to Australia. Initially, Joy Nicholas and Jimmy Edwards did not care too much for each other. As Jimmy wrote, "I had the feeling that the blonde young lady didn't like me, and I certainly didn't think our careers would later be so completely intertwined."[3] By 1949, Joy Nichols was so popular that when she appeared at the London Palladium, she was billed as "The First Lady of Radio."

Dick [Charles Walter] Bentley (1907-1995) was already fairly successful in his native Australia when he first came to England in 1938. He returned to Australia at the start of World War Two, but came back to Britain again in 1946. Frank Muir and Denis Norden wrote two later series for him, *Gently Bentley* for Australian radio in 1951, and the 1954 BBC television series, *And So to Bentley*, in which he co-starred with Peter Sellers. In 1960, Bentley returned to Australia, and was active on screen there, before briefly returning again to the U.K. in 1978 for guest appearances in the BBC television series, *Some Mothers Do 'Ave 'Em.*

Joy Nichols.

The material for Joy Nichols and Jimmy Edwards was written by Frank Muir, while Dick Bentley's contribution was the work of Denis Norden. Thanks to the strong audience response to the final season of *Navy Mixture*, producer Charles Maxwell[4] was able to persuade the BBC to sponsor a new comedy series featuring the three new arrivals at *Navy Mixture.* As Muir and Norden later recalled, Maxwell took them both out for lunch at an expensive Italian restaurant on Jermyn Street, and invited them to put together the new show. Norden worked as a staff writer for comedy scriptwriter agent Ted Kavanagh, while Muir was currently working on a radio series with Vic Oliver, titled *Oliver's Twists.* Because it was closer, the two men adjourned after lunch to Norden's office and decided to work on the new series in the evenings at the latter's flat, which he shared with his wife and baby son; wife Avril also cooked supper for both men.

Frank Muir (1920-1998) and Denis Norden (born 1922) are unquestionably the two most influential figures in Jimmy Edwards' career, although of the two, it was certainly Muir with whom Edwards had a particular affinity.

Jimmy Edwards, Frank Muir and a Great Dane during filming of Innocents of Paris.

Norden began his writing career while serving in the R.A.F. during World War Two; while getting ready for a troop show in 1945, he went with Eric Sykes and Ron Rich to a prison camp in search of some form of equipment suitable for stage lighting, and instead discovered the horror of the Bergen-Belsen Concentration Camp. The partnership with Frank Muir ended in 1964, but Norden continued as a writer and radio and television presenter. He also wrote a number of films, including *Buona Sera, Mrs. Campbell* and *The Bliss of Mrs. Blossom* (both released in 1968).

Frank Muir also served in the R.A.F. during World War Two, working as a photographic technician; he also wrote some plays and scripts with the encouragement of a fellow officer, Arthur Howard (who was later, of course, to be closely associated with Jimmy Edwards). After the war, Muir embarked on a scriptwriting career, although his first work for the BBC was not in that profession but as master of ceremonies for a 1947 television revue, celebrating the twenty-fifth anniversary of the corporation. This led to his being hired as compère of a series titled *New to You*, which introduced Norman Wisdom and Ian Carmichael. Aside from *Take It from Here*, Muir also wrote a one-episode, trial radio show titled *Ghastleigh Manor* for Jimmy Edwards, which was apparently never broadcast. With Denis Norden, he continued to write for Jimmy Edwards in television, and the pair also wrote the Ian Carmichael series, *Brothers-in-Law*. Frank Muir became assistant head of BBC Light Entertainment in the early 1960s, and this led to his being appointed Head of Entertainment at the commercial television network, London Weekend Television in 1969.

Both men were well known to British audiences as broadcasters, working as contestants on radio's *My Word!* (1956-1988) and *My Music* (1967-1994), competing against each other with various invited guests. Additionally, Frank Muir appeared on television's *Call My Bluff* (1965-1988), and hosted *TV Heaven* in 1992 on Channel 4, among other television appearances. Both Denis Norden and Frank Muir took part in episodes of *Take It from Here*, contributing various disguised voices, credited to an "actor" named Herbert Mostyn, which was actually made up from the middle name of each man.

The two men obviously complemented each other very well. In a way, they were somewhat old-fashioned, devoted family men (unlike Jimmy Edwards) and prolific writers, always ready with an idea or a joke, even if some seem rather antiquated in retrospect. They were good at puns and spoofs, and if required, they could lampoon current events, with cutting edge humor, as did Frank Muir later with his script material for David Frost's *That Was the Week That Was*. As Denis Norden recalled,

"Come right down to it, Frank and I could not have been more different in temperament…While he always laughed when the cast were rehearsing a script we had written, genuinely enjoying hearing our words, I was known as 'The Miserable One,' sitting there scowling and worrying….

"In spite of these differences, we spent so many years sharing an area of our lives that could not be shared with anyone else, we took on the kind of affinities you associate with long-married couples. These included a form of non-verbal communication that enabled us to exchange complex messages without a word being spoken. You have no idea how many pungent remarks I was glanced."[5]

"More than any other script-writing team," wrote one critic, "they caught the mood of the post-war public and they have kept their fingers on the pulse-beat ever since. They hit on a formula which appeals to the masses and attracts the minorities."[6]

Take It from Here was first heard on the BBC's Light Programme[7] at 7:30 P.M. on Tuesday, March 23, 1948, which just happened to be Jimmy Edwards' 28th birthday. The show was to prove a very good, and lasting, present for the comedian. The title song, performed by the close-harmony group, the Keynotes,[8] accompanied by Frank Cantell and the "Augmented" BBC Revue Orchestra,[9] for all the mediocrity of its lyrics, was a welcoming chorus for radio listeners of the 1940s and the 1950s:

> *"Take it from Here!*
> *"Don't go away when you can*
> *"Take it from here,*
> *"Why don't you stay and maybe*
> *"Join in the fun now,*
> *"The Show has begun.*
> *"Half-an-hour of laughter beckons,*
> *"Every minute packed with seconds!"*

As was explained in the BBC weekly program guide, *Radio Times*, "[the] opening scene…will be set, appropriately enough, in a broadcasting studio, and when we meet the company they will be about to go on the air minus script or producer. The location was obviously supposed to be, or at least based on, Radio Luxembourg, a commercial radio station broadcasting to Britain and elsewhere from 1933 onwards.[10]

The BBC soon adopted a well-loved three-part structure for the series, although it was not fully developed in the early shows. "They [Muir and Norden] re-shaped it as it went from programme to programme,"[11] wrote Jimmy Edwards. Two musical spots would feature the Keynotes in one and Joy Nichols, sometimes joined by Dick Bentley, in the other. The first of the three parts consisted of the three stars conversing and telling jokes. The second part was described by Norden and Muir as the "gimmick," a sketch embracing a new idea each week, and finally, in the third segment, there was a spoof of a film or something similar. Each of these spoofs took its title from a play on words; for the first show, it was *The Trial of Madame Z* (as opposed to *The Trial of Madame X*). Other sketches from the first series were titled *Matinée on the Bounty*, *The Wimpoles of Barrett Street*, *Stooge Coach*, *TIFH with Father*, and *The Best Years of Our TIFH*. When *Take It from Here* was broadcast from *HMS Indefatigable* at Spithead on June 15, 1953, it was *The Cruel B.B. Sea*.

The first season of *Take It from Here* did not generate a wide audience, but the BBC was sufficiently pleased to renew the show for a second season, which began airing on December 28, 1948. There were changes. Initially, additional character voices had been provided by Wilfred Babbage. For the second season he was replaced by Clarence Wright, playing the role of Henpecked Harry Hickory, always trying to avoid his

Take It from Here: *Wallas Eaton, Jimmy Edward, Dick Bentley and June Whitfield.*

wife with the catchphrase, "Sh! What? Thought it was her for a minute!" The second show in the new season, airing on January 4, 1949, introduced a second new player to the cast in the person of Wallas Eaton (1919-1975). He was an established stage actor with frequent film appearances, often appearing in the West End while the series aired, and remained with *Take It from Here* through the years. Obviously, contact with his Australian co-stars impacted on Eaton in that he moved to that country in the 1970s, appearing on television soap operas. Wallas Eaton was given to catchphrases relating to Jimmy Edwards. The first was a plea for his return to his supposed roots in London's East End and drop his upper-class accent, "Come 'ome, Jim Edwards!" The other, first heard in the fourth season, which began on October 24, 1950, was a suggestion that he "Take the plunge!" Perhaps the best-known character introduced by Wallas Eaton was "Disgusted of Tunbridge Wells," a stereotypical resident of that Southern, upper-middle class town who would sign off letters to the newspaper with this phrase, introduced with the seventh season, first broadcast on November 12, 1953.

Rather as playwright Joe Orton did in inventing outraged middle-class individuals who would fulminate in what he wrote and propagandized, so would Jimmy Edwards in later years contemplate a character named "Mrs. Maria Smudge," with a column titled, "Society News Revealed."

The most important impact on the second series of *Take It from Here* did not originate with the show or its players, but rather with the demise of the most popular radio show in British history, *It's That Man Again*, with its title abbreviated, as with *Take It from Here*, as *ITMA*. That program entertained listeners throughout World War Two, first being heard in July 1939, and it starred a beloved entertainer, Tommy Handley, whose name is strangely forgotten in Britain today and unknown in the United States. Handley died three days after broadcast of the last *ITMA* show on January 6, 1949. Radio audiences switched their collective affection to *Take It from Here*, and, perhaps more importantly, with the demise of *ITMA*, its repeat slot on Saturday lunch time became free and was given to *Take It from Here*.

The show was recorded in front of a live audience on a Sunday evening, at the BBC-owned Paris Cinema on Lower Regent Street,[12] and was not always broadcast on a regular night or at a regular time during the week. The cast would convene at the studio at 4:00 P.M. to read through the script for the first time. The recording began at 8:00 P.M. with a warm-up by Frank Muir, leading into an introduction of Dick Bentley, who would then introduce the remaining members of the cast. Amazingly, the BBC was actually concerned at the reaction of a live audience, particularly when applause was appropriate. Michael Standing, the BBC's Director of Variety prepared a leaflet on the subject, circulated for the first time at the *Take It from Here* recording on June 12, 1949.

"The leaflet asks audiences to applaud only in the appropriate places.

"In a list of 'don'ts' it cites 'clapping for individual gags or jokes during an act or scene.' This, it says, often spoils the show for listeners.

"Catcalls, whistles and cheers are described as making a horrible noise on the air.

"Laughter is welcomed at any time, and 'we hope for your applause, but in appropriate places only.' "[13]

There was one widely reported censorship issue in regard to *Take It from Here*, and that occurred on January 1, 1951 with a joke about the Coronation Stone or the Stone of Scone. Not the most famous of pieces of British heritage perhaps, but in 1950 it was stolen by a group of Scottish students from under the chair in Westminster Abbey upon which the British monarchs are crowned, and where it had sat since 1296, when taken from Scotland. The students repatriated it, and later the Stone was returned to Westminster Abbey until 1996, when it officially returned to Scotland. The BBC allowed the initial reference to the Stone, a portion of a parody of *The Thing* to be broadcast, but then deleted it from the rebroadcast of the episode. The following week, Wallas Eaton referred to *The Thing* and asked, "Have you heard about that one?" Jimmy replied, "Heard about it? We are still explaining." Unfunny as it might seem today, the remark was greeted with prolonged applause.

"The facts of life are sometimes cruel," wrote Jimmy Edwards, and *ITMA*'s great tragedy proved *Take It from Here*'s greatest gain. Our show caught on and more and more people seemed to be repeating our catch phrases."[14]

Just as *ITMAS*'s catchphrases — most notably "Can I do you now sir?" and "Don't forget the driver" — had moved into the common currency of the language so did those of *Take It from Here*. With *ITMA*, *Take It from Here* was the only radio program known by its initials. "It has taken the place of *ITMA* in the public imagination," wrote one critic.[15] At its peak, Jimmy Edwards and his co-stars drew a radio audience in excess of twenty million.

The success of *Take It from Here* is evidenced by its three stars being installed in waxworks form at Madame Tussauds in April 1950 — Jimmy, Joy Nichols and Dick Bentley were present for the unveiling — and its overwhelming 1949 win as best radio show of the year at the annual National Radio Awards, sponsored by the British newspaper, the *Daily Mail*. The program received the accolade for a second time in 1951. The award consisted of a life-size silver microphone, and the stars and writers were also given a silver replica, one-and-a-half inches tall, "too small to mount on a stand and too big to make into a cuff link, but encouraging to have," as Frank Muir pointed out.[16]

At the awards presentation, Dick Bentley offered to sing a few songs, assuming he was appearing before the "East Finchley Working Men's Institute and Social Night." Jimmy Edwards interrupted to explain that the cast would go on there afterwards; "This is the one we do for nothing."

As Eric Midwinter has written so perceptively,

"Like all art forms that attract both critical and popular acclaim, the award winning *TIFH* also suited the immediate mood perfectly. For all its cruel horror, World War II had widened the horizons of the British people....many turned, wiser and more mature, to what they hoped would be a fruitful future. They did so with some decent optimism, but with a restrained anticipation of what 'Reconstruction' could deliver. There were neither the heroic broken promises nor the excited doomed hopes of 1918. *TIFH* deftly touched the pulse of the confident, intelligent but genially skeptical victors of 'the People's War.'

"Frank Muir was very conscious of this refusal not to talk down to audiences, for he recognized that, perhaps compared with the pre-war listenership, they had a much wider frame of reference. He wrote, particularly of the film and book parody, that it was 'a small breakthrough in radio comedy because as far as we knew it was the first time in a prime-time series that the listener was credited with being at school, taken a newspaper and read a few books.'

"As a sixth-former when *TIFH* hit the airways in the late 1940s, I relished the treat of leaving my academic labors for that sublime thirty minutes each week, and reliving its smart phrases with compatriots at school the following morning. All these years on, and the lines of Muir and Norden have lingered as long as those of Chaucer and Sheridan, and have proved, justly, to have been as potent an influence."[17]

Frank Muir credits the success of the writing to an American influence, noting, "We had a lot to learn from American radio comedy in those days, such as Fred Allen's brilliant use of odd but real characters popping in, and fresh satirical techniques from Henry Morgan."[18]

From the beginning, many of those lines were given to Jimmy Edwards, who would begin his monologue with "Greetings, gentlefolk." If the "gentlefolk" in the live audience did not laugh with sufficient force, he would resort to his schoolmaster guise, and yell, "Wake up in the back there!" Much of Edwards' humor, as provided by Muir and Norden, was directed at Dick Bentley, with jokes as to his age. Bentley was his oldest friend: "There are friends I've known longer, but you're the oldest." There were gags about his inability to count the candles on Dick Bentley's birthday cake because the heat drove him back, and that the comedian was invited to participate in a radio broadcast in honor of the coronation of Queen Elizabeth II because he was the only BBC performer to have been an Elizabethan twice. Edwards would constantly be remarking, "Gently, Bentley" or "Black mark, Bentley!"

Jimmy would also participate with the warm-up, or at least the last ten seconds of it, by suddenly announcing as the show was about to record that he had left his script in "the reading room" (i.e. the toilet), explaining, "I always read in there." He was happy to co-operate, but, apparently, resented the discovery that the script contained a straight line: "'What do you expect me to do with 'How do you do that?' he would mutter. 'What's funny about How do you do that?' "[19]

Denis Norden recalled a BBC special featuring the biggest names on radio and titled *Christmas Night with the Stars*. It was broadcast live and involved the host's being at the Aeolian Hall studio in Bond Street all day. One year, Muir and Norden were invited to write the show with Jimmy Edwards being the host from rehearsals to live broadcast. The only problem, and it was a problem for Jimmy, was that the BBC would permit no alcohol in the studio. An angry Edwards read the closing speech, which began, "Well, listeners, that's about all we have time for. But our party will be continuing here in the studio as we hope yours will be out there. So please join us in a final chorus of 'Auld Lang Syne' by imagining there is a hand stretching out from your wireless set and that hand belongs to the BBC."

He veered offscript to continue, "Get an axe…"

Take It from Here is best   *Denis Norden.*
remembered for an ongoing sketch which, perhaps surprisingly, was not introduced until the seventh season, which began with the 200th show on November 12, 1953. That season is also important in that Joy Nichols is no longer one of the three stars. In 1949, she had married American singer/actor Wally Peterson, who was appearing in the U.K. stage production of *Oklahoma!* Joy Nichols was quite busy in the 1950s, co-starring at the London Palladium in 1952 with Max Bygraves in a revue titled *Wonderful Time*, representing Australia in the BBC's 1953 "Dominion's Salute" for the Queen's coronation, and co-starring opposite Edmund Hockridge at the London Coliseum in 1955 in *The Pajama Game*. At the end of season six, she left the show to have a baby daughter, Roberta, with Sally Rogers briefly taking over, and then went with her husband to America in the unfulfilled hope of a starring

career on stage, although she did appear on Broadway in the 1959 musical, *Fiorello*. After divorcing her husband, apparently she returned to Britain, playing a small role as a singer in Chaplin's *A King in New York* (1957), and it is reported she was working as a shop assistant in later years. At the time of her death, she was back in the United States, living in New York.

The ongoing sketch is, of course, "The Glums," which became the main feature of the series, and which has its origins perhaps with Joy Nichols earlier character of Miss Arundel, associating each remark with her red-blooded fiancé Gilbert, and Dick Bentley's poetic character and his love. "Oh Mavis," he would declaim, "How ravishing you look in your nee-glige with its tantalizing glimpses of vest."

It was presumably not that big a leap for Frank Muir and Denis Norden to the Glum family, a typically British family, as it was described, a far remove from the "wholesome" families presented in such BBC comedy series of the time as *Life with the Lyons*, starring Ben Lyon and Bebe Daniels, and *Meet the Huggets*, starring Jack Warner and Kathleen Harrison and based on the 1947 film, *Holiday Camp*. "As an antidote we invented a repugnant family," wrote Frank Muir.[20] The Glum family consisted of Pa Glum, played by Jimmy Edwards, based on the landlord of the comedian's local pub in Barnes, "The Market Gardener." Each segment with the Glums would open with Pa Glum at the local pub just as the landlord was calling "Time" (meaning he was about to lock up and customers would have to drink up), and perhaps to slow down the closing process, Pa Glum would begin recounting his latest problem with Ron and Eth. As commentators have noted, Pa Glum is a male chauvinist of the first order, similar to the cartoon character, Andy Capp, created by Reg Smythe for the British newspaper, *The Daily Mirror*. A typical comment might be, "Ron, run upstairs and fetch me your mother's toothbrush — I've got my new suede shoes on and I've trodden in something."

Brainless son Ron, perhaps best described by the British term "gormless,"[21] is played by Dick Bentley, actually older in real life than Jimmy Edwards, while his "intended" or fiancée is played by June Whitfield. When Joy Nichols left the show, she was replaced not by one but by two female leading ladies. June Whitfield handled the comedy roles, and, of course, has become a legendary entertainer both in the U.K. and in the U.S.A. (in the latter thanks largely to *Absolutely Fabulous*). "Miss Whitfield is a revue artist of a familiar type," it was explained. "She cannot be herself with success but she is wonderful at doing 'people'. Every Saturday morning, when she gets her script, she sits up in bed and spends an hour practicing her voices on a portable tape recorder."[22]

The singing was taken over by Alma Cogan, a popular vocalist, known as "The Girl with a Giggle in Her Voice," who died young, at the age of thirty-four, in 1966. Alma Cogan also played Pa Glum's wife, who actually spoke in the first episode of "The Glums," but in later episodes is represented only by the occasional and muffled moan or whine from an upstairs room. Alma Cogan left the show after season eight, and subsequently Ma Glum was nothing more than a vague shuffling across the floor above.[23]

Also considered for the female lead in *Take It from Here* were Betty Marsden and Prunella Scales. It is, of course, intriguing to consider how each would have approached the character; can one really conceive of Basil Fawlty's wife, Sybil, in the role of Eth?

Episode one of "The Glums" has Ron introducing his intended, Eth, to the family, which, it is revealed also includes a grandmother who had been living with them since the war: "The zeppelins frightened her, you know." When Ron explains to his father that he and Eth are to get married and have modern ideas, Jimmy

June Whitfield.

responds, "Is this the golden-haired boy in the sailor's suit what used to climb onto his dad's knee and recite *Goblin Market?*"[24] To which Ron responds, "I've grown up dad — That was last Christmas! I've met Eth now and become a man." Each episode would generally have Eth sitting beside Ron on the living room couch, crying, "Oh Ron." Pa Glum would always manage to enter a room just as Ron was about to embrace Eth, and the first words out of his mouth would be "Ullo, Ullo, Ullo," rather like some stereotypical British policeman. Through the series, with some episodes introduced in the form of reminiscences by Pa Glum, Ron and Eth never got any closer to a marriage ceremony. They were just going steady, leading Pa Glum to remark, "Any steadier and they'd be motionless." Eth's efforts at persuading Ron to be more romantic would generally prove abortive, with a typical response from Ron being, "Wouldn't it 'elp if I turned my cap back to front?"

Spoken humor does not particularly work on the printed page, but Frank Muir selected a couple of examples of a typical conversation between Ron and Eth for his autobiography, and at least one is most certainly worth reprinting here:

> ETH: Come on, there must be something you don't like about me. Something tiny.
> RON: No, Eth.
> ETH: Some little thing…?
> RON: Well, there is something.
> ETH: Come on, then — out with it.
> RON: You're a bit ugly.

What is undoubtedly the greatest conversation between Ron and Eth never made it on air, for obvious reasons, but it is recounted by June Whitfield, and definitely deserving of wider distribution. The scene is the bedroom on Ron and Eth's wedding night.

> RON: I'm going to get undressed now, Eth. You're not to look.
> *[Eth is unpacking her suitcase and hold ups her pretty new nightie.]*
> ETH: Ooh, Ron, isn't it lovely. All pink and crinkly.
> RON: I told you not to look, Eth.

While Mrs. Glum did not appear, she was often the subject of conversation. As an example,

> PA: Do you remember them earrings your mum lost last summer?
> RON: Yes, dad?
> PA: Well, she's had her hair washed and guess what? They were there! In there all the time. Found two stubbed-out fag ends as well. I must give up smoking in bed.

"The Glums" and *Take It from Here* continued as part of British radio history with Frank Muir and Denis Norden writing every script through the twelfth series, which ended on March 12, 1959. The pair decided it was time to move fully over to television, much to the dismay of the BBC Radio Variety Department. Muir and Norden, who actually owned the copyright in *Take It from Here*, agreed to allow the series to continue but with new writers. Those new writers were Barry Took and Eric Merriman, who had previously written *Beyond Our Ken*, featuring Kenneth Horne and Kenneth Williams, and which was first heard on July 1, 1958. The two writers worked independently of each other, and it was Took who wrote "The Glums" episodes, assisted by Marty Feldman, who was uncredited. The thirteenth season of *Take It from Here* proved to be an unlucky one in that it was the last, with the final broadcast on March 3, 1960, and the Glums about to immigrate to Australia.

Take It from Here might be over on radio, but "The Glums" continued with a 1960 Fontana release of a 45 r.p.m. record of "Jimmy Edwards Sings 'Pa Glum.'"[25] The album consisted of four songs, with piano accompaniment, "I've Never Seen a Straight Banana," "Across the Bridge," "I'm Forever Blowing Bubbles," and "Rhymes." The last was nothing more than a series of limericks set to music and two, "There Was a Young Lady of Gloucester" and "There Was a Young Guardsman of Reading," sufficiently upset the BBC bureaucracy that the recording was banned from radio. "Jimmy Edwards Sings 'Pa Glum'" was not Jimmy's only recording. In 1974, he recorded a single of "Time Gentlemen Please" and "Was It Something I Said" on the Spark label.[26] Ken Mackintosh and His Band provided accompaniment on this and on the L.P., "Jimmy Edwards at the Top of the Pubs" (1974), which also featured pianist Joe Henderson. There were also original cast recordings featuring Jimmy in *Cinderella* (1959) and *The Maid of the Mountains* (1972), as well as "The Cream of Take It from Here," with Jimmy, Joy Nichols, Dick Bentley, and Wallas Eaton on the Fontana Label.[27]

And, of course, he, Dick Bentley and Joy Nichols enjoyed considerable success with their 1953 Columbia single, "Little Red Monkey,"[28] which gave Jimmy the opportunity to play his euphonium, and which was coupled with "Me an' Johnny." Composed by Jack Jordan, with added lyrics by Stephen Gale, "Little Red Monkey" had been the theme song for a six-part BBC television thriller, broadcast at the beginning of 1953, and starring Honor Blackman and Donald Houston. It had tremendous impact, identified as one of the best of the genre up to that time, and I can personally attest to how scary it was as an eight year-old-boy who was too terrified to go to bed alone after viewing it. The series was adapted into a feature film of the same title in 1955, directed by Ken Hughes and starring Richard Conte and Rona Anderson, with an American release title of *Case of the Little Red Monkey*. An American "cover" version of the song was recorded by Rosemary Clooney.

On November 15, 1962, Jimmy Edwards and June Whitfield reunited, in company with Ronnie Barker as Ron, for the first episode of the six-part

BBC television series, *Six Faces of Jim*, titled "The Face of Fatherhood." "The Glums" were back by public demand as a regular segment of the 1978 television series, *Bruce Forsyth's Big Night Out*, with Jimmy Edward reprising his original role, Patricia Blake as Eth and Ian Lavender (from *Dad's Army*) as Ron. The following year "The Glums" were given their own television series on London Weekend Television, with the same cast,

and with Michael Stainton as pub landlord Ted. The scripts were adapted by Frank Muir and Denis Norden from their original radio scripts. Those television scripts were published by Robson Books in 1979 (and later reprinted in paperback by Penguin Books).

Jimmy explained that he had spent some time considering Pa Glum's appearance now that he would be brought to life visually on television. The scripts had his demanding, "Pass my bowler," and so a bowler hat was an obvious accessory. Jimmy decided that Pa Glum would wear a suit and a shirt collar with studs. He would also be a "red-necked type of beery chap," and Jimmy needed no special make-up for that role.[29] In reality, as far as alcoholic beverage of choice, Pa Glum might enjoy his beer, but Jimmy much preferred wine.

While "The Glums might mean nothing to Americans, the name has become part of British popular culture. It is so legendary that the musical, *Les Misérables*, is often described as "The Glums" by members of the British entertainment community.

Jimmy Edwards and June Whitfield were again reunited for a couple of episodes on the BBC Radio 2 series, *Jim the Great*, heard on Saturdays at 1:00 P.M. There was a pilot episode, broadcast on February 14, 1976, with six episodes in series one, beginning on March 26, 1977, and eight episodes in series two, beginning on August 26, 1979, each thirty minutes in length. Written by Andrew Palmer and produced by Edward Taylor, *Jim the King* was a "pseudo-historical romp" with Jimmy as the chauvinistic, hunting and drinking King and Joan Sanderson, perfectly cast, as his wife.

As an announcer explained, "it was said his majesty would spread into the four corners of the earth — if he didn't cut down on the beer." June Whitfield guest starred in series two, episode one, "Fit for a Queen," as Queen Boadicea, and was also featured in series two, episode seven, "The Camelot Caper." Somewhat unkindly *Television Today* (August 30, 1979) described the show as "a series from one of the oldest of old timers."

Indirectly, some of the gags from *Take It from Here* continued with life in the Talbot Rothwell scripts of the "Carry On" films. Frank Muir and Denis Norden gave Rothwell (who had contributed a sketch titled "Friends, Romans and Countrymen" or "What a Sphinx!" to the stage production of *Take It from Us*) permission to use some of their old scripts, and the most famous line borrowed from *Take It from Here* occurs when Julius Caesar played first by Jimmy Edwards, and later on screen by Kenneth Williams, declaims, "Oh, infamy! Infamy! They've all got it in for me." According to Denis Norden, "Of the two deliveries, I would judge Kenneth Williams' cry the more heart-stricken; Jimmy Edwards' declamation the more thunderous."[30] Another exchange from the same *Take It from Here* routine, but perhaps not in a "Carry On" film:

QUESTION: "Where's me army? Where's me army?"
ANSWER: "Just off the coast of Florida."

Take It from Here also found life on stage. During the third season, the three stars, along with Wallas Eaton, appeared top of the bill at London's Victoria Palace and later the Prince of Wales Theatre. As Jimmy has written in his autobiography, "From now on I was to be almost continually engaged in stage shows."[31] The show enjoyed a summer season in Blackpool, and returned to London's West End and the Adelphi Theatre on October 30, 1950, now titled *Take It from Us*, and running for some 580 performances. Only Jimmy Edwards appeared during the entire run of the show, which he thought should have been retitled *Take It from Me*. A second show, with two sketches, "A Seat in the Circle" and "Polly Does Everything," by Frank Muir and Denis Norden, opened on April 12, 1952, under the title of *London Laughs*, again at the Adelphi Theatre, but with only Jimmy Edwards from *Take It from Here*, and with Tony Hancock substituting for Dick Bentley, and with the addition of Vera Lynn. The show was revived, with new material, at the Adelphi in November 1954, under the title of *The Talk of the Town*.

That revival included a sketch set in a lighthouse with Jimmy as the aged lighthouse keeper, proclaiming, "Ninety days without relief," and a young Tony Hancock staring into space, and announcing, "I can't stand it." One performance, in an effort to get Hancock to laugh, Jimmy came on stage with a black eye patch. Hancock did not respond until, on leaving the stage, he turned to Jimmy and asked, "Something wrong with your eye, old boy?" During the run of *The Talk of the Town*, Jimmy was asked to cut short his act in order that impresario Jack Hylton might try out a

new act." As Jimmy explained, he never minded doing less work for the same money. He saw the act, a singer, and announced, "She'll never make it." The singer was Shirley Bassey.

Frank Muir recalls,

"Jimmy by then had become a very strong theatre performer, and his schoolmaster act — which Denis and I helped put together for him — was successful and reliable. For theatre purposes we had given him much more visual comedy. He strode on stage in gown and mortarboard, swishing his cane and glowering at the audience as though they were a difficult class, and went straight to a tall stand-up desk which had two hand bells on its top. He took one of these off and rang it vigorously, shouting, 'Quiet, everywhere! Fags [cigarettes] out! Pay attention!' He put down the hand bell and pulled at the handle of the other bell. It was a beer pump. He pumped a few strokes then lifted the desk lid and produced a frothing half pint of bitter. 'Cheers!' he said.

"He glanced out of the window and noticed somebody. 'It's our dear matron' he exclaimed to the audience. 'She's going to watch the cricket match sitting on her shooting stick.' He smiled benignly and looked out of the window again. Shock, horror!

"'Matron! No!' he yelled out of the window, then mimed turning the shooting stick round the other way."[32]

It was classic Jimmy Edwards, paving the way for the next advance in his career — television and *Whack-O!*

1. Two excellent websites for *Take It from Here* are hosted by Dave Brown, providing a complete listing of all episodes, and Mark McKay's Laughterlog, which documents which of the shows are still extant in the BBC Archives.

2. Jimmy Edwards, *Take It from Me*, p. 149.

3. Ibid, p. 159.

4. Scotsman Charles Maxwell (1910-1998) has been described by *The Stage* (August 20, 1998) as "one of the most innovative and pioneering BBC radio producers." *Navy Mixture* was his first major success.

5. Denis Norden, *Clips from a Life*, p. 84.

6. "Show That Hopes to Beat ITMA Record," p. 3.

7. The BBC Light Programme, as the name suggests, was the corporation's radio channel for light entertainment and popular music. It was so named from 1945 through 1967, when it became BBC Radio 2. Among the other popular, and fondly remembered, comedy series that it broadcast are *The Clitheroe Kid* (with Jimmy Clitheroe), *Educating Archie* (with Peter Brough and Archie Andrews), *Hancock's Half Hour*, *Life with the Lyons*, *Much Binding in the March* (with Kenneth Horne), *The Navy Lark* (with Leslie Phillips), *Ray's a Laugh* (with Ted Ray), and *Round the Horne* (also with Kenneth Horne).

8. Johnny Johnson, Alan Dean, Terry Devon, and Renee King. The group was earlier called the Harmony Heralds, and Johnson and Dean had also been billed as The Song Pedlars.

9. The orchestra was later conducted by Robert Busby, Charles Shadwell, and Paul Fenoulhet, and for most of the 1950s by Harry Rabinowitz.

10. In 1939, with the outbreak of World War Two, Radio Luxembourg was closed down by the Luxembourg government, but re-opened after the German occupation of the country as a propaganda tool.

11. Jimmy Edwards, *Take It from Me*, p. 165.

12. The Paris Cinema at 12 Lower Regent Street was taken over by the BBC as a theatre for radio broadcasts in 1939. It was very much the home of BBC Radio comedy until it closed in 1995.

13. "B.B.C. Audiences Told When to Applaud, p. 1.

14. Ibid, p. 168.

15. Peter Chambers, "Show That Hopes to Beat ITMA Record," p. 3.

16. Frank Muir, *A Kentish Lad*, p. 151.

17. Eric Midwinter, "Take It from Here," p. 7.

18. Frank Muir, *A Kentish Lad*, p. 146.

19. Denis Norden, *Clips from a Life*, p. 105.

20. Frank Muir, *A Kentish Lad*, p. 151.

21. One critic somewhat kindly describes the character as "intellectually challenged."

22. "Show That Hopes to Beat ITMA Record," p. 3.

23. For a brief period American-born Toni Eden was heard as a singer on the show.

24. A controversial poem, sometimes identified as feminist, by Christina Rossetti. And what a strange reference to use in this context.

25. Phillips Fontana Label, AA 465 128 2E.

26. Spark Label, SRL 1116.

27. Fontana Label, TFL 5103.

28. Columbia Label R3684.

29. "Jim Is So Glum About His Whiskers."

30. Denis Norden, *Clips from a Life*, p. 264.

31. Jimmy Edwards, *Take It from Me*, p. 175.

32. Frank Muir, *A Kentish Lad*, p. 196.

CHAPTER SIX

Bottoms Up!

As Denis Norden has commented, one of the ingredients most appealing to English humor is a reference to "bottoms."[1] Jimmy Edwards always insisted that one of his favorite lines, written by Muir and Norden, was "His name was Winterbottom. A cold, stern man." The television series *Whack-O!* managed to adopt and glorify bottoms as the receiving end of a cane, part of the ritual of flagellation, the English vice as it was described in Victorian times when it was extremely popular with many intellectuals as well as lesser beings. The poet Swinburne took delight in being caned and was fascinated by this form of punishment, even writing an ode on the subject as applied to the boys of Eton school:

> *"Lad by lad, whether good or bad:*
> *"Alas for those who at nine o-clock*
> *"Seek the room of disgraceful doom to smart like fun*
> *on the flogging-block!"*

The 1960 film version of *Whack-O!* was simply titled *Bottoms Up!*, and conveniently or perhaps inconveniently its release coincided with Arthur Howard's arrest for importuning or "cottaging," as it is known in the gay community, in a public toilet.

Whack-O! represented Jimmy's first major foray into television. He was not an advocate, and in the first episode of series nine of *Take It from Here*, broadcast on October 11, 1955, he had taken the "mickey" out of television, in part perhaps because both June Whitfield and Alma Cogan had recently embraced the medium

All in all, Jimmy Edwards' major television series debut was somewhat controversial, although admittedly most of the controversy is in retrospect, and unknown or unperceived by the British viewing public. *Take It from Here* was described by one critic as "a programme of brilliant surrealist comedy."[2] As already noted, there was definitely something surreal about *Whack-O!*, even if it was not comedic.

The genesis for Jimmy Edwards television series was simple and obvious. As Frank Muir recalled,

"He would revert to his original comic character of a venal, boozy, devious and incompetent headmaster of a small, tatty public school. We

invented a name for the school which sounded vaguely unreliable — Chiselbury — and we called the series *Whack-O!*."[3]

Credit for the series should also go to the BBC's Head of Light Entertainment Ronnie Waldman,[4] who was the first seriously to discuss Edwards' breaking into television, and, of course, to Jimmy himself whom one feels sure was happy to use his old stage act as the basis for a television characterization.

The concept of a comedy set at a British public school was nothing new. In the 1930s, Will Hay (1888-1949) had appeared as an exasperated, confused and bespectacled headmaster in a series of comedy features, including *Boys Will Be Boys* (1935), *Good Morning, Boys* (1937) and *The Ghost of St. Michael's*, although as a schoolmaster rather than headmaster (1941). Denis Norden recalled that he and Frank Muir were asked to rewrite the script of *Boys Will Be Boys* as a vehicle for Jimmy Edwards, but "It was such a perfectly constructed and characterised piece of comedy, neither of us wanted to be party to altering a word of it."[5]

On the distaff side, Ronald Searle's cartoons concerning an anarchic girls' school, St. Trinian's, had been filmed in the 1950s and later, and obviously had its basis in the 1950 film, *The Happiest Days of Your Life*, several cast members of which were to appear in the series. The first two, *The Belles of St. Trinian's* (1954) and *Blue Murder at St. Trinian's* (1957) were the best of the series, in very large part because of the casting of Alastair Sim as the Headmistress. Irene Handl played the Headmistress in *The Pure Hell of St. Trinian's* (1960), Dora Bryan was the Headmistress in *The Ghost of St. Trinian's* (1966), and Sheila Hancock essayed the role in *The Wildcats of St. Trinian's*. A second, and somewhat pointless series, consisting of *St. Trinian's* (2007) and *St. Trinian's 2: The Legend of Fritten's Gold* (2009) cast Rupert Everett as the Headmistress.

Interestingly, when Ronald Searle collaborated with Geoffrey Williams in 1953 on *Down with Skool!*, featuring Williams' character Molesworth, a schoolboy at St. Custard's, it boasted a comment by Jimmy Edwards: "The boy who left this subversive book on my desk will be expelled. Once I picked it up I was unable to put it down and thus wasted the whole of Latin Prep. Young Molesworth should go far — he would go farther still if I had my way."[6]

Jimmy Edwards had the perfect physical and vocal attributes for the part. He was large, and thus threatening, he was loud-mouthed and thus bullying. He was an alcoholic and thus could play drunkenness without any apparent effect on his demeanor. He might at times obviously forget his lines and, in all honesty, his timing is sometimes off, but it really did not matter.

There are those who have suggested that the Jimmy Edwards character, in terms of the scheming in which he is involved, owes much to Phil Silver's Sergeant Ernest G. Bilko, the sitcom that ran for many years on CBS from 1955 through 1959 under the titles of *The Phil Silvers Show* or *You'll Never Get Rich*. The series had certainly been seen in the United Kingdom, but, personally, I am dubious as to the similarity.

As to the wielding the cane, there is nothing to suggest that Jimmy was attached to that weapon of punishment in private life, either as a giver or taker. But surely he could play the role as if he enjoyed the act of caning, and present it as nothing more than a spot of harmless fun, particularly as in episode six of the third series (broadcast October 28, 1958) in which the "TERRA," a caning machine is introduced after the headmaster loses use of his caning arm in a football accident. The canings could also work to Jimmy's detriment as in episode two of season five, in which schoolboy Crombie (played by Jimmy Ray) decides to take the headmaster to court for his excessive cruelty, claiming that the six strokes that he actually received were in reality 347 strokes.[7]

It might well be argued that audiences at the time had no problem at finding amusement in the physical abuse of the Chiselbury boys, with the Headmaster's study identified as "The House of the Swinging Bamboo." After all, these were the offspring of members of the upper class (albeit perhaps lowly ones), and working and middle class Britishers could enjoy the spectacle of this snobbish minority taking a beating.[8] Are audiences today too sensitive, too politically correct to enjoy the on-screen canings here? Personally, I doubt they are. After all, there is no hint of sympathetic pain felt in a viewer's nether regions while watching *Whack-O!* It is all a joke, and one is very much aware that the boys are not suffering — and even if in real life, at the time, the boys had been punished in this fashion, then surely the marks on their buttocks would have been a mark of honor to share with their fellow schoolboys.

Contemporary critics even joked about the canings, with one writing that "I have a very definite soft spot for Chiselbury School — I bet the boys have a few soft spots too — thanks to the Professor!"[9]

Not that the boys could not wreak an appropriate revenge for the beatings. A sketch from *Whack-O!* featured on the BBC's December 25, 1959 special, *Christmas Night with the Stars*, and described by *The Stage and Television Today* (December 31, 1959) as the "highlight of the whole show," opens with a shot of the headmaster's study and the sign, "Flogging in Process." It transpires that Jimmy had assumed the three boys visiting his study had come for a caning, of which they receive 300 apiece, when, in fact, they had come with a gift for him. Before opening the gift in private, Pettigrew arrives wearing a very fetching bonnet which makes him look exceedingly effeminate and bearing his own gift for the headmaster, a bottle of parsnip wine. When Jimmy does retire to his private abode, he opens the boys' gift, which proves to be a bomb, but, perhaps in the spirit of the season, the blame for the climactic explosion rests on the parsnip wine and its surprising kick.

As the BBC's own website so aptly puts it,

"These days it'd be hard to make a long-running series based on a schoolmaster who took pleasure in thwacking his charges and swindling everyone. Fortunately, in olden days sense prevailed."[10]

The comedy of a caning was raised to a whole new, sadistic and unthinkable height by Rowan Atkinson in a stage sketch in which he is the headmaster and he has called parent Angus Deayton (Atkinson's regular straight man) into his office. As he explains to Deayton, with a level of callousness which only Rowan Atkinson could accomplish, the son is dead. "Tommy is in trouble and if he wasn't dead I'd have had him expelled."

Tommy has apparently been caught removing a library book without registering the loan on his library card. "I administered a beating during which he died," explains the headmaster. "One moment he was bending over, the next he was lying down." To add to how aggrieved Atkinson is by the whole matter, he continues, "In order to accommodate the funeral I've had to cancel afternoon school on Wednesday."

The sketch, "Fatal Beatings," is brilliant in the manner in which it captures the attitude of a public school headmaster, such as Jimmy Edwards portrays, in dealing with parents, who have failed in their duty. As Atkinson explains to Deayton, if the boy had been beaten a few more times earlier in life he might have turned out a lot different.

The closest that *Whack-O!* came to "Fatal Beatings" is with an episode in which Jimmy proudly invents what he described as the ultimate deterrent, a mechanical boy-thrasher. Here, as *The Guardian* (July 11, 1988) pointed out, Jimmy echoes the characters of Captain Hook and Mr. Squeers (in *Peter Pan*) and Captain Grimes (the Benjamin Britten opera).

The opening credit sequence for *Whack-O!* ends with a shot of the school gates, and a sign reading, "Chiselbury School for the Sons of Gentlefolk, Headmaster, Professor Jimmy Edwards." Below is the school motto, "They Shall Not Pass," suggested by Muir and Norden with some help from producer Douglas Moodie. Prior to the shot of the school gates are credit titles on a blackboard, each of which concludes with the whack of a cane across the board. Again, the emphasis appears deliberately to be on the cane and its impact.

Chiselbury was the worst example of what a British public school (the American equivalent of a private school) might be. It was no Eton or Harrow, and at times might resemble some of the educational establishments to be found in the novels of Charles Dickens:

"A visitor to this venerable seat of learning (so called because it has no standing) will first notice the surrounding high stone wall, designed to keep the undesirables *in*. A sign on the gate proclaims 'Chiselbury School, for the sons of gentlefolk.' With good reason too — at 110 guineas a term, not including extras (such as food, bedding and use of the bathroom), it seems only the nobility can afford to send their sons here. Naturally doors open instantly to school leavers — specifically those of the labor exchange and Pentonville [Prison]."[11]

The character of the headmaster needed an ensemble cast both to bully and to threaten the cozy existence that Chiselbury might have offered. Obviously, the boys were important, although often seen in only a secondary capacity, compared to those supposedly teaching them. There was a matron, providing potential sexual interest for the headmaster and the teachers. The matron was played variously by Barbara Archer, Elisabeth Fraser and Charlotte Mitchell. Among the more prominent teachers were Kenneth Cope (as F.D. Price-Whittaker), John Garside (as G.D. St. John Dinwiddie), and Edwin Apps (as geography teacher L.J. Halliforth).[12] One of the most endearing, and amusing pedagogical characters was the P.T. (Physical Training or Gym) teacher, Mr. Dinwiddie played by the aged Gordon Phillott and later by Harold Bennett, remembered fondly as Young Mr. Grace on *Are You Being Served?* with his catchphrase, "You've all done very well."

In *Bottoms Up!* one of the Chiselbury boys is played by John Graham "Mitch" Miller (1946-2008). The character name is Wendover, as in "Bend over Wendover." Miller later became drummer with the Jimi Hendrix Experience, and was named one of the greatest rock drummers of the 1960s. Another musician who played a Chiselbury boy is Michael Des Barres, who later had a small role in the 1967 Sidney Poitier vehicle, *To Sir with Love*. Initially, boys in the series were recruited from London's Arts Educational Schools, and from the third series onwards, also from the Italia Conti Stage School.

Some contemporary celebrities also made guest appearances in the series; on September 30, 1958, Eamonn Andrews, the host of the British version of *This Is Your Life*, appeared as Edwards attempted to have deputy headmaster Pettigrew featured on the show; another television host, of the quiz show *Break the Bank*, Jerry Desmonde appeared on May 20, 1960; singer Max Bygraves was hired to appear in a Grand Variety Concert at Chiselbury village hall on June 17, 1960; television personalities Cliff Michelmore and Derek Hart appeared on the December 13, 1960 show; and, most prominent of all, legendary singer Vera Lynn is persuaded to attend Dinwiddie's bedside and sing "The Chiselbury Boating Song" on December 15, 1959.

A number of British comedians relied on a straight man or a stooge as part of the act. Sid Field, for example, had a masterly foil in Jerry Desmonde,[13] while Arthur Haynes, on television would rely on Nicholas Parsons, who would without embarrassment strip down to his shorts as part of a gag. Ken Dodd is perhaps unique in that he treats his entire audience as his collective straight man. Some stooges were always silent on stage, such as Frankie Howerd's[14] aging pianist/accompanist or Hylda Baker's tall companion, Cynthia (in reality a man in drag). For *Whack-O!*, Jimmy Edwards had the perfect stooge in Arthur Howard, and he was certainly far from silent as, with timidity, he nervously fluttered around, desperately trying to contain the headmaster's latest burst of fury or a ploy/plot littered with potential trouble. As deputy headmaster Pettigrew, Arthur Howard often appeared effeminate but never gay. He had the appearance of a perennial bachelor for whom female companionship was unthinkable and far too difficult with which to deal.

There were some critics who compared Edwards and Howard to Laurel and Hardy, and Howard, who really saw himself as a serious actor, had to admit to a reporter with the *Bristol Evening World* (January 22, 1960) that "This idiotic comedy business seems to be what I do best."

Concurrent with what was to be the last season of *Whack-O!*, Frank Muir and Denis Norden wrote an internal BBC memorandum, noting,

"It isn't surprising, but worth noting, how popular Arthur Howard's 'Mr. Pettigrew' character is with the public...I feel that we mustn't underestimate the hold this Jim-Pettigrew relationship has on the public's affections when we get down to planning a new format."[15]

Reviewing Arthur Howard's work in another, and later, BBC television series, *The Whitehall Warriors*, created by Alan Melville, a critic in *The Stage and Television Today* (January 19, 1967) summed it up so perfectly: "Arthur Howard is such a funny worried man, doomed to play the underdog."

Arthur Howard (1910-1995) was the son of a British mother and a Hungarian-Jewish father; the family name was Steiner, later anglicized to Stainer. He was the brother of matinée idol Leslie Howard, and made his screen debut in his brother's film, *The Lady Is Willing* in 1933. His next film came in 1947 with *Frieda*, in which he played a clerk issuing ration books at the local town hall. He was to continue to play similar roles throughout his screen career, best suited to portrayals of vicars or judges; Howard appeared in two school-related comedies, *The Happiest Days of Your Life* (1950), in which he played a science teacher somewhat similar in mannerisms to Mr. Pettigrew, and *The Belles of St. Trinian's* (1954), in a non-academic role. Other screen roles include Arthur, the butler in *Trail of the Pink Panther* (1982) and *Curse of the Pink Panther* (1983), and a small role in the 1979 James Bond film, *Moonraker*.[16] Aside from *Whack-O!*, Arthur Howard appeared in a number of television programs, with the last being *The Last Englishman* (1995).

Arthur Howard as Mr. Pettigrew.

It might be said that he left *Whack-O!* under a cloud, involved in what was in reality only a minor scandal, discussed below, but the BBC's initial reaction to what had transpired did not hurt the actor's later career in television, on screen or on the stage, where, ironically in view of what had happened, he appeared for a number of years in the popular farce *No Sex Please We're British*.

Arthur Howard not only had a famous brother but an equally famous son, Alan Howard (1937-2015), whose career is primarily associated with the stage as represented by the National Theatre and the Royal Shakespeare Company. On screen, Alan Howard will always be remembered for Peter Greenaway's 1989 production of *The Cook, the Thief, his Wife and Her Lover*, in which he is a mild-mannered bookshop owner whose affair with a gangster's wife leads to his being roasted in the oven and served up to the gangster and his family for dinner. Strangely, it was almost embarrassing to watch Alan Howard frontally nude, the shock almost being equal to the suggestion of his father similarly unattired.

Frank Muir first met Arthur Howard when the latter was entertainments office at RAF Warmwell during World War Two. It was Howard who encouraged Muir to write material for the company's revues. The partnership broke up when Muir was posted to Iceland and Howard to Cairo, but the two reunited to be demobbed at RAF Henlow at the end of the War.

It was Muir who persuaded Denis Norden that Arthur Howard might be ideal for the role of Pettigrew:

"Arthur and his actress wife, Jean Compton-Mackenzie [niece of the novelist] were then going through the experience which most actors have to endure during their working lives — a sticky patch financially....Arthur was kipping down at a friend's flat and Jean was in a Soho hostel for actresses. When their young son Alan...came home from school they hired a room so that the family could be together for the weekend."[17]

Arthur Howard was appearing at the Pitlochry, Scotland, Theatre Festival, sharing accommodation with actor Edwin Apps, who recalls Howard's joy on receiving a letter from Frank Muir advising him that he was to play the assistant headmaster in *Whack-O!* Edwin Apps was later to play in the radio adaptation of the show and also in the television version, from the fifth series onwards, thanks to some lobbying by both Arthur Howard and Jimmy Edwards: "The BBC booking department explained that, as the part would be small, they couldn't pay me my normal fee, but proposed 15 pounds a show. 'Make it guineas' I told my agent, which got me fifteen shillings extra. Jimmy was paid 1000 pounds a show."[18]

While not documented, the figure of 1000 pounds per show is probably correct in that by 1960 or 1961, the BBC was paying Tony Hancock a similar amount per show, but the salary was kept secret in that the Corporation feared that the British public, the people who were forced to pay an annual license fee to watch the programming, might have objected. In reality, the BBC was compelled to pay higher and higher salaries to prevent some of its biggest stars defecting to the commercial ITV network, financed through advertising.

Pettigrew was often the principal character as far as the plots were concerned. In episode six of series two, after the headmaster is fired, he is promoted and introduces new "progressive education" policies. In season four, episode six, he must put on athletic attire and win a race at the headmaster's insistence. In season seven, episodes one, Pettigrew wins 38,000 pounds on that peculiarly British fixation, the football pools, and is forced to sample what the fleshpots have to offer in order to dissuade him from giving the money away to the Four-Footed Friends Fund.

Perhaps the classic Mr. Pettigrew line is "I may be a fool, but…" To which the headmaster responds sharply, "No buts about it Pettigrew!"

In another episode, Pettigrew becomes so overwhelmed with anger at the headmaster's hitting his bandaged head that he kicks him in the rear. In horror, he whimpers, "I wish I was dead!" "That can be arranged" is Jimmy's response.

As Frank Muir wrote, it "rapidly became a classic comedy partnership of the strong but not honest big man and the inept but thoroughly decent little man."[19]

There were initially seven series in black-and-white, beginning on October 4, 1956 and ending on December 27, 1960. The first series of six episodes was broadcast fortnightly on Thursday evenings at 7:30 P.M, 8:00 P.M. or 7:45 P.M. Series two through five were seen weekly, on Tuesday evenings, at 7:30 P.M. Series six was seen Friday evenings at 8:30 P.M., and series seven was broadcast on Tuesday evenings at 7:30 P.M. To promote the 1957 season, Jimmy and Arthur Howard appeared in character in a BBC special, *These Are the Shows*, which aired on September 28, 1957.

For rehearsals, the BBC rented the Sulgrave Boys Club on the Goldhawk Road in West London; *Whack-O!* was in rehearsal on the ground floor, while the popular police series, *Dixon of Dock Green* was in rehearsal on the floor above. Both series were produced by Scotsman Douglas "Dougie" Moodie, a heavy smoker given to coughing fits. Rehearsals would begin on a Tuesday morning with the reading of the script. On Fridays, Muir and Norden would arrive and there would be a run through, first for them, and then for the technicians, setting up the camera angles. Sunday mornings and afternoons, there would be further run-throughs for the cameras, followed by a final rehearsal at 6:00 P.M., after which the company would be informed if the show was running too long and what cuts had to be made.

"The first rehearsal was usually hilarious," recalls one of the Chiselbury boys, Keith Nichols. "Jim was drunk on several occasions…I remember one time when he insisted on sitting in a waste paper basket (for effect) while reading the script. After the first rehearsal, work started seriously.… Jim was on perfect behavior…a total professional. I don't remember any particular attitude towards younger actors. He was fine to the boys.…To me and the other boys he and Arthur Howard were great actors — comic geniuses."[20]

Edwin Apps recalls that the company lunched at Oddie's Club, a basement room under an Italian restaurant on Goldhawk Road:

"The clientele appeared to be restricted to the Light Entertainment Section of the BBC. The other company we lunched with regularly was *Hancock's Half Hour*.

"The pattern was that the first person to arrive bought a round of gins-and-tonic, the second did the same, as did the third and so on. This meant that we each consumed at least four gins-and-tonic, more if there were guests that week. We then sat down to a hefty Italian lunch with several bottles of Beaujolais, after which we would stagger back to rehearsal."

Whack-O! was broadcast live from the Shepherd's Bush Empire, a former music hall, in West London. The stage was divided into two, with a different set on each half and a curtain closing off the half not in use from the audience's gaze. The most used set was the headmaster's study, and that always occupied the left-hand side of the stage. While a scene was taking place there, stagehands might well be changing the scenery on the right-hand side, and this required Muir and Norden to write scenes long enough to permit the scenery change to take place.

Prior to the broadcast, the audience was treated to a warm up by Muir and Norden, followed by a second warm up from Jimmy Edwards.

Live broadcasts [21] did, of course, present problems, particularly if something should go wrong. Frank Muir recalled a scene in which Jimmy Edwards was required, supposedly by accident, to reach across his desk and bang a telephone down on a school inspector's spectacles. He was then to comment, "I'm so sorry, I seem to have accidentally dented your spectacles." Of course, the spectacles failed to break, and Edwards resorted to a series of vicious thumps on the spectacles, eventually throwing them on the floor and stamping on them, to the growing amusement of the audience, until finally the spectacles were nothing more than twisted wire and plastic.

Producer/director Douglas "Dougie" Moodie was noted for the insulting remarks he would make to "bit" players and even to the writers, whom he would sometimes refer to as Gilbert and Sullivan. He was in fact so strict that none of the actors, not even Jimmy, would dare disobey him. Moodie would carefully rehearse the camera movements and the actors to such an extent that little needed to be done while the show was broadcast. In fact, he would generally go to a local restaurant for a few gins and tonic, return to the theatre as the show was about to start, sit down in the control room and do nothing.

The Shepherd's Bush Empire was also used for a one-off show, *The Sound of Jim*, written by Muir and Norden, and broadcast on October 7, 1961. It was described in the *Radio Times* as "A Cacophony in which Jimmy Edwards (professor of music) conducts an Enormous Orchestra, demonstrates instruments both Large and Small, introduces Guests of a Certain Distinction, and plays upon your ignorance of Music in General." As he had done for later episodes of *Take It from Here*, Harry Rabinowitz conducted the orchestra.

Among the endless frustrations that headmaster Edwards had to deal with on *Whack-O!* was forcing the teachers to dress as boys in order to win a quiz program (October 16, 1956); having only one novel, *Piccadilly Gun Moll*, and seventeen dust jackets for the school's prize giving (December 13, 1956); a Sunday newspaper investigates corruption in private schools

(September 23, 1958); the school's playing fields are sold for industrial development (May 19, 1958); the boys rebel at the suggestion they participate in a floral dance at the Chiselbury village fete; the headmaster is fired after a photograph of a naked lady, with the caption, "Proposed new addition to hobbies room," is published in the school magazine (May 27, 1960); a visit to the Tate Gallery results in the loss of one of the boys and a sculpture (June 10, 1960); etc. The storylines are often predictable but always original in concept, and, no matter what issues arise with the pupils (particularly those of the Lower Third), the under-paid teachers, the antagonistic board of governors, and unimpressed parents, headmaster Jimmy Edwards, the ultimate sociopath, survives for another week. It is a remarkable series to a certain extent that the headmaster is at war both with the students and with the teachers, with the exception, of course, of Pettigrew.

It was not merely the plots that were ingenious and entertaining, but equally, and more importantly, the lines and the delivery, with such dialogue always proving that the headmaster was never lost for words.

When an inspector from the Ministry of Education visits the school, he examines the account books…

> AUDITOR: Can you explain this entry, Headmaster? "Owed to turf accountant…"
> HEADMASTER: Alas, we had to have the first eleven cricket pitch returfed.
> AUDITOR: But the entry goes on: "For my losses on the Oaks, 80.00 pounds." Is the Oaks not a horserace, Headmaster?
> HEADMASTER: I don't listen to gossip, sir, I am a man of the Arts. The entry refers to my selling two of our oak trees to a furniture manufacturer who refused to pay up as trees were riddled with the dread Hungarian gunge beetle.

A frequent combatant that the Headmaster faced was the chairman of the school governors who also happened to be the Lady of the Manor…

> HEADMASTER: *(closely examining an oil painting on her drawing-room wall)* Exquisite, milady! Quite exquisite! All hand-colored, I'll warrant.
> MILADY: *(Acidly)* It's a Constable.
> HEADMASTER: Really? *(He peers closely at the picture)* In plain clothes, I see…

As a result of his success on *Take It from Here* and *Whack-O!*, Jimmy Edwards was the subject of *This Is Your Life*, which aired on the BBC on October 6, 1958, hosted by popular Irish-born television personality, Eamonn Andrews. Surprised at the BBC's Piccadilly 1 Studio, Edwards proved to be the type of subject any host might want to avoid as he showed no emotion and poked fun at all the guests, including June Whitfield, Max Homan, Frank Muir, Denis Norden, Charles Maxwell, Dick Bentley, and, via film, Joy Nichols. The only pause in Jimmy's non-stop comedic tirade came when his sister from Australia was brought over by the *This Is Your Life* crew.

Looking at his large family after the show, Jimmy exclaimed, "A worse dressed bunch you never saw."[22] He was outraged that the BBC had provided only one bottle of gin in the way of refreshment, and even more outraged that he was forced to take his family out to dinner at his expense.

(Jimmy also appeared on *This Is Your Life* as a guest on January 28, 1981, when Melvyn Hayes was honored, appearing on stage riding a horse. Jimmy Edwards appeared as a guest on the Eric Sykes tribute on November 29, 1979. He provided a filmed tribute for June Whitfield's show on March 19, 1976.)

After broadcast of the seven *Whack-O!* television series, the BBC adapted various episodes for three seasons on radio, to be aired on the Light Programme, the first time a television series was to have a later life on radio. Series one (May through October 1961) consisted of twenty episodes, series two (March through May 1962) of twelve episodes and series three (April through July 1963) of thirteen episodes. Jimmy Edwards, of course, headed the cast and was reunited with June Whitfield, playing the matron.[23] Others in the radio version were Roddy Maude-Roxby (as Aubrey Potter, replacing the Arthur Howard character), Frederick Treves (as Alfred Tennyson), Edwin Apps (as Arnold Hallforth) Roy Dotrice and Roger Shepherd (both as Lumley), and John Coxall (as Fenner). The Muir and Norden scripts were adapted by David Climie, and the radio series was produced by Edward Taylor.

Arthur Howard was not invited by the BBC to participate in the radio version of *Whacko-O!* because of an unfortunate incident that took place in Brighton in 1961. He had been arrested for importuning in a public lavatory, "cottaging," as it is called in the gay community. He was remanded for a week in Brixton Prison, and at his trial on June 2, 1961, looking like Mr. Toad in *Wind in the Willows*, he was fined twenty-five pounds. Both Frank Muir and Denis Norden spoke on his behalf, and the two writers stood surety of one hundred pounds apiece for Howard's good behavior over the next six months. At the time, there was a witch-hunt for gay man, and that may well be why Howard was forced to spend a week in jail rather than being bailed the next day as would have been routine for such a minor offense.

As Frank Muir explains in his autobiography, Arthur Howard was basically unable to cope with ordinary life. He was very obviously a sweet, kindly, unprepossessing gentleman, with an inferiority complex. He explained to Frank Muir and his wife why he had taken to "cottaging." He would attend dinner parties at which the participants were all more talented and had achieved far more in their careers than had he. Sad at what he perceived as his failure in life, he would leave the parties and go "cottaging," which made him feel as if he was somebody, somebody who had a secret that others at the dinner table did not know.

Arthur Howard was invited by Frank Muir and his wife to stay with them for a week after the hearing. The couple were amused that he could not even cope with eating a boiled egg for breakfast. Howard entertained Muir and his wife with stories about the hardened criminals he had met in Brixton, all of whom protected him and showered him with kindness. He would read the newspapers each morning, checking on their trials, delighted to learn if they had been found not guilty.

Missing, of course, from Howard's defense "team" was Jimmy Edwards, who, according to Frank Muir, was "furious and unforgiving"[24] as he regarded Howard as a selfish and stupid individual, responsible for the end of *Whack-O!* on television. Similarly, Edwin Apps claims that Jimmy's attitude was "unforgiving" and that he would never permit Howard's name to be mentioned.[25] In all probability, the comedian was very much aware that perhaps his own career was in jeopardy should he be identified as gay, something which, in reality, Arthur Howard was not. Indeed, Glenn Mitchell writes, "I do know Edwards was distressed and frustrated by his inability to help…Arthur Howard…He couldn't risk being exposed himself."[26]

The Chiselbury boys were totally unaware of Howard's bisexuality. Keith Nichols recalls,

"We (the boys) found Arthur Howard to be a charming completely professional actor. He was friendly and polite to the boys (I spoke to him briefly a couple of times) but he did not take any special interest in any of us. When we were doing the show, we had no idea he was gay. After the court case in 1961, it was common knowledge….As far as I could see, Jim's relationship with Arthur Howard was a totally professional one. Jim himself of course went both ways, so it was reported later. But to me and the others boys he and Arthur Howard were great actors — comic geniuses."[27]

Earlier, the title *Whack-O!* had been exploited for a summer show, *Wacko, Southsea*, which opened for six week on the South Parade Pier, Southsea, on July 21, 1958. Jimmy, of course, topped the bill, assisted by the Dunja Twins, Dennis Spicer, Harriet and Evans, and Ronald Chesney. Acting as Jimmy's stooge was Tommy Godfrey. According to *The Stage* (July 31, 1958), Jimmy was "in his usual fruity robust form with his ability to get laughs at the twirl of a moustache and clever wisecracking."

From November 1971 through February 1972, the BBC remade some thirteen of the original scripts in color. Jimmy Edwards was joined by Julian Orchard as Pettigrew, Peter Greene as Halliforth, Harold Bennett as Dinwiddie, Gary Warren as Taplow, and Greg Smith as Potter, and the series aired on Saturday afternoons at 5:30 P.M. In response to a question as to how difficult it was to replay the role, Jimmy said, "to play this frightful character is no effort at all." While a handful of the black-and-white episodes exist in the BBC Archives, none of the color episodes are known to have survived.

Happily what has survived and is still legitimately available is *Bottoms Up!*, the feature-length version of *Whack-O!*, although some of the critics pointed out that it was little more than a thirty-minute TV sitcom spun out to ninety minutes. Also complaining as to the length, was the [Melbourne, Australia] *Age* (July 28, 1961) which described Jimmy's performance as "a caricature act which should be taken only in small doses." *Variety* (March 30, 1960) complained that "often the gags and the situations have to be flogged to produce the frequent yocks," amusingly adding, "'Flogged is, perhaps, the operative word," and suggesting the film might have been retitled *The Cane Mutiny*. But who cares? All the fun of the television series is there, and there is seldom a dull moment. Truth be told, *Bottoms Up!* is actually considerably more funny than any of the television episodes of *Whack-O!*, in part because some of the dialogue and suggestive comments would not have been approved of by the BBC.

Bottoms Up! was shot at Elstree Studios, and released in the U.K. by Warner-Pathe in April 1960. Direction was in the reliable hands of Italian-born Mario Zampi, whose career included the co-founding in 1942 of Two Cities Films (producer of such serious classic dramas as *In Which We Serve* and Laurence Olivier's *Henry V* and *Hamlet*) and production/direction of the 1950s comedies, *Laughter in Paradise* (1951) with Alastair Sim and *Too Many Crooks* (1959) with Terry-Thomas. Zampi was also uncredited producer of the 1950 school-based comedy *The Happiest Days of Your*

Life, and so had the right credentials for tackling *Bottoms Up!*. While neither Frank Muir nor Denis Norden were responsible for the storyline, with Michael Pertwee (whose brother, Jon, had impressed in *Murder at the Windmill*) receiving screenplay credit, both Muir and Norden did provide some additional dialogue. Aside from Edwards and Howard, the cast included such British stalwarts as Martita Hunt, Sidney Taffler, Reginald

Jimmy Edwards and Arthur Howard surrounded by the boys in Bottoms Up!

Beckwith, Raymond Huntley, and a bespectacled Richard Briers (prior to his own success in television sitcoms).

At its opening, over the credit titles, *Bottoms Up!* offers something new in the form of a school song, written by Sid Colin, and sung by what appear to be a choir of happy, untrained boys. Jimmy Edwards appears in typical style, sitting in his car for which he has failed to purchase gasoline, and which must now be pushed by Mr. Pettigrew. "I am trying," he whines to the headmaster, who responds, "You're never anything else."

The storyline involves the new chairman of the board of governors (Martita Hunt) issuing an ultimatum that either there must be a vast improvement at the school or Jim must resign. "Goodbye Mister, you've had your chips," as he later comments. Jimmy comes up with a scheme to take as a new boy, Cecil Biggs, played by Melvyn Hayes, to whose father, bookie Sidney Taffler, he owes money. "The little sheik" as Jimmy describes him. The headmaster pretends the new boy, now in blackface, is Prince Hassid of the oil-rich Arab nation of Giwak, impressing the new chairman. In the meantime, the Foreign Office sends the real prince (played by Paul Castaldini in blackface) to Chiselbury, the last place anybody would voluntarily send a boy to be educated. Soviet kidnappers arrive to capture the prince and take him to Russia, but they are foiled thank to a revolt by the boys, led by Wendover, a revolt in part brought on by Cecil Biggs' exploitation of them and challenge to Wendover's leadership.

There is no actual caning of the boys, with Jim's practicing on a cushion — "the old arm hasn't lost its cunning" — and taking out his anger, via the cane, on poor Pettigrew. On Founder's Day, there is to be a public flogging of Wendover and four other boys, unfairly blamed for the actions of Cecil Briggs. Somewhat embarrassingly, Mr. Pettigrew inspects the boys' bottoms for hidden articles that might soften the blows. Jimmy has all four boys bend over as one, and produces a cane long enough to reach each bottom — "a five-seater model."

Bottoms Up!! is a fun film, and I write that as someone who has, as of writing, sat through it three times. The last third is very reminiscent of Lindsay Anderson's *If...*, almost as if Jimmy and company were prescient enough to produce a comic version of the anti-establishment drama. Certainly, the boys here are fighting the establishment as much as the three boys, and one girl friend in *If...*, but without real guns, and limited to water cannon, arrows with rubber tips, eggs, and flour. As *Variety* noted, it "is a piece of genuine slapstick," but as to the "purely local appeal," which the trade paper describes, I would disagree and suggest it should have appeal in most of the English-speaking world, and, yes, as Jimmy's 1940s friend and film critic Alan Dent wrote in the *Illustrated London News* (April 30, 1960), it would be "Unimaginable without this maestro of fun."

Whack-O! may represent Jimmy Edwards' best-known and best-loved television work, but there were certainly other appearances and other series. The BBC television service resumed after the end of World War Two on June 7, 1946, broadcasting from Alexandra Palace in North London. In creative charge as director and producer was Cecil Madden (1902-1987), who had been at the BBC since 1933 and with its television division from its inception in 1936. Madden wrote,

"In my eternal search for new talent I had always haunted the Windmill Theatre and on their glass stage there was always new talent. However one always had to brace oneself for endless arguments with Vivian Van Damm who ran it dictatorially."[28]

One Windmill comedian who made it to the BBC and Cecil Madden was Jimmy Edwards. Madden sent his agent, Kenneth Bandy, a letter, dated August 26, 1946, booking the comedian and noting, "I hope you will impress on him that the act must be absolutely clean material from our point of view," adding, presciently, "I hope this will lead to many dates for him in television." On August 30, 1946, Jimmy sent the producer a script for his trombone act. "I won't prove a disappointment," he promised, adding, "There's a great deal of music involved which will have to be arranged 'On the stand,' as they say. I warn you, not ALL musicians like that!"[29]

Within a year of completion of the initial run of *Whack-O!*, the comedian appeared in the BBC's seven-episode series, *The Seven Faces of Jim* (broadcast from November through December 1961), as well as two sequels, *Six More Faces of Jim* (broadcast from November through December 1962)[30] and the six-episode *More Faces of Jim* (broadcast from June through August 1963), all written by Frank Muir and Denis Norden. June Whitfield and Ronnie Barker were Jimmy's co-stars as each self-contained episode had Jimmy facing up to a different situation in life. For example, in the first episode of the first series, "The Face of Devotion," he is a devoted husband fearful that he is losing his wife, June Whitfield, to her fixation with ballroom dancing. Popular orchestra leader Victor Sylvester guest starred.

In his autobiography, Frank Muir particularly remembers the fifth episode from the first series, "The Face of Duty," a parody (as were many of the episodes) of the Michael Powell film, *A Matter of Life and Death* (released in the U.S. as *Stairway to Heaven*). Jimmy Edwards is retired wing-commander Frobisher who operates a minicab company with one cab and one driver (Richard Briers, who appeared in three episodes from the first series). In a thick fog, the company's dispatcher (June Whitfield), with direction given over her microphone, has to guide the lone driver back to the office. "Exactly on time, the minicab crashed through the brick wall of the minicab office and came to rest a few inches from June."[31]

That first series earned Muir and Norden the award for the "Best Work in Television Light Entertainment Series" from the Screenwriters' Guild of Great Britain.

For the first two series, the episodes were all titled "The Face of" whatever (including Guilt, Fatherhood, Wisdom, and Retribution). For the third series, the episodes were all titled "A Matter of" whatever, and ranged from subjects as varied as Amnesia and Empire.

In 1962, aside from the first two series of the "Faces of Jim," the star appeared in one episode of the American television series, starring Danny Thomas, *Make Room for Daddy*; titled "A Hunting We Will Go," the thirty-minute comedy also featured a couple of other prominent British performers, Raymond Huntley and Peter Butterworth, and was filmed in part at Henley-on-Thames. As early as 1959, a former CBS executive had

Jimmy Edwards with Danny Thomas and Marjorie Lord, filming Make Room for Daddy *on location at a pub of course.*

noted that Jimmy Edwards could be a big success in the United States,[32] but always his appeal here was limited.

One new series followed another for Jimmy Edwards, with none really intended to air beyond the initial first run. At the rate of one per year, for the BBC, he starred in fortnightly episodes of *Bold as Brass* (April through June 1964), ten episodes of *I Object* (April through June 1965), eight episodes of *Mr. John Jorrocks* (July through September 1966), and six episodes of *The World of Wodehouse: Blandings Castle* (February through March 1967). *Bold as Brass* was based on a BBC comedy-drama, *Man o' Brass*, which aired on November 28, 1963, and starred Jimmy Edwards as Northerner, Ernie Briggs, whose principle interest in life was the local brass band, founded by his great-grandfather, much to the annoyance of his wife, Bessie, played by the brilliant comedienne Beryl Reid; "a glorious partnership," reported *The Stage* (April 9, 1964). Beryl Reid was good for Jimmy in that she would demand he learn his script; "No, you can't go and play polo, you've got to learn your part. We can't have you here not knowing the words."[33] She was ideally cast in that like her character she didn't care for brass bands. Reid did, however, find amusing a line that Jimmy used here and had often used on other occasions: "I must take my bicycle-clips off, otherwise I shan't feel the benefit when I go out!"

The brass band featured in the show was the Ulverston Town Band,[34] with location filming at Stanley Park, Liverpool. With his love of the trombone, and his involvement with the City of Oxford Silver Band, the part was perfect for Jimmy, although he did admit to having a problem with accents, such as that here from the North of England. The program also reunited him with Wallas Eaton from *Take It from Here*. Writer Ron Watson used his original script as the basis for the series, again with Beryl Reid, and with Ronnie Barker, who was becoming almost a regular co-player in Jimmy Edwards television work.

Beryl Reid and Jimmy Edwards worked together on stage in S.H. Newsome's *Spring Review* at the Coventry Theatre in April 1962, which became S.H. Newsome's *Autumn Spectacular*, when it played the Palace Theatre, Manchester in October of the same year. In her autobiography, Beryl Reid recalls that a horse called Tunis, who appeared in the show, was obviously attracted to her and would achieve a giant erection whenever she climbed on his back. Jimmy would be required strategically to place his bowler in front of the horse and shield the audience from the engorged member.

As the title character in *Mr. John Jorrocks*, Jimmy is a cockney grocer who abandons his store to become squire and master of fox hounds of the village of Handley Cross. (Location scenes were shot at Atheralls Farm.) Playing his wife was Angela Baddeley, best known to American audiences as the cook, Mrs. Bridges, on *Upstairs, Downstairs*. The series was based on *Jorrocks' Jaunts and Jollities* (1838) by the popular Victorian novelist, R.S. Surtees, and the character must have appealed to Jimmy in that not only was he somewhat vulgar but, and far more importantly, he loved to ride with the hounds in search of a fox.

Jimmy's then-agent Sonny Zahl wrote David Attenborough, controller of BBC2 that the series "proved a turning point in Jimmy Edwards' career, and was a subject that he has wanted to portray for many years."[35] Sadly, Attenborough responded, "At the moment we have no plans for another *Jorrocks* series, delighted though we are with the programmes themselves."[36]

Another well-known novelist provided the source material for Jimmy's next series, *The World of Wodehouse: Blandings Castle*. It was based on a succession of books by P.G. Wodehouse, which did not feature his best-known characters of Jeeves and Wooster, but rather Lord Emsworth (played here by Ralph Richardson), with Meriel Forbes as his wife, Lady Constance. Jimmy was cast as Sir Gregory Parsloe-Parsloe, a name which surely must have appealed to him in its alliteration.

Jimmy Edwards has another connection to P.G. Wodehouse, with *Oh! Clarence*, a Wodehouse adaptation, that played the Grand Theatre, Leeds, in December 1970, with the comedian appearing opposite Cicely Courtneidge, with Robertson Hare in support, and the entire production under the direction of Courtneidge's husband, Jack Hulbert.

I Object was not a sitcom, as one might assume, but rather a parlor game or quiz show, broadcast as a series of ten episodes in 1965, that brought together three great British comedians, Jimmy Edwards, Ted Ray and Charlie Chester in a courtroom setting, with Jimmy as the judge and the other two as opposing barristers. All three were stand-up comics who had enjoyed major success on radio, with an argument once having been made that Ted Ray had been heard on radio more times than any other British comedian. Jimmy also starred in another quiz-type show, *The August Game*, which aired in eight episodes on London Weekend Television in August and September 1968, and with Barry Cryer, Ted Ray, Les Dawson, and others, he starred in *Jokers Wild* on Yorkshire Television in June 1969. Jimmy was obviously at ease and enjoyed this type of programming, unscripted and unrehearsed; minimal effort as far as he was concerned for a reasonable payment, and as early as September 1955, he had appeared on a trial panel game, *Bury the Hatchet*, for the commercial television outlet, Associated Rediffusion.

Another short-lived series in the tradition of game shows, this time a little more upmarket, was *The Auction Game*, produced by Humphrey Barclay for London Weekend Television in 1983. Very much a precursor to the popular afternoon programs currently on the BBC, in which antiques are bought, sold and valued, *The Auction Game* had three contestants bidding for antiques with the winner being the one with the biggest profit. As host, Jimmy enjoyed himself inviting the contestants to take a glass of port with him at opportune moments.

The World of Wodehouse: Blandings Castle marked the end of Jimmy Edwards' exclusive connection to the BBC, as he moved on to appearances on commercial television. For London Weekend Television, he was James Fossett, a writer of cheap, popular fiction or "penny dreadfuls" in *The Fossett Saga*, a period piece set in Victorian England, shown as a series of seven thirty minutes episodes in January through February 1969. Another period piece was *Sir Yellow*, a six-part series for Yorkshire Television set in the 13th Century, with Jimmy as the anti-hero, a cowardly, womanizing, beer-swilling knight, to whom chivalry was truly dead. The series, which was both a critical and an audience flop, aired in six episodes from June through August 1973. *The Galton and Simpson Comedy*, which aired on London Weekend Television in April and May 1969, presented a series of comedy shorts, with potential for adaptation as series. Jimmy starred in episode four, airing on May 10, 1969, opposite Pat Combs, as Mr. and Mrs. Croucher, and titled "Don't Dilly Dally on the Way."[37]

Here the Crouchers are about to leave the home that they have just sold and move on to another, "Mill stone mark two," as Jimmy describes it. But Joyce Croucher decides she does not want to move and locks herself in the toilet, much to the fury of husband Arthur and the newlyweds who have purchased the house and are moving in to take possession. There are jokes about the dry rot and rising damp in the house, which only sold this year "because we had a dry summer," that "more than memories will start coming back if it starts to rain," and the Crouchers' cat buried in the garden under the carrots.

As an added bonus, newlywed Gordon is played by a young David Jason, familiar and highly regarded by British television viewers for the comedy series *Only Fools and Horses*, the police drama *A Touch of Frost* and the comedy-drama, *The Darling Buds of May*.

"Don't Dilly Dally on the Way" was not picked up as a series, nor was another pilot, *Heirs on a Shoestring*, in which Jimmy Edwards appeared. Co-starring Clive Dunn (best known to television viewers for *Dad's Army*), the thirty-minute sitcom, written by Dave Freeman, who had provided a 1952 script for Jimmy on *Workers' Playtime*, aired on BBC One on June 9, 1967, with Jimmy expecting a substantial inheritance from his uncle, only to discover there was another potential claimant. The show was not well received by the critics, with *The Stage* (June 15, 1967) noting, "Jimmy Edwards seemed very subdued as though unhappy at being forced to stick to dialogue as pedestrian as this instead of ad-libbing wildly....This show was neither good enough to appeal to those who prefer wit nor bad enough to appeal to those who like their comedy to be obvious. It was merely tedious."

Jimmy and Clive Dunn had also worked together on another pilot, *Gentleman Jim*, written by Jimmy Grafton and David Climie, which was broadcast by the ABC commercial company on February 16, 1967, in the Midlands and the North of England only. With Jim as Squire Jim and Clive Dunn as his butler, Jim Bules, the show had actually been recorded almost two years earlier, in April 1965.

Jimmy's ability to ride a horse was probably the only reason for his being cast as Sir William Barry in one episode of the children's television serial, *Brendon Chase*, which aired for thirteen episodes beginning at the end of December 1980. He was his usual irascible self, as another player in the film, Liza Goddard, writes,

"I remember being on the set one morning at about 7am and David [her husband] has a polystyrene cup full of coffee in his hand. Jimmy appeared and said: 'Blimey, David, that looks a bit hot. Let me sort it out for you.' With that, he reached into his pocket, produced a hip flask and proceeded to pour a very generous measure of brandy into David's cup."[38]

Liza Goddard worked later with Jimmy on stage in the Ray Cooney farce, *Wife Begins at Forty* (1985), and once walked past Jimmy in the theatre. In response to her question as to how he was, Jimmy replied, "I am completely pissed." Somehow, he still managed to appear on stage and get through the performance. "Back in the day, people turned a blind eye. As long as the actor in question didn't let the people down, they were allowed to get away with it."[39]

Jimmy Edwards' last major contribution to television was, in reality, a continuation of his last major contribution to radio, and that was *Does the Team Think?* The concept was a simple one: that of having members of the studio audience pose questions to a panel of comedians. When the show first aired on radio, beginning on October 20, 1957, the panelists were magician David Nixon, actor David Tomlinson (who the previous year had co-starred with Edwards in the screen adaptation of *Three Men in a Boat*), Jimmy Wheeler (a comedian who had first been heard on radio in the 1920s), and, of course, Jimmy Edwards himself. BBC announcer Peter Haigh was the original chairman of the panel.[40] To regulars on the show, it was also known simply and affectionately as *Stinks*.

For the second season, which began June 1, 1958, Peter Haigh was replaced by fellow BBC announcer McDonald Hobley, who had been the BBC's chief staff announcer but by this time had actually defected to commercial television. There were three new panelists, diminutive Arthur Askey, Tommy Trinder (who would always refer to his audience as "You Lucky People") and Larry Adler (a brilliant harmonica player who had been forced to leave the United States and emigrate to England as a result of the blacklist in the 1950s). When the 100th show of *Does the Team Think?* was aired on March 4, 1963, Edwards and Trinder were joined by Ted Ray (whose radio show, *Ray's a Laugh*[41] was heard from April 4, 1949 through January 13, 1961) and Cyril Fletcher (known for his "odd odes").

Tommy Trinder had been featured on a 1955-1956 show titled *My Wildest Dream*, and heard on the BBC Light Programme. It was similar in many ways to *Does the Team Think?* Tommy Trinder was not a favorite of Jimmy's, often dominating the proceedings, and at one point, he was told, "Tommy, instead of always saying the first thing that comes into your head, why not try the second?"

Does the Team Think? was brought to television by the BBC in 1961, with twelve shows airing between May and August of that year. Joining Jimmy were Ted Ray, Bernard Braden, Frank Muir, and Kenneth Horne. The program was revived by commercial broadcaster Thames Television, with nine shows televised between January and March 1982 and six shows broadcast in May and June 1983. The panelists were Frankie Howerd, Beryl Reid, Tim Brooke-Taylor, and Willie Rushton. The last was co-founder of the satirical weekly *Private Eye*, and has the distinction of having brought back from Australia the ashes of Tony Hancock, in an Air France carry-on bag. *Does the Team Think?* is a reminder that throughout Jimmy Edwards' career, so many of the same names pop up, be it Frank Muir, Beryl Reid or, in indirect fashion, Tony Hancock

1. Denis Norden, *Clips from a Life*, p. 104.

2. "And We Applaud," p. 205.

3. Frank Muir, *A Kentish Lad*, p. 225.

4. Ronnie Waldman (1914-1978) is credited with the discovery of Morecambe and Wise, and was married to actress Lana Morris, who was well-known in her native country.

5. Denis Norden, *Clips from a Life*, p. 186. The script was the work of Robert Edmunds, Will Hay and J.B. Morton; the latter was best known for the "Beachcomber" column in the *Daily Express*.

6. *Down with Skool!* was published by Max Parrish and Co.

7. Corporal punishment was banned in all British state schools in 1987; in 1999, it was banned in private schools in England and Wales; in 2000 in private schools in Scotland; and the following year in private schools in Northern Ireland.

8. "Beating Their Privileged Bottoms," an article in *The Times* (October 18, 1973), provides a good overview of canings in British public schools.

9. Guy Taylor, "Not Good — But You Mustn't Blame the BBC for Trying," p. 16.

10. "Whack-O!," *http://www.bbc.co.uk/comedy/whacko/*.

11. Mark McKay, "Whack-O!," *Laugh Magazine*, p. 2.

12. Later played by Peter Greene. Actor Edwin Apps was also responsible, with his wife, Pauline Devaney, for the popular BBC television comedy series, *All Gas and Gaiters*, which aired from 1966 through 1971.

13. As already noted, Jerry Desmonde (1908-1967) was a perfect stooge for Sid Field. In later years he was associated with Norman Wisdom. Jerry Desmonde committed suicide, depressed at the death of his wife, Peggy Duncan, the year previous.

14. In 1971, Frankie Howerd and June Whitfield recorded a parody of the Serge Gainsbourg/Jane Birkin hit, "Je t'aime, Je t'aime."

15. Memorandum, undated but written circa 1960, in BBC Written Archives.

16. One of the strangest of Arthur Howard's films and the only one in which he starred is *Paradisio*, written and directed by H. Haile Chace, in which he plays a college professor who is given a pair of spectacle that allow him (and the audience) to see clothed people in the nude and in 3-D. Eva Waegner, the German Brigitte Bardot, co-starred in this romp through European tourist locations. The film was released in the U.S. in the summer of 1962, and described by the *Baltimore Sun* (July 2, 1962) as "a combined comedy, thriller, travelogue and peep show, in none of which capacities is it any good."

17. Frank Muir, "A Little Foil to Big Jimmy," p. 32.

18. Edwin Apps, *Pursued by Bishops*, p. 279.

19. Ibid, p. 32.

20. Keith Nichols to Anthony Slide, e-mail dated February 6, 2017. Keith Nichols is now an award-winning jazz pianist and arranger, and is on the faculty of the Royal Academy of Music.

21. Prior to 1957, the only means by which the BBC could record a live show was through telerecording or the use of a kinescope (as it was described in the U.S.). In April 1958, the BBC introduced its own videotape system, VERA or Vision Electronic Recording Apparatus. It was abandoned about six months later, and the BBC acquired an AMPEX recorder from the United States, but it was more than a year before a second AMPEX recorder was purchased. Thus, there was only very limited videotape use at the BBC by late 1959. Surprising as it might be, it was more expensive in the 1960s to videotape a show than to film it. For this reason, the BBC routinely wiped videotapes and re-used them, thus resulting in the loss of such a large quantity of its programming. As Glenn Mitchell points out, what little archival policy the BBC had seemed to favor keeping black-and-white telerecordings, irrespective of the program's original format.

22. Edwin Apps, *Pursued by Bishops*, p. 302.

23. Various actresses had played matron in the television series, most notably Liz Fraser in series two. In her autobiography, she recalls that Jimmy would frequently forget his lines, and once, while trying to fill in with her next line, he held up his hand and declaimed, "Back, Matron, Back!" He had just remembered the forgotten line. "It was a very happy show" (p. 49).

24. Frank Muir, *A Kentish Lad*, p. 247.

25. Edwin Apps, *Pursued by Bishops*, p. 288.

26. Glenn Mitchell to Anthony Slide, e-mail dated January 23, 2017.

27. Keith Nichols to Anthony Slide, e-mail dated February 7, 2017.

28. Cecil Madden, *Starlight Days*, p. 256.

29. Correspondence from the BBC Written Archives.

30. There was also a fifteen-minute special, *The Christmas Face of Jim*, part of *Christmas Night with the Stars*, broadcast on December 25, 1962.

31. Frank Muir, *A Kentish Lad*, p. 252.

32. Margaret Cowan, "Britain As a Market, Is Important to the U.S.," p. 7.

33. Beryl Reid, *So Much Love*, p. 97.

34. Ulverston is, of course, famous as the birthplace of Stan Laurel.

35. Sonny Zahl to David Attenborough, July 28, 1966, BBC Written Archives.

36. David Attenborough to Sonny Zahl, August 2, 1966, BBC Written Archives.

37. The episode was remade in 1996 as a vehicle for Paul Merton.

38. Liza Goddard, *Working with Children and Animals*, p. 135.

39. Ibid, p. 140.

40. Peter Haigh (1925-2001) joined the BBC in 1952 and was better known for his work on television, where he was dubbed "Television's Most Eligible Bachelor."

41. Like so many Englishmen of my generation, I can still recall with affection the theme song, which began "Ray's a Laugh! Ray's a Laugh!/When you're feeling sad and blue just/Ray's a Laugh!"

CHAPTER SEVEN

The Stage

For most of his career, Jimmy Edwards was as busy on stage as he was on radio and television. He was an enthusiastic performer in summer shows at British seaside resorts and in that peculiarly British tradition, the pantomime, in which the principal boy was always played by a girl and the "dame" always played by a man. Perhaps because of the moustache, there was no suggestion that Jimmy don drag and appear as a pantomime dame; he was usually cast as the king or the baron or some such relatively decent character.

He played pantomime in small and large venues, beginning with *Mother Goose* at London's Golders Green Hippodrome for seven weeks in 1948-1949, playing the village mayor. Jimmy managed to introduce his euphonium[1] into the story. He co-starred with up-and-coming young singer-comedian Freddie Starr[2] in *The Sleeping Beauty* at the New Theatre, Oxford, during the 1970-1971 Christmas season. On a grander scale, he starred in *Puss in Boots* at the London Palladium in 1962-1963, playing Jimkhana, Duke of Monte Polo, and was, according to *The Stage* (January 3, 1963) "in his element." In one memorable pantomime, *Babes in the Wood*, at the Hippodrome, Brighton, which opened on December 24, 1956, the comedian appeared as Jimmy the Good Robber, and rode a horse on stage.[3] Another memorable appearance, many years later was in the 1983-1984 Christmas season at the Theatre Royal, Lincoln, where Jimmy stumbled around the stage with script in hand. "It seemed to add entertainment for the adults," commented *The Stage and Television Today* (January 12, 1984). A similar problem occurred the following year in the pantomime, *Jack and the Beanstalk*, at the Theatre on the Green in Richmond, when Jimmy, as the father did not seem able to remember his daughter's name and could only reference her as "that ginger-headed girl."

The Richard Rodgers and Oscar Hammerstein II musical, *Cinderella*, was originally written for television, and first broadcast on CBS on March

31, 1957. For its British debut over the 1958-1959 Christmas holiday season, from December 18, 1958 through April 11, 1959, it was presented as a pantomime, with some additional songs and rewriting of the book, at the London Coliseum (later the home of English National Opera). The show featured an all-star cast, with Kenneth Williams (as one of the ugly sisters), Betty Marsden, Yana (as Cinderella), Tommy Steele (as Buttons

Jimmy with his nephew Rolly Wilkinson at a rehearsal for the 1951 Royal Variety Show.

and making his pantomime debut), Bruce Trent (as the prince), and Jimmy Edwards, in the lesser role of the King. In large part because of its presentation as a pantomime rather than a typical musical comedy, it ran for only 160 performances. There was a 1961 Christmas revival of *Cinderella* at London's Adelphi Theatre, and again Jimmy Edwards was the King, with Janet Waters in the title role. The show also marked a nice reunion for Jimmy with Mr. Pettigrew, as Arthur Howard was cast in the role of the Lord Chancellor. Both Arthur Howard and Jimmy had also appeared in a 1959/1960 production of *Cinderella* at the Bristol Hippodrome.

Throughout the 1950s, Jimmy Edwards was a staple of the Royal Variety Performance, held on an annual basis at various London theatres on a rotation basis, and usually attended by Queen Elizabeth II and Prince Philip. His first appearance before the Royal Family, the future Queen and her father, George VI, was at the Victoria Palace on October 29, 1951, on a bill that included Vera Lynn and the great African American singer and longtime London resident Adelaide Hall. He shared the bill at the London Palladium on November 3, 1952, again with Vera Lynn and Maurice Chevalier, no longer maligned as a World War Two collaborator;[4] it was the first time that the Queen and Prince Philip attended together.

"I have to deal with an old Queen at the Palace," says the Duke of Edinburgh, "Do I have to deal with another one on the polo field."

On November 2, 1953, at the London Coliseum, with Britain's new Queen and ruler in attendance, he harangued members of the audience with shouts of, "Sit up, boy, and look at me. Don't keep staring at your new ruler." It brought the biggest laugh of the evening.[5] Certainly, Jimmy did not seem to concern himself with offending royalty, perhaps because he played polo with the Duke of Edinburgh. On television in 1968, celebrating the 50th anniversary of the Royal Air Force, he made a few jokes about playing polo with the Duke. After the show, the Duke met the performers, but pointedly ignored Jimmy, who responded to the slight with "Sir. You've missed me out." "What do you expect," replied the Duke, adding, "Don't worry. I'll get my own back on the polo ground!"[6]

The Queen would also appear to have been kindly disposed towards the comedian. Royal convention has it that she must always wear gloves when shaking hands with her subjects. However, there are photographs of her greeting Jimmy Edwards with ungloved hands. It might appear trivial, but it was major break with propriety.

Jimmy's friendship with members of the Royal Family was such that in the 1960s, at a Concert Artistes Association royal concert in the presence of Princess Margaret and Lord Snowden, when organizer Cyril Fletcher was having difficulty in getting the Royal party back into the auditorium after intermission, he turned to Jimmy Edwards. Edwards came on stage and yelled, "Ma'am! Overtime and beginners! We are about to begin the second half!" "How enjoyable," replied Princess Margaret as she returned to the Royal Box.[7]

In *Big Bad Mouse*, Jimmy would make reference to "'im" whose married to "'er," adding that "'im" and Jimmy played polo (or 'orse 'ockey as it was called in Cockney slang) together, and that "'im" had been told to stay close to Jimmy if he wanted to get his photograph in the newspapers.

When I asked "'im," better known to lesser mortals as H.R.H. The Duke of Edinburgh if he had anything to relate in regard to Jimmy Edwards, I was informed that "he doesn't have any recollections…that would be of any significance or interest."[8]

Jimmy would share the bill for the Royal Variety Performances with the best of British entertainers and a sampling of American stars, such as George Jessel, Lena Horne and Johnnie Ray at the November 7, 1955 Victoria Palace performance. Significantly, after years of sharing the bill with his contemporaries or older members of the profession, on May 16, 1960, at the Victoria Palace, he was on the same stage as newcomers, Lonnie Donegan, Cliff Richard and Adam Faith, offering a very different style of entertainment, as well as competing with Americans Liberace and Sammy Davis, Jr. (who proved to be the hit of the evening).

At the 1955 performance, Jimmy appeared as a judge, hearing a breach-of-promise case. "How do you plead?" he asked the accused. And when the poor man burst into tears, Jimmy responded, "My God, you are a miserable pleader, aren't you?"

Despite his aversion to the city, Jimmy Edwards was considered a steadfast member of the group of comedians who played Blackpool each summer on a regular basis. The group included many names little known today, such as Charlie Cairoli, Freddie Frinton, Nat Jackley, Jimmy James, Albert Modley, Gladys Morgan, and Jack Storey, as well as better-known comedians, such as George Formby, Tony Hancock, and, perhaps surprisingly, Terry-Thomas. As early as July 1950, Jimmy and his co-stars on *Take It from Here* appeared at Blackpool's Winter Gardens Pavilion. It was Blackpool that gave Jimmy his first opportunity to appear on independent, commercial television, with ABC's *Blackpool Night Out*, broadcast on July 5, 1964.

It was on the London stage that Jimmy enjoyed his greatest successes, all at the Adelphi Theatre. First with *Take It from Us*, which ran for 570

performances from October 31, 1950 through October 6, 1951. Next came *London Laughs*, which ran for an incredible 1,112 performances from April 4, 1952 through February 6, 1954, with a brief break in July/August 1952. There was a "closed" performance at 8:45 P.M. on August 17, 1953, when the show was televised. Finally, there was *Talk of the Town*, with 656 performances from November 17, 1954 through December 10, 1955.

Take It from Us was performed twice nightly, at 6:00 and 8:30, and Jimmy was featured in Act One in a sketch "with interruptions" by Wallas Eaton. In Act Two, Jimmy had a solo spot, with "Wake Up at the Back," and the show concluded with *Friends, Romans, Countrymen*, written by Talbot Rothwell (of "Carry On" fame) from radio scripts by Frank Muir and Denis Norden.

In *London Laughs*, Jimmy shared the stage with Tony Hancock and World War Two forces' sweetheart Vera Lynn, performing two shows a night at 6:00 and again at 8:45. During the course of the long run, Hancock had three nervous breakdowns, while the imperturbable Miss Lynn remained calm and spent free time in her dressing room either knitting or tapestry embroidering. Jimmy noted that he might also have suffered a mental collapse had it not been "for the grace of Scotch." One night, with an attack of the flu, he told producers George and Alfred Black that he could not go on. Following instructions to go to the theatre and do his best, he found a bottle of Johnny Walker whisky in his dressing room with a note attached from the Blacks with the words, "You'll manage, Jim." As he confessed, "They knew their Jim."[9] Both Jimmy and Hancock were heavy drinkers, but the former always had his alcohol consumption under control unlike Hancock, who once told Jimmy, "For me, the best drink of the day is the vodka in the bath before breakfast."[10]

Act One began with Vera Lynn and Jimmy Edwards saying "Hello to You" to the audience. Jimmy was joined by Tony Hancock for the sketch, "A Seat in the Circle," written by Frank Muir and Denis Norden. The writers also provided the Second Act sketch, "Polly Does Everything," also with Jimmy and Tony Hancock. Jimmy Edwards had a solo spot, again titled "Wake Up at the Back There," and the entire cast appeared on stage for the concluding "Al Jolson Memories," with Jim singing, "About a Quarter to Nine."

London Laughs was widely praised by the critics, with R.B. Marriott writing in *The Stage* (November 6, 1952) that "Mr. Edwards pricks the bubble of solemnity and neatly mangles all sorts of familiar pretenses."

It was around this time that Jimmy designed a familiar stage prop, the schoolmaster's desk that was to become a staple of his act. Fellow comedian Nat Jackley helped in the creation of the desk, which famously included a bottle of beer where the inkwell should be. It was possibly first used in *London Laughs*, against a backdrop of school room, with windows looking out to the playing fields and cloisters of a school named St. Lucifer's. For the stage act, Jimmy would have the audience as his class, rather than actual boys on stage (not wanting, he maintained, to so obviously imitate Will Hay).

When Jimmy Edwards tried to appear in a straight musical — he never attempted a dramatic legitimate play — he was generally unsuited for the role, as with his performance as General Malona in the old-fashioned revival of the 1917 operetta *The Maid of the Mountains* at London's Palace Theatre in May 1972. Jimmy was, as *The Stage* (May 4, 1972) noted, "a simple buffoon, an act out of variety, not a character in *The Maid of the Mountains.*" The problem was, as the comedian tried to explain, the only role he was qualified to play was that of Jimmy Edwards.[11] However, his musical ability, coupled with comedic delivery, did provide him with the occasional unique experience, such as narrating "Tubby the Tuba," the children's story for orchestra and narrator by Paul Tripp and George Kleinsinger, as part of a semi-classical program at London's Royal Festival Hall in June 1957. *The Stage* (July 4, 1957) reported that Jimmy's delivery was "highly diverting, visually and aurally." Some years later, on May 25, 1960, on the BBC Television *Music for You* program, Jimmy reprised his performance.

What was arguably Edwards' first straight part in the West End was at the Queen's Theatre in September 1968, when he took over from Robert Morley as General Mallalieu FitzButtress in Peter Ustinov's *Halfway Up the Tree*. The plot concerns the character's having to deal with teenage hippy children. *The Stage* (October 3, 1968) wrote,

"In the first scene Mr. Edwards is rightly, carefully restrained; in the later scenes, when the character assumes comedy-farce proportions, he retains a basic restraint and develops the characterization while adding layers of exuberant comedy."

Concurrent with Jimmy's appearance in *Halfway Up the Tree*, the first London production of *Hair* opened, taking advantage of the abolition of stage censorship. How strange it must have seemed to the comedienne to realize that his career as a star had begun with *Take It from Here*, and that he was still a star but in a very much changed world.

One very interesting role for Jimmy, and one that he would appear to have played only once, is Sheridan Whiteside in a production of *The Man Who Came to Dinner* that was seen at the Richmond Theatre, West of London, on October 12-24, 1970. The character of Sheridan Whiteside was created by Moss Hart and George S. Kaufman, using the prototype of Alexander Woollcott, and became a stage and screen vehicle for Monty Woolley. How one wishes that Jimmy's performance might have been recorded for posterity, if for no other reason than discovering if he could actually adopt an American accent (which seems unlikely).

Jimmy Edwards was back in the West End, at the Criterion Theatre, in November 1972 in the sex-themed revue-type *Hulla Baloo*, set in a lavish public toilet. (The London theatre had moved on from the relatively restrained production of *Hair*.) Female impersonators, Michael Rogers and Ray Starr were the stars. Jimmy co-starred, and R.B. Marriott in *The Stage* (November 9, 1972) noted that he performed without the aid of a

Hulla Baloo: *Female Impersonators Michael Rogers and Roy Starr at left and right, with Jimmy Edwards and Chelsea Brown in the middle.*

musical instrument and was "in top form, more amusing than I have seen him for sometime, simply because there is an air of freshness about all he does."

In *The Guardian* (November 1, 1972), critic Michael Billington provides a good record of Jimmy's performance:

"the ebullient Jimmy Edwards enlivens the party whether inviting us to sing a blatantly racialist hymn to Enoch [Powell], slapping knees, thighs and buttocks as a hairy Tyrolean songster or appearing in full drag looking like some raddled Boadicea….Mr. Edwards is a comic who needs, in every sense, ample room to manoeuvre and time to bully, cajole and harass the audience in his peculiar hectoring style. Here he seems cabin'd, cribb'd, fin'd."

The "Doctor" series of feature films, based on the novels by Richard Gordon, and with either Dirk Bogarde or Leslie Phillips in the leading role, were popular with moviegoers from 1954 through 1970. A stage adaptation, *Doctor in the House*, based on the original 1954 film, was to become a staple of British repertory theatre. Jimmy Edwards took over the role of Sir Lancelot Spratt, played on screen by James Robertson

Justice, in a touring version in 1978, which began in Hull in January of that year, moving on to York in February. Despite a script by an eminent writer, Ted Willis, Jimmy could not resist extensive ad-libbing. The youngish male lead was played by dancer Lionel Blair, a familiar figure on British television, and he and Jimmy turned the play at its conclusion into a cabaret act with a musical interlude on the trombone and Blair's tap dancing. Critical response indicates that Blair stole the show. The Dirk Bogarde character, Simon Sparrow, was played by Andrew Knox, the son of Hollywood stars, Alexander Knox and Doris Nolan, and the matron was played by Chili Bouchier, a British silent star often compared to Clara Bow. All in all, it would appear to have been a fun production, and one wishes it might have been captured on film.

Not content to appear in the work of others, Jimmy wrote his own starring vehicle in 1979, *Oh! Sir James!* There was little question as to whom the leading character, with his love of horses and the bottle, was based. The plot revolved around Jimmy's effort to hang on to a potential legacy from his grandfather in Australia by adopting the image of a virtuous, abstemious, God-fearing grandson. Helping in the characterization and the humor was Kenneth Connor as faithful servant, Soames. *Oh! Sir James!* Opened at the Towngate Theatre, in Poole Dorset, and subsequently toured. The critic for *The Stage* (May 24, 1979) wrote that "Impresario Paul Elliott described himself not so much as director but as referee, and once the rough edges have been trimmed, the play word perfect and the ad libs can flow, *Oh! Sir James!* will be a great success." It was not, with dates seemingly limited to seaside resorts such as Weston-Super-Mare (the birthplace of John Cleese, a British comedian who does not seem to have realized that he is no longer funny).[12]

While by no means did it signify the end of Jimmy's acting career on stage, it seems somehow appropriate to conclude this overview of Jimmy's stage career with *Big Bad Mouse*. I am probably one of the few around who was friendly with the man ultimately responsible for the play, the one who came up with the original idea, adapted to play form by Phillip King and Falkland Cary. And that man was Ivan Butler (1909-1998). When I knew Ivan, he walked with a limp and the aid of a stick, and he was known to film buffs of the day for the wide variety of books he had published.[13] He also had another claim to fame as one of the actors in the original, 1929 British stage production of *Dracula*. Ivan played Lord Godalming and also understudied Dracula, whom in later productions he was actually to play. It never bothered Ivan that his play was being destroyed by its actors; after all, it simply meant a healthier return on his work thanks to inflated box office receipts.

In 1966, Jimmy was signed by producer Martin Codron to star in *Big Bad Mouse*, which would have a six week tour of the provinces and then open in London. The play had already been staged, first with comedians Dave King and Charlie Chester, and then with Terry Scott and Hugh Lloyd (hugely successful as a duo on television), and been a dismal failure. Edwards called Eric Sykes, a friend with whom Jimmy shared similar right-wing, Conservative views, and told him that he only wanted to take on the part if Sykes was involved. Asked what the play was about, with typical lack of concern, Jimmy replied, "No idea, I haven't read it yet."[14]

The tour was not a success, with theatre staff often outnumbering the audience, and after the fifth week, Sykes, playing downtrodden employee Mr. Broome, and Edwards, playing factory owner Price-Hargreaves, agreed that the mistake they had made was in actually doing the play, which had only one set, the offices of Chunkibix Ltd., a biscuit factory. They had realized that their joint curtain speech, in which they would apologize for the play and their performances, was better received than the play itself. For the sixth week of the play — in Manchester — they decided to enjoy themselves. Jimmy was seen drinking a glass of cold tea and smoking a cheroot, and instead of reading the lines from the play, he turned to the audience and said, "You'd think on our last week they'd give me real whisky…and a real cigar. In response, Sykes said, "I wish they'd give me a real actor."[15]

The authors of the play, King and Cary, had obviously expected this might happen and threatened a lawsuit if any word from the original script was altered. The comedians avoided court action simply by keeping in all the original dialogue, but also adding their own to the play.

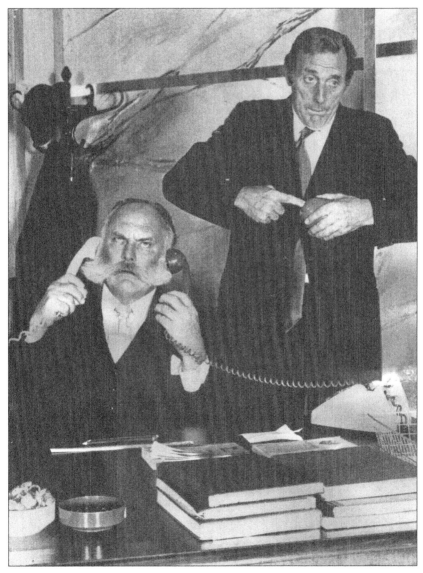

Jimmy Edwards and Eric Sykes in Big Bad Mouse.

Suddenly, *Big Bad Mouse* was a success, and when it opened in London at the Shaftesbury Theatre on October 17, 1966, under the direction of Alexander Doré, it was intended simply as a vehicle for the Edwards-Sykes double act. Unfortunately, that was not to be in that Sykes became ill and his role was taken over by Roy Castle, much younger than Eric Sykes but an accomplished comedian. The critics did not seem to know exactly what to make of it; in *The Illustrated London News* (October 29, 1966), J.C. Trewin, one of the most distinguished of his group, reported it "has no virtue whatever as a farce," adding, "the night is more than a little unruly." "As *The Times* (July 7, 1988) wrote in Jimmy's obituary, he and Eric Sykes "created a wandering flight of fancy which grew in the course of two years from 1966 to 1968, from a harmless romp into a wild, but controlled chaos, designed to amuse two players of contrasting but undeniable funniness."

Audiences must have been confused at times to discover the stars in a pub across Shaftesbury Avenue from the theatre, enthusiastically imbibing as it got closer and closer to curtain time. When those in the pub started to check their watches, Jimmy responded, "It's no good looking at the time. They can't start without us."[16]

In December 1972, Thames Television broadcast the play, with Edwards and Sykes, as a made-for-television movie, shot at London's Prince of Wales Theatre. John Robins directed. Earlier, in December 1966, the BBC had broadcast scenes from the original London production. It is not known if the BBC used the *Big Bad Mouse* theme music, written by Carl Davis (now associated with music for silent films), and recorded by Fenella Fielding. It's a jolly song, with Fielding's pleading "Don't look at me that way, Big Bad Mouse," and asking "See what the mouse in the back room will have."[17]

Viewing the television adaptation, which clearly contains what might be described as rehearsed ad-libs, with Jimmy making his first appearance on stage, being dissatisfied with the audience response and demanding a repeat of his entrance, and a little later haranguing two members of the audience for arriving late, it is Jimmy who is responsible for the majority of the laughs with Eric Sykes unable to compete with someone who is obviously a master of stand-up comedy. The late arrival of the audience members allows Jimmy to provide a truncated version of all that has preceded their appearance; it is a funny routine, later used and with much more ingenuity and comic effect by Ken Dodd.

Ken Dodd recalls meeting Jimmy Edwards only in once, in the company of Eric Sykes, and notes "they were both very charming men." He kept in touch with Eric Sykes, but not Edwards.[18]

After eighteen months on the London stage, the play, sometimes described as the most successful flop in theatrical history, embarked on tour after tour, with Eric Sykes back as co-star, whenever its stars had nothing else to do, playing not only around Britain but also in Australia, Hong Kong,[19] Canada, Singapore, Rhodesia (Zimbabwe), and the United States. Producer/director Paul Elliott would be listed in the program as "referee," in that direction was almost non-existent, not that much refereeing was necessary. As *The Stage* (February 28, 1980) noted, "Audiences, quickly involved in the clever shambles, love it and respond like kids at a pantomime to the blandishments of the irrepressible Jimmy and to the poker-faced artistry of Eric Sykes (memories of Buster Keaton of silent movie days?)." *Big Bad Mouse* was, in the words of Eric Sykes, "a peg on which Jim and I had hung our overcoats."[20]

The reference to the silent days of the motion picture is somewhat relevant in terms of Eric Sykes' performance here and elsewhere. He was not only legally blind, but also severely deaf. He would lip read and insert his lines when his opposite number stopped speaking. The problem in *Big Bad Mouse* was that Jimmy Edwards was very much aware of this and would deliberately turn his back to his co-star while delivering his lines. When Sykes would accidentally interrupt a speech, Jimmy would angrily respond, "I haven't finished talking yet."

Eric Sykes thought he might have gained the upper hand when he realized that the muscles in the back of Jimmy's neck would respond to his lip movement. When the muscles stopped moving, then Eric Sykes knew it was time for his lines. In turn, Jimmy then figured out how to control the muscles in his neck. And so it went on, performance after performance — with the comedians entertaining one another rather than the audience.

In a 1974 Australian tour, beginning in Melbourne, *Big Bad Mouse* was promoted as "London Flop Becomes Australian Success."[21] There was also a television special, filmed there in March 1974, and titled *The Making of a Disaster or the Sweet Mouse of Success*. Prior to the Australian visit, *Big Bad Mouse* had two presentations at the O'Keefe Centre in Toronto, Canada, in December 1973 and then a repeat visit in January 1974 (which Edwards described as a stopover on the way to Australia). While Sykes told the audience that his mother-in-law was Canadian, Jimmy proudly recited every town in Canada, explaining that he had been in them all during World War Two, and also noting that he had made his first radio broadcast there, in North Battlefield in a take-off of a Canadian show, *The Happy Gang* (a CBC musical variety show heard from 1937-1959).

Later that same year, Edwards and Sykes had a limited tour with the play in the United States, appearing in Chicago, Boston, Fort Lauderdale, and Washington, D.C. (four weeks at the Kennedy Center, beginning July 1, 1974). "Well, that was scarcely an ovation," Jimmy would comment on his first arrival on stage, while Eric Sykes would check out members of the audience in the orchestra in the hope of purloining chocolates or candy. At a matinée, Jimmy might play his trombone and cajole the audience into singing "I'm Forever Blowing Bubbles."

For the program, Sykes wrote Jimmy's biography and Jimmy wrote Eric's. "What might he not have accomplished as a house painter, a grocer, a joiner or a cotton mill operative," asked Jimmy, noting also that Sykes had "a bottle of rather inferior whiskey." Eric explained that he did not remember Jimmy at the Windmill; "when the girls left the stage I used to read." His hobby was listed as "drinking my Scotch."

A 1976 American tour was a disappointment in terms of audience numbers and reaction. Writing in his diary on January 25, 1976, while in Detroit, for a four-week run at the Fisher Theatre, from January 6 through February 7, Jimmy complained,

"There is absolutely nothing to do in this god-forsaken city except eat and drink….The hotel is dull…full of old people who walk slowly and irritate you in the lifts….I got two very sticky audiences going…with not even a ripple of applause at my first entrance…but was it worth all the effort? Where is the fun?….There is no fun left in this touring, especially with *BBM*. It is too much like hard work."[22]

In retrospect, it is very obvious that *Big Bad Mouse* was not quite the production one might believe. It did not provide Edwards and Sykes with an incredible opportunity to display their original comedic talents, night after night, with new dialogue and jokes at each performance. It was very obviously rehearsed ad-libbing, the type of ad-libbing for which British comedian Frankie Howerd was well-known. Every night Eric Sykes would get his tie caught in a desk drawer and someone in the wings would have to hand him a pair of scissors with which to free himself. Fellow actors on stage would giggle uncontrollably at the same ad-libs, unable to keep a straight face, night after night. But the giggles and the inability to deliver their lines was always predictable and at the same place in the play. It was actor Michael Simkins, whose credits are many and who is also an accomplished author and *Guardian* columnist, who first pointed this out, after taking respective girlfriends to see the play a year apart:

"I marked with disgust the helpless mirth of the fellow actors at each successive prank. Only one interpretation was possible: they were even faking that. From soup to nuts, it was obviously rehearsed down to the last snigger.

"With the hindsight of more than 20 years in the business, including several long runs, I now see both occasions in a more forgiving light. An ordinary play was transformed into an unforgettable experience, simply because the actors managed to convince the paying public that they were watching this extraordinary foolery for the first time. For which many thanks.

"George Burns once said, 'Acting is all about honesty — if you can fake that you've got it made.'"[23]

Big Bad Mouse continues to be revived. A British touring version from May through August 2008 starred the comedy duo of Tommy Cannon and Bobby Ball. In October 2016, it was given its Houston, Texas, premiere at Theatre Suburbia.

Outside of the United Kingdom, Jimmy Edwards had limited stage exposure. His films might be screened, albeit in limited fashion, abroad, but theatregoers could basically have the opportunity to enjoy Jimmy only in the United States, the Middle East, Canada or Australia.

In 1977, to celebrate the Queen's Silver Jubilee, Jimmy Edwards and Tessie O'Shea ("magnificently large," as Jimmy described her)[24] joined forced to star in *Tessie and Jim's London Music Hall*, created by impresario and entertainment consultant David Stones, which opened at Boston's Colonial Theatre on May 17, and subsequently was to have played Detroit, Chicago, and Los Angeles in the United States, and Victoria, Vancouver, Hamilton, and Ottawa, in Canada. The show was devised and directed by John Gratton, with choreography by Irving Davies. A press release explained,

"If you can't go to London to celebrate the Queen's Silver Jubilee, why not let London come to you.

"Music Hall has always been a particularly English institution, and now two of its greatest stars, Tessie O'Shea and 'Professor' Jimmy Edwards join forces to celebrate Queen Elizabeth's Silver Jubilee in an exciting and memorable music hall experience created especially for this occasion!

"The London Music Hall Show combines the best of Britain's Music Hall tradition with contemporary variety entertainment in a full production show that features top British singing stars the New Faces, the London Music Hall Dancers, compere-singer Tony Wells, Argentine gaucho dance attraction les Renquales, and the Burt Hardin Band.

"As the curtain ascends, through the fog you will see a typical London street scene complete with hot chestnut sellers, barrel organs, lamp-lighters, flower sellers and English Bobbies as the sights and sounds of London in the 1920s come to life.

"You will also see a dance spectacle based on the popular TV series *The Avengers* featuring the suave sophistication of Steed and the indomitable Purdy and Emma!

"In turn, Tony-award-winning Tessie O'Shea and the incomparable Jimmy Edwards will make you feel good all over with their unique brands of laughter and song.

"The entire company — in top hats and tails — will round off a smashing evening and a visit to London that you'll never forget.

"The best of British to you."[25]

It was truly a production of which any Carnival or Cunard cruise ship would have been proud. What Jimmy thought of it is not recorded; he was remarkably quiet at least in public. He must have been aware that his co-star, Tessie O'Shea (1913-1995) was far better known in America than was he. With her theme song of "Two Ton Tessie from Tennessee," O'Shea was a plump and enthusiastic entertainer, combining comedy with singing and playing the banjolele. She had been active since the 1930s, but gained American fame in 1963 when she won a Tony for her performance in Noel Coward's *The Girl Who Came to Supper*, together with an appearance on *The Ed Sullivan Show* (repeated the following year when she co-starred with the Beatles). American film appearances include *The Russians Are Coming, the Russians Are Coming* (1966) and *Bedknobs and Broomsticks* (1971).[26]

Tessie and Jim's London Music Hall was a disaster in every possible way. It folded after only fourteen days, David Stones absconded with the cash it generated (and was subsequently arrested and tried in the U.K.), and the British Consulate in Boston had to help repatriate most of the cast back to Britain.

Jimmy was not particularly happy playing the United States because he was little known and not immediately recognizable to most Americans. However, June Whitfield recalls,

"He went on the *Johnny Carson Show*, and the next day a cab driver eyed him in the mirror and said, 'Hey, weren't you on the *Carson Show* last night?' Jimmy then relaxed and felt at home."[27]

Australia was a more popular destination for Jimmy, with appearances not only in theatres but also nightclubs. And there was also the added attraction of young Australian males, whom the comedian appears to have found particularly appealing.

A typical Australian appearance was at the Tivoli Theatre, Melbourne, in the spring of 1966, in a show named in his honor, *The Jimmy Edwards Show*, produced by Stanley Willis-Croft, and with Jimmy's billing as "The

Emperor of English Comedy Entertainment Himself." (Both *Take It from Here* and *Whack-O!* enjoyed a major following in Australia, and Jimmy had first appeared there live on television in *Top of the Town* in March 1960, airing on Channel 9 in Sydney and Channel 7 in Melbourne.) When he returned to Australia the following year, on March 18, 1961, his arrival in Sydney was worthy of coverage by the Australian Broadcasting Commission.

The supporting bill at the Tivoli Theatre consisted of ventriloquist Arthur Worsley, Peter Maxwell, "The Piano Playboy," and Gita Rivera, "Glamorous Rising Singing Star." Arthur Worsley (1920-2001) was a brilliant Ventriloquist, hailed by Ed Sullivan no less as "the world's greatest," who spoke not one word on stage but allowed his dummy, Charlie Brown, to do all the talking. He was truly funny, maintaining a straight face as a more and more agitated dummy shrieked abuse at him. One critic quoted in *The Daily Telegraph* (July 20, 2001) commented that "Looking at Arthur Worsley's lips is like watching a play by Chekhov: nothing happens." At the Tivoli, Worsley and Jimmy appear on stage together, with Worsley coming on stage with a dummy in the form of a duck, which carries on a hilarious conversation with Jimmy. At the conclusion Jimmy and the duck sing a confused version of "Old McDonald Had a Farm."

In 1983, Jimmy brought a touring production of the musical *Oliver!* to Australia, with his playing Mr. Bumble, a role created on screen in 1968 by Harry Secombe, who had also made his professional debut at the Windmill Theatre. Prior to the Australian tour, *Oliver!* had toured the U.K. with Roy Hudd as Fagin.

In view of his at times extreme Conservative views, it is something of a surprise that Jimmy should have ventured into the Soviet Union. But in 1959, in his capacity as chairman of the Variety Arts Federation, he flew with a party of stage performers to Moscow and Leningrad. With what might be termed typical arrogance, he broke the trip halfway through for a weekend return to the U.K. Jimmy's report makes the obvious comment that "Most of the comedy had a propaganda motive."

1. As Jimmy described the euphonium, it differs from the trombone, with its tubes sticking straight out and a hazard to fellow musicians, in that the tubes of the euphonium are bunched together; "when you first see it, you think it's just a handful of bent piping. When you hear me play it, you're sure it is."

2. Freddie Starr was the subject of what is considered the most famous, and outrageous, tabloid headline in British history, "Freddie Starr Ate My Hamster," published by *The Sun* on March 13, 1986.

3. It is not clear if he did this at every performance or just the opening night.

4. After World War Two, Chevalier had initially been banned from appearing in the U.K. because of his collaboration with the Nazi occupiers of his country.

5. That bill included Tommy Cooper and Jimmy James, together with Stubby Kaye and the original London cast of *Guys and Dolls*.

6. Peter Dacre, "It's Back to the Old Tuba Again for Jimmy Edwards."

7. Cyril Fletcher, *Nice One Cyril*, p. 27.

8. Captain Frederick Moynan, Assistant Equerry to H.R.H. The Duke of Edinburgh to Anthony Slide, March 7, 2017.

9. Jimmy Edwards, *Six of the Best*, p. 103.

10. Ibid, p. 104.

11. James Towler, "The Forgotten World of Musical Comedy," p. 20.

12. Barry Cryer makes the interesting point that John Cleese has now become one of the characters he and the Monty Python troupe used to pillory.

13. Ivan Butler's film books are: *The Horror Film* (1967, revised in 1970 as *Horror in the Cinema*), *Religion in the Cinema* (1969), *The Cinema of Roman Polanski* (1970), *The Making of a Feature Film* (1971), *To Encourage the Art of the Film: The Story of the British Film Institute* (1971), *Cinema in Britain* (1973), *The War Film* (1974), and *Silent Magic: Rediscovering the Silent Film Era* (1978).

14. Eric Sykes, *Eric Sykes' Comedy Heroes*, p. 57.

15. Ibid, p. 57-58.

16. Eric Sykes, *If I Don't Write It, Nobody Else Will*, p. 372.

17. Columbia 1966 recording, DB 8056, with the song "Later" on the reverse.

18. Ken Dodd to Anthony Slide, November 25, 2016.

19. In Hong Kong in 1971, Jimmy played polo, captaining his own team, against one comprised of members of the cavalry regiment, the Queen's Own Hussars.

20. Eric Sykes, *If I Don't Write It, Nobody Else Will*, p. 375.

21. *The Stage*, April 11, 1974, p. 24.

22. Diary pages in the possession of Jim Pennington.

23. Michael Simkins, "An Actor's Life," p. A15.

24. Jimmy Edwards, *Take It from Me*, p. 177.

25. "Tessie and Jim," *The Stage*, p. 3.

26. Tessie had co-starred in a 1956 BBC series, *Tess and Jim*, but the Jim was not Jimmy Edwards but Jimmy Wheeler.

27. June Whitfield, *...And June Whitfield*, p. 142.

CHAPTER EIGHT

The Screen

Asked in 1949 to describe his early film appearances, Jimmy responded, "Dreadful."[1] He bemoaned the fact that the only way to become an international star was by making more films: "And that's my problem, trying to find the right scripts."[2] Certainly, he was never a major screen figure, often appearing more in cameo parts than leading roles. "Film was not his medium," notes Barry Cryer,[3] but Jimmy should not have felt ashamed for any of his film roles or for the films themselves.

While playing at the Golders Green Hippodrome, prior to *Take It from Here*, Jimmy was asked if he would like to play a part in a film. He visited the J. Arthur Rank Studios at Highbury in North London, and was asked that in lieu of his making a screen test, he would agree to play a small part in a film already in production. "I was supposed to be the editor of a great, national daily newspaper, and all I had to do was sit in my imposing office and have a conversation with my cartoonist on the telephone. There was, however, no comedy in the part and I did not feel the character at all," he recalled.[4] The scene did not appear in the final, unidentified film, but Jimmy did not particularly care as in each take he was required to drink heavily from a glass of beer.

The discarded footage did lead to the official beginning of a film career in 1948 with what is certainly a minor effort, *Trouble in the Air*, directed by Charles Saunders, a former film editor, and produced by George and Alfred Black,[5] who also provided the original story. Only fifty-five minutes in length and barely qualifying as a feature, the film is obviously intended to exploit its star, BBC commentator B. Barrington Crockett, who, while visiting a small village community and broadcasting the work of the church bell ringers there, manages to foil the criminal activities of a group of low-life and low-level British gangsters or "spivs." Joining Jimmy in the cast are Freddy Frinton, Bill Owen, Sam Costa, and Jon Pertwee (who also wrote the screenplay). Bill Owen is perhaps best-known to American audiences for appearances in the "Carry On" films and the television series, *The Last of the Summer Wine*. Sam Costa, with a handlebar moustache as impressive as that sported by Edwards, was well-known to Britishers thanks to his work on radio in *It's That Man Again* and *Much Binding in the March*. Jon Pertwee, of course, is best remembered as Doctor Who.

A star of Music Hall and Variety, Freddy Frinton is pretty much forgotten everywhere except for Scandinavia and Germany, thanks to a sketch, recorded in 1963, titled *Dinner for One*, which is shown there on television at every New Year. In the eleven minute sketch, Frinton plays the butler of a lonely old lady, May Warden, hosting a New Year's Eve dinner for her long-dead admirers, all of whom are played by Frinton as the butler. "The same procedure as last year, Miss Sophie," asks Frinton, who is getting more and more inebriated thanks to the wine he must drink in the guise of each non-existent guest. "The same procedure as every year," is the response. When the dinner is over, the butler accompanies his mistress to her bed.

While *Trouble in the Air* might be unimportant, it did lead to Jimmy's being given a five-picture, three-year contract with J. Arthur Rank, but the Highbury studio was closed down and the contract cancelled prior to coming into force.

Vivian Van Damm had been approached on a number of occasions as to the possibility of featuring the Windmill Theatre in a film production. Eventually, in 1949, he agreed, in large part because the potential producer was his son-in-law Daniel M. Angel (1911-1999), who was married to Betty Van Damm. So close were the couple that she died two days after his passing. Angel was confined to a wheelchair thanks to polio, and *Murder at the Windmill* was his first film, but neither the poor production values in the feature nor his handicap prevented his going on to produce some major British pictures, including *The Sea Shall Not Have Them* (1954), *Reach for the Sky* (1956), and *Carve Her Name with Pride* (1958). (This is a book about a comedian, and so I will not restrain myself and mention Noel Coward's reaction to seeing a marquee in Leicester Square for *The Sea Shall Not Have Them* and its stars, Michael Redgrave and Dirk Bogarde. "Why not," asked Noel. "Everybody else has.")

Prolific filmmaker Val Guest was responsible for both the direction and the screenplay, and also contributed two of the featured songs. Rehearsals took place at the Windmill Theatre, but the film was shot in part at Walton-on-Thames Studios, beginning January 1949, with replicas of the dressing rooms, canteen and Van Damm's office built there. Later in January, the company moved to the Windmill Theatre itself and

filmed stage sequences after the last public performance. The film cost
a mere 40,000 pounds to produce, and Daniel M. Angel hoped that it
might prove the Britain could make good, low-price musicals. It couldn't
and it didn't.

In the United Kingdom, the film was released in May 1949 on a
double bill with a reissue of the 1942 Marlene Dietrich vehicle, *The Lady
Is Willing*, a strange combination. In September 1949, low-budget producers, the King Brothers acquired the film for American distribution, and
it was released by Monogram in April 1950. Perhaps became American
audiences would not understand the reference to the Windmill, the title
was changed to *Mystery at the Burlesque*. Reviews were lackluster, with the
critic for the *Los Angeles Times* (April 14, 1950) commenting,

"No strip tease, and not even one of those slyly naughty music hall
songs which Marie Lloyd, Elsa Lanchester and their followers did and do,
over here. But the show far more than makes up in subtle English humor,
beauty, and ingenuity what it lacks in saltiness. At that there are a couple
of numbers that are saline enough….The English cast leaves nothing to
desire in its acting."

The trade papers were neither unkind nor wildly enthusiastic. *Boxoffice*
(April 29, 1950) wrote that "Considering what they [the producers] had
in the way of talent, bankroll and story, they did well in turning out a wee
parcel of supporting fare which can be booked with topsider without fear
of offending the ticket buyers." As far as the *Independent Film Journal*
(April 22, 1950) was concerned, "The title of this English-made film is
about all the attraction the picture possesses." *Variety* (April 19, 1950)
thought it "a mild little musical whodunit….[that] moves along okay."

None of the reviewers considered it necessary to comment on Jimmy
Edwards or his act. Perhaps because the film provides only a partial record
of his performance, limited to the opening few minutes. How one wishes it
might have been more in that it does hint at a burgeoning talent. The U.S.
release version of the film relies on a narration at the start and conclusion,
perhaps reducing the role of Eliot Makeham, a talented British character actor, here playing what might be described as the villain although a
semi-reasonable explanation for his carrying out the murder is provided.
Aside from Makeham, there are good performances from Gary Marsh
as the investigative detective, Jon Pertwee as his loquacious sergeant, and,
particularly, Jack Livesey as Vivian Van Damm.

Unquestionably, *Murder at the Windmill* is an entertaining film, illus-
trating how small was the stage at the Windmill, but, sadly, providing little
suggestion of how its nude tableaux might have looked to an audience.

One song in particular, "I'll Settle for You," stands out, with various imper-
sonations of Hollywood stars, including Veronica Lake, Dorothy Lamour,
Danny Kaye, and James Stewart.

Murder at the Windmill was followed by *Helter Skelter*, a seldom-seen
film with a reputation as the British answer to the 1941 Olsen and Johnson
vehicle, *Hellzapoppin*. Produced in 1949 by Gainsborough Pictures, the
film's plot involves an heiress (Carol Marsh), who desperately needs to
stop hiccoughing, and who is helped by her would-be boyfriend (David
Tomlinson) with visits to a haunted house, watching a silent film, etc.
The Tomlinson character is a radio detective, which provides opportunity
for appearances by various radio personalities, including Terry-Thomas
(as a disc jockey) and Jimmy Edwards. Tomlinson points out that the
girl acquired the hiccups from laughing too much at a ventriloquist in a
nightclub, and that laughing too much at "a fellow on a BBC show called
Jimmy Edwards" might reverse the effect. *Helter Skelter* is narrated by
Richard Hearne in his character of Mr. Pastry (which I, for one, as a child
never found funny).

Helter Skelter was the third production to be directed by Ralph Thomas,
who was later to make the "Doctor" series of films. Interestingly, at one
point in the film, the heiress is shown a silent film as a cure, and it is
the 1929 feature, *Would You Believe It*, directed by and starring the much
under-rated Walter Forde.

Treasure Hunt, directed by the reliable if uninspired John Paddy
Carstairs, boasted a somewhat obvious and conventional storyline involving a group of eccentric characters who inherit an Irish manor house, only
to discover there is no land and no money included in the inheritance and
they must open the hall to paying guests. Jimmy Edwards heads the cast,
which also includes Naunton Wayne and Athene Seyler, and played a dual
role of the dead Sir Roderick Ryall and Uncle Hercules. The film provides
him with the opportunity to play his trombone, a gift for which audiences
should be grateful, as equally they should be grateful for the presence of
co-star Martita Hunt.

Argentine-born and resolutely British Martita Hunt (1900-1969)
enjoyed a career as a character actress both on stage and screen in Britain
and the United States from the early 1930s onwards. She was wonder-
fully superior in manner with the ability to glare with such ferocity that
could put down all who confronted or contradicted her. Jimmy had the
good fortune as an actor and the bad fortune as a screen character to play
opposite her not only in *Treasure Hunt*, but also *Three Men in a Boat*, in
which she is Mrs. Willis, and *Bottoms Up!*, in which she is school governor,

Lady Gore-Willoughby. She was at her best perhaps as Miss Havisham in the 1946 production of *Great Expectations*, repeating a role she had played in Alec Guinness' 1939 London stage adaptation. In real life, she could be equally aloof and superior, as actress Anna Lee once told me.

Treasure Hunt is based on a 1939 play of the same name, by M.J. Farrell and John Perry, and it is Martita Hunt's character of Aunt Anna Rose

Athene Seyler and Jimmy Edwards in Treasure Hunt.

(played by Dame Sybil Thorndike on stage) who saves the day with the discovery of the rubies she had earlier hidden in her fancy hat.

Something of the lack of commercial interest in *Treasure Hunt* may be assumed from *Variety*'s failure to review the film, which was acquired for a minimal U.S. release by Souvaine Selective Pictures.

Treasure Hunt was followed a year later — in 1953 — by *Innocents in Paris*, one of those films with an all-star cast which might seem a good idea on paper, or in the vision of a producer, but fail to deliver to an audience. As Howard Thompson wrote in the *New York Times* (March 5, 1955), "What a cast!…If it all sounds too good to be true, it is." Joining Jimmy in the film were Claire Bloom (as the ultimate innocent young thing attracted to a flirtatious French man), Margaret Rutherford (as an amateur painter anxious to purchase a copy of the "Mona Lisa"), Alastair Sim (as a stuffy diplomat), Laurence Harvey (as a waiter), the Band of the Royal Marines, and the Can Can dancers from Moulin Rouge, not to mention assorted British character players such as Ronald Shiner and Richard Wattis, and the Paris scenery.

Innocents in Paris was written and produced by Anatole de Grunwald, who was later to write a couple of other films with the similar notion of all-stars casts, *The V.I.P.s* (1963) and *The Yellow Rolls Royce* (1967). Directing was Gordon Parry, with a handful of minor screen credits from the late 1940s through the late 1950s, along with a few episodes of television's *The Adventures of Robin Hood*.

On its British release, the film garnered little enthusiasm from the critics, with William Whitebait in the *New Statesman and Nation* (July 18, 1953) describing it as "almost fascinating in its staleness." The British reviewer for *Variety* (July 29, 1953) was a little kinder, while admitting that "There is little that is new in the idea," but "the treatment is fresh and snappy, and is modelled strictly for pop tastes."

Innocents in Paris opened in America at the Palace Theatre, New York, on March 4, 1955, and the Paramount Theatre in Hollywood on March 31, 1955. "The treatment is fresh enough and the situations amusing enough to provide a fair measure of light entertainment," wrote Jesse Zunser in the New York entertainment guide, *Cue* (March 5, 1955). The *New York Times* dismissed the film as "a dreary, banal excuse for a romantic frolic.... Mr. de Grunwald has assembled a highly personable band of 'innocents,' only to leave them stranded." In *The New Yorker* (March 12, 1955), John McCarten thought the film "has an amusing moment or two, but it is thin stuff generally, and a terrible waste of the valuable time of actors like Alastair Sim, Claire Bloom, and Margaret Rutherford." The anonymous critic in the *Los Angeles Times* (April 1, 1955) noted that "Mark Twain's *Innocents Abroad* is no funnier, or anyhow not much more comical, than the new English-made comedy."

The Jimmy Edwards character is a typically xenophobic Englishman who visits Paris and spends his entire time there drinking English beer in an English bar. The critics did take note of Jimmy's performance and generally liked what little he had to do. Damning with faint praise was the *New York Times* critic who wrote, "Jimmy Edwards, a raucous patriot who dives into a neighborhood bar and stays there, makes all too convincing a bore."

Equally misusing a good cast was Jimmy's next film, *An Alligator Named Daisy*, directed by J. Lee Thompson, and released in the summer of 1956. At least *Innocents in Paris* uses its players to some comedic advantage, while in *An Alligator Named Daisy*, Donald Sinden, Jeannie Carson,

James Robertson Justice, Diana Dors, Roland Culver, Stanley Holloway, and Margaret Rutherford are simply wasted. The story involves Donald Sinden's acquiring an alligator from a sailor, played in an uncredited role by Jimmy Edwards, and the comedy involves his taking care of it. One might possibly believe the storyline of *Innocents in Paris*, but the implausible plot here is impossible to identify with.

Laurence Harvey, Jimmy Edwards and David Tomlinson in Three Men in a Boat.

At last, with *Three Men in a Boat*, Jimmy Edwards gets the opportunity to star, or rather co-star with David Tomlinson and Laurence Harvey, in a film with a plot that nicely mixes comedy with some vague dramatic intensity. David Tomlinson and Jimmy Edwards must surely have got along in that the former had served in the R.A.F. in Canada and, like Jimmy, he would often fly (although apparently he did not own a plane himself). In a situation in which one would have thought to find Jimmy, during the making of *Three Men in a Boat*, Tomlinson was taken to court accused of dangerous flying, after crashing a De Havilland biplane, Tiger Moth at the bottom of his garden.

The novel by Jerome K. Jerome provides the basis for a pleasant boating holiday in the late 1800s, at the end of the Victorian era, on the River

Thames undertaken by Harris (Edwards), Jim (Tomlinson) and George (Harvey), along with their dog Montmorency,[6] each anxious to get away from the trials, both personal and professional, in their private lives. The production also has the advantage of three elderly actors whose presence immediately evokes pleasure, Miles Malleson, A.E. Matthews and Ernest Thesiger, as veteran fishermen and cricketers.

Three Men in a Boat is not great cinema, but, as Bosley Crowther wrote in the *New York Times* (July 29, 1959) a day after the film opened in New York at the 68th Street Playhouse, it is "clean, simple fun of an order that you don't see much of these days." The film opened in London at the Carlton Theatre in December 1956, obviously intended for the Christmas market, and the trade paper *Variety* (January 2, 1957) was somewhat uncertain as to its box-office potential beyond the elderly seeking out nostalgia: "Story seems slow and artificial in development and background but marquee names may help put it over." *Variety* did single out Jimmy Edwards' performance for comment:

"Jimmy Edwards, popular revue and radio comic, twirls his outsize moustache and rolls his eyes effectively when ogling girls, subsiding under the collapsing tent and falling overboard. While bombastically protesting his superior knowledge as to the inner workings of the maze at Hampton Court Palace, he nearly gets lynched by the pack of near hysterical folks who have trustingly followed him."

Three Men in a Boat is a pleasant, light entertainment; the comment by the Edwards character that a holiday on the River Thames is "some sort of a breather" might also be used to describe the film, which as an added attraction has character comedy actor, Robertson Hare, as a photographer and speaking his catchphrase, "Oh Calamity." Laurence Harvey plays the banjo and sings, rather badly, a few bars of Stephen Foster's "Way Down upon the Swanee River" (also known as "Old Folks at Home"). Jimmy gets the opportunity to entertain a group of society types, performing a song from a Gilbert and Sullivan opera, but with some confusion as to what song and which opera.

From a purely salacious viewpoint, one must note a nude bathing scene involving the three leading men, although none are seen from below the waist. Jimmy looks very hairy-chested, although not as overweight as he was to become. David Tomlinson is rather flabby, while Laurence Harvey is much too skinny. I am afraid that this display of male flesh probably did and does nothing for audience members of either sex.

It is a puzzle why Ken Annakin, who directed the film from a script by Hubert Gregg, ideal for this type of storyline, and Vernon Harris, chose not to mention either it or its stars in his autobiography.[7] However, after completion of filming, the director did note that, "He [Jimmy] may be difficult to cast, of course, like so many comedians whose appearance is almost a trademark, but what I saw of him while making *Three Men in a Boat* interested me because of the way he fitted naturally into the framework of the script."[8]

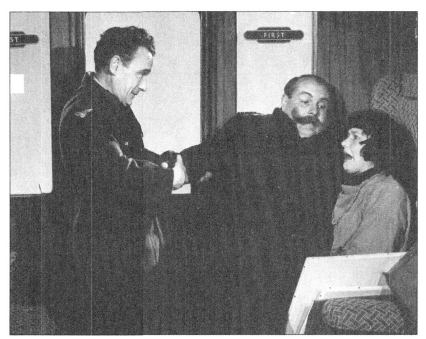

Kenneth Connor, Jimmy Edwards and Charlotte Mitchell in Nearly a Nasty Accident.

Jimmy Edwards was to make six films in the 1960s his busiest decade as far as his screen career is concerned. The first, *Bottoms Up!*, is discussed elsewhere. Two of the films represent a change in direction as he appeals to a new audience. Only the first two actually provide him with starring roles.

Nearly a Nasty Accident, released by British lion in the U.K. in May 1962 is very much in the tradition of the "Carry On" films. Bertram Ostrer produced, Don Chaffey (later to be known for fantasy films such as *Jason and the Argonauts*, *Creatures the World Forgot* and *Pete's Dragon*) directed, and the script by Jack Davies and Hugh Woodhouse was based on a play, *Touch Wood*, by David Stringer and David Carr, which was probably unproduced. One of the three stars, Kenneth Connor, had a busy career appearing in the "Carry On" films, beginning with *Carry On*

Sargent (1958) and was brilliantly comic as Monsieur Alphonse in the television series *'Allo 'Allo*. Shirley Eaton was a blonde sex symbol of the decade, there to provide sex appeal and little else, with *Variety* (May 24, 1961) unkindly noting she proved that "a winning smile is not enough to disguise somewhat shaky thesping ability." She was, of course, a Bond Girl in *Goldfinger* (1964) and at her best dead and covered in gold paint.

And then there is Jimmy Edwards as Group Captain Kingsley a R.A.F. officer in search of the accident-prone Kenneth Williams in order to get him out of the service. Some reviewers were not kind, with *Variety* describing Jimmy as "a radio funnyman who has yet to find the right niche in films. A little of him goes a very long way. In this case, he has to carry much of the burden of the comedy and it's a hard fight for Jim to survive." *Boxoffice* (April 6, 1962) described his performance as "apoplectic." In *The Guardian* (May 13, 1961), an anonymous critic commented,

"The player who really holds the piece together is Jimmy Edwards…. Mr. Edwards's moustache is a splendid growth — a great tree, as it were, under which lesser comedians nestle comfortably; his fruity voice dominates all else in the orchestration and his bulky presence is a galleon, with smaller craft trailing in its wake. Thanks very largely to him and to the swift, relentless boisterousness with which the nonsense is conducted by all concerned, this farce becomes surprisingly funny."

Similarly, Howard Thompson, reviewing the film on its U.S. release by Universal-International, in the *New York Times* (June 28, 1962) was sympathetic:

"This middling British job has a couple of assets. One is a truly funny portrait of a bellowing pompous captain by Jimmy Edwards. The other is the whirlwind succession of slapstick disasters."

"Middling" is a kind way to describe *Nearly a Nasty Accident*, set in Wales for no apparent reason except that it provides Jimmy Edwards with the opportunity to make a scathing remark in regard to Welsh licensing laws for the sale of alcohol. An unfunny pre-credit sequence warns of what lies ahead: bad comedy, bad dialogue, and bad over-acting, which, of course, is what one might expect from Jimmy. It is almost as if he now believes that larking about, as he would have called it, is what audiences preferred rather than real acting. Certainly he demonstrates the appropriate stature and standing of an R.A.F. officer, and there is one mildly amusing sequence in which somehow he becomes caught in the equipment used to eject mail bags from moving trains and finishes up tangled in a net. Otherwise, there is nothing funny in the manner in which Kenneth Connor manages to destroy an office, crash a plane, smash dishes, and drive a lorry into a canal.

Nearly a Nasty Accident is hardly the "slam-bang, slapstick farce," described by the critic for *Motion Picture Herald* (April 25, 1962).

Ronnie Stevens as Flight Lieutenant Pocock plays the role very much with the same characteristics as Arthur Howard played Mr. Pettigrew. Otherwise, he and a familiar cast of British character players, including Richard Wattis, Joe Baker and Terry Scott, are wasted. The only line worth recording for posterity is Jimmy's description of himself as "a blithering great moustache bristling with rage.

The Children's Film Foundation (now the Children's Film & Television Foundation) was established as a non-profit entity in 1951 to produce films for children that might be screened at the children's matinees presented by many British theatres on a Saturday morning, when the building might otherwise be closed, for children only at a nominal admission fee. Although still extant, it is no longer active. The films produced were intended as wholesome entertainment, with any comedy aspects determined as appropriate for children by adults who were in all probability out of touch with modern kids and their behavior. As a result, films from the Children's Film Foundation were generally greeted with scorn and derision by a young audience, with the noise from that audience far in excess of the sound emanating from the screen.

The choice of Jimmy Edwards to star in four films is evidential of his popularity with a wide range of individuals, both old and hopefully young. The first film, *A Ghost of a Chance*, released in 1968 has both children and a group of ghosts joining forces to save a historic mansion from demolition. Jimmy Edwards was joined by an illustrious group of comedy performers, including Ronnie Barker, Bernard Cribbens, Patricia Hayes, Terry Scott, and Graham Stark.

The second film *Lionheart,* also released in 1968, was produced, written and directed by Michael Forlong, and stars his son, James, as a young boy helping to save the life of an escaped lion. Jimmy is guest starred, along with Wilfrid Brambell and Irene Handl. The third production, titled *The Magnificent Six and ½*, was a serial released in 1971, and advertised as "The misadventures of six children and a young girl." Finally, in 1972, Jimmy appeared in *Anoop and the Elephant*, in which Rani, the elephant, decides to adopt a young boy played by Anoop Singh.

In direct contradiction to the Children's Film Foundation productions are the three films that Jimmy Edwards made at the end of his career — *The Plank*, *The Bed Sitting Room* and *Rhubarb* — all of which show an independence of spirit and an originality in regard to content and presentation.

While it is often described as being a silent film, *The Plank*[9] actually does have dialogue from the actors, but presented in a slightly zany fashion. There is music, whistling, footsteps, and other sound effects. The story is nothing more than a series of jokes involving the antics of Eric Sykes and Tommy Cooper trying to get a plank of wood across town, from a timber yard to a new housing development, with Jimmy Edwards as a gen-

Jimmy Edwards and Roy Castle in The Plank.

erally bumbling and unhelpful police officer on a bicycle. He is actually not particularly funny. The first word heard on the soundtrack is "Wood," the opening credits are sung as well as being visually presented on screen. The star is definitely shown to be a plank of wood, with the actors co-starring. Unkindly, one might be tempted to suggest that some of the performances are as wooden as that plank. Others in the cast include Roy Castle, in a fairly prominent role, Stratford Johns as a policeman (in obvious tribute to his role on the popular BBC TV police series, *Z Cars*), Jim Dale as a housepainter, Hattie Jacques (glimpsed only slightly in a window with a rose on her ear), and Graham Stark as a van driver.

It is something of a puzzle why Tommy Cooper was chosen to play alongside of Eric Sykes as this is far from his usual characterization of an incompetent magician. The film does, however, allow Cooper to introduce his distinctive laugh.

An Associated London Films production from Jon Pennington and Beryl Vertue, *The Plank* would appear to have been shot in the Royal Borough of Kingston upon Thames, just South West of London. (A garbage truck with the city's name is seen twice onscreen.) There are a number of references to Malthouse Passage, but there is no such address in Kingston, but such a street does exist in Barnes, and perhaps Eric and Jimmy were indulging in a small (very small) in-joke. The house that Sykes and Tommy Cooper are building is part of the Caversham Park Estate in Reading.

Contemporary reviewers noted the amount of time that it took for the film really to get started and be funny, and this is certainly true, although it is obvious that the producers were aiming for a slow approach in what they must have assumed was silent style.

The Plank was screened out of competition at the Cannes Film Festival in 1967, and reviewed there by *Variety* (May 10, 1967). The trade paper declared that the film should be "a profitable bundle of laughs," but questioned if its fifty-eight minute running time would make it difficult to pair with another feature. "Technically, effort is first rate, with color, music [by Brian Fahey] and…editing all working together towards a continually chucklesome and very often hilarious effect."

The theatrical version of *The Plank* is actually the second of three that Eric Sykes made. The first, *Sykes and a Plank*, was a thirty-minute episode of the BBC seres, *Sykes and a…*, broadcast on March 3, 1964. The third version, also titled *The Plank*, was an ITV Television production, broadcast on December 17, 1979. Replacing Tommy Cooper as Eric's assistant is, of all people, Arthur Lowe, and in support are Lionel Blair, Diana Dors, Harry H, Corbett, Bernard Cribbin, Charles Hawtrey, Frankie Howerd, Wilfrid Hyde White, Joanna Lumley, boxer Henry Cooper, and, of course, Jimmy Edwards.

A surreal black comedy, *The Bed Sitting Room* is assuredly the most eccentric of all of Jimmy's films. Filmed in May through July 1968 on location at Chobham Common, a 400-acre nature reserve, desolate in appearance and used for military training during both World War One and Two, *The Bed Sitting Room* was directed by Richard Lester, who had already gained international fame for his direction of the Beatles in *A Hard Day's Night* (1964) and *Help!* (1965). It was produced for United Artists release, but because of its eccentric quality, it was eventually released, two years after production, by the distributor's foreign releasing arm, Lopert Films.

Based on a play by Spike Milligan and John Antrobus, the film is set in a post-apocalyptic Britain, and boasts a cast of familiar British comedy names (listed in the credits in order of height), most of whom are wasted in their roles: Peter Cook, Marty Feldman, Roy Kinnear, Spike Milligan, Dudley Moore, Harry Secombe, Frank Thornton, and Jimmy Edwards (sixth billed) and definitely redundant. The principal players are Arthur Lowe, Mona Washbourne, Rita Tushingham, and Richard Warwick, as a family living on the Circle Line of London's tube. They are very much the clichéd English middle-class family; "We don't want to cause any trouble," whines Mona Washbourne as the mother. Also in principal roles are Michael Horden, as Bules Martin, in love with the Rita Tushingham character, and Ralph Richardson, as Lord Fortnum of Alamein, who is slowly transforming into the bed sitting room of the title and worried that he will be completely changed in an inappropriate neighborhood of the city. Once he has become a bed sitting room, Mona Washbourne is transformed into a wardrobe.

Jimmy first appears as someone abandoned in left luggage; he hides in a trunk (affectively removing himself from the story) and appears only at the film's conclusion reunited with the Michael Hordern character, with whom, it would seem, he had been in a relationship and who had abandoned him at the left luggage office. His voice is also heard, crying fire, as the trunk is accidently left to burn. Heavily whiskered, with there being no line between unkempt beard and moustache, Jimmy is more than merely unused in the part, which could have been played by anyone — even an extra. The only truly amusing moment is at the film's conclusion when Dandy Nichols as Mrs. Ethel Shroake of 393A High Street, Leytonstone and elevated to Queen (thanks to the Royal family being destroyed in the nuclear blast) is serenaded with the National Anthem while seated on a horse.

Variety (July 16, 1969) reviewed the film at the Cannes Film Festival, and was surprisingly enthusiastic in that it described the production as a "characteristically off-beat anti-war film.....this is a very special little picture worth a discriminating look-see." The problem was that discriminating American critics, such as Stanley Kauffman in *The New Republic* (October 18, 1969) described *The Bed Sitting Room* as "a weak humanist gesture," and urged Richard Lester to move on.

Ultimately, one wishes that one might like *The Bed Sitting Room*, but it simply is not funny and the situations do not make sense even to a semi-crazed mind. Presumably, a fan of *The Goon Show* might appreciate or a Monty Python aficionado.

Rhubarb is supposedly the semi-intelligible word spoken by extras in crowd scenes to signify a general atmosphere of noise, either negative or positive. It is also the title of a 1969 British short subject, released to theatres in 1970, written and directed by comedian Eric Sykes, and starring himself, Harry Secombe and Jimmy Edwards, with additional appearances by Kenneth Connor, Hattie Jacques and Graham Stark. It was remade in 1980, with the title appropriately changed to *Rhubarb Rhubarb!*, as a television production by Thames Television, again with Sykes and Edwards, but with Bob Todd (a familiar face to fans of Benny Hill) replacing Harry Secombe as the Vicar, and with Hattie Hacques as the only remaining member of the supporting cast. The 1980 version was shot at the Ottershaw Golf and Country Club in Ottershaw, Surrey, and first shown on Thames Television on December 15 of that year.

The plot of each film is identical, with the only word used being "Rhubarb" or the abbreviation thereof, "Rhu". It is nothing more than a silent film, with musical accompaniment, with Eric Sykes as a police inspector determined to win a golf match against the vicar (either Secombe or Todd), with the aid of Jimmy Edwards as a police constable on his bicycle. The action takes place at the Royal Rhubarb Golf Club. Hattie Jacques is a nanny whose charge in a pushchair accidentally gets switched with a golf bag filled with golf clubs.

The first version is not available for re-evaluation, but one assumes that the remake is pretty much the same, with some humor derived from the vicar's receiving help with his game from God. At one point, he walks on water to the strains of the hymn "Jerusalem." Viewed today, *Rhubarb Rhubarb!* seems rather tame and lacking in much unrestrained comedy, despite the obvious enjoyment of a live television audience. It has been described as "Chaplinesque," but if it is influenced by Charlie Chaplin it is more the Chaplin of 1915 short films rather than the maker of sophisticated feature comedies in the 1920s and 1930s.

Jimmy and Eric Sykes were reunited in 1972, when the former appeared in episode eight, series one, of *Sykes*, produced by the BBC. Eric Sykes was the star, but in the role of his twin sister, Hattie Jacques is just as much deserving of the title of co-star. Jimmy appears as the boss of the factory where Hattie works and where she has persuaded him to hire brother Eric. Unfortunately, Jimmy must deal not only with an incompetent employee but also with an implacable union organizer who is determined that Eric may not be sacked, despite his creating problems for all the other workers in the factory.

In 1973, two Irishmen, Joe Lynch and Martin Cahill (not to be confused with the infamous Irish gangster of the same name) formed Lyncah International to produce "family entertainment." The first production was to be *You'd Better Go in Disguise*, written by, directed and starring Eric Sykes, with Hattie Jacques, Arthur Lowe, Jimmy Edwards, and producer Joe Lynch, but nothing came of the project.[10]

1. As reported in the *Yorkshire Evening Post*, August 6, 1949.

2. Godfrey Winn, "Life Is So Full, and Yet...," p. 8.

3. Anthony Slide interview with Barry Cryer, February 6, 2017.

4. Jimmy Edwards, *Take It from Me*, p. 161.

5. The names of George and Alfred Black are synonymous with British entertainment, particularly in connection with variety and the London Palladium. In that George Black died in 1945, one must assume the men credited on the film are actually his sons, George Black, Jr. and Alfred (named for his brother).

6. The actual title of the 1889 novel is *Three Men in a Boat (To Say Nothing of the Dog)*.

7. The BBC remade the film for television in 1976 with Michael Palin in the Jimmy Edwards role, Tim Curry and Stephen Moore.

8. Dick Richards, "A Whack-O Bang-On Type," p. 13.

9. For his performance in *The Plank*, Edwards was promised one percent of the net profits.

10. The film is referenced in *The Stage*, August 9, 1973, p. 10.

CHAPTER NINE

Sex and the Comedian

The English are noted for their reticence in discussion of sex, in all its variety; after all, was there not a popular farce titled *No Sex Please We're British*. While an argument certainly can be made that there is a far less prudish attitude towards sex and nudity in the United Kingdom than there is today in the United States, such was not the situation in Jimmy Edwards' day. As Ian McKellen so aptly puts it, "For most people in England, sex is a tricky topic."[1] A gentleman did not discuss such matters, and no-one was more circumspect or disposed to silence when it came to his sex life than Jimmy Edwards. "Jim kept his private life Private," comments June Whitfield, "and I hope you understand if I leave it at that."[2]

Not only was Jimmy secretive as to his sexuality, as he openly admits in his second volume of autobiography, *Six of the Best*, also he was and remained a prude by some standards, old-fashioned in many ways, and he was not self-indulgent as to sex. He recounts while stationed in North Africa during World War Two having a night out, "a bit of 'togetherness,'" with members of his crew. After enjoying French food and local wine, he was persuaded to experience something more "piquant," in the form of a sex show involving "woman and woman,"

"My stomach began to turn. I groped my way to the door, thinking I would wait outside until it was all over. Damn. The door was locked. What could I do? I was trapped…Nothing would induce me to watch the obscenities being perpetrated in front of this grotesque gang of malodorous males. I leaned my head against the door and counted the minutes, and after what seemed like hours, the door opened. I was first out."[3]

His revulsion is very different in comparison to later encounters with prostitutes in the Red Light district of Sydney, Australia, in the early 1970s, for which he had acquired considerable notoriety among Australians. "This was before he was outed," notes writer Glenn Mitchell. "I rather imagine he'd either done it as a smokescreen or else sought out some company as an alternative to going back to empty, lonely accommodation — rather as the Marx Brothers recalled doing in vaudeville days, when the local brothels were about the only places where traveling actors would be welcome for a drink, a meal and a song or two, irrespective of whether or not they were there for sex."[4]

In later years, once his homosexuality was no longer a private matter, he seems to have been more relaxed in regard to gay socializing. In 1977, he visited a gay club, the Nightingale, on Witton Lane in the Aston district of Birmingham, signed his own name in the guest book and paid the fifty pence entrance fee.[5] What happened inside the club remains, as it should be, known only to Jimmy and those with whom he socialized.

The family was certainly aware of Jimmy's homosexuality, but their response was not helpful. Nephew Roy Pennington, the son of Jimmy's older sister, Margaret Aline, who was known as "Girlie," notes that after Jimmy's death, brother Alan said, "Yes, we knew, but we didn't talk about it much. We didn't want it thrust in our faces."[6] Niece Anne Gravett (Alan's daughter) continues,

"You will most certainly appreciate that in my uncle's 'hey day' the public attitude towards homosexuality was a world away from where we stand now. Let's just say that my father's stance on the matter did not change with the times! Of course he knew Jimmy was gay but it was not publicly discussed and this may have made it more difficult for Uncle Jimmy to 'come out' of his own volition."[7] Similarly, Fletching villagers remember Alan as "well involved" in social life there, but "old fashioned."[8]

In a BBC radio documentary, for perhaps the only time Alan talked of his brother's homosexuality:

"Brothers don't talk to one another about their sexual lives. He had another side of his life that he decided to keep away from us and he did."

"He was never blatant about it," recalled Alan's wife Betty. "Although it was in the open he didn't want to mix just with a lot of homosexuals because he didn't really get on with them. He was not the sort of person to lead a totally homosexual life."

As sister Libby told the BBC, "When it all came out he did try to say something like you don't understand men can love one another. I don't want to know — I didn't."[9]

In 1881, homosexuality replaced the crime of buggery in Great Britain, and homosexuality remained a crime until 1967, when the Sexual Offences Bill became law and decriminalized homosexual acts between men over the age of twenty-one. It was not until 1972 that the country held its first Gay Pride Parade in London and its first gay newspaper, *Gay*

News, was founded, and it was not until 1984 that Britain's first openly gay M.P., Chris Smith, was elected to Parliament. Jimmy Edwards would have been aware of the highly publicized October 20, 1953, arrest of actor John Gielgud for importuning in a London public toilet, and he should also have been aware that when he appeared on stage shortly after his arrest and conviction, the theatre audience gave him a standing ovation.[10] The comedian may not have been aware that the number was 250,000, but he must have known that quite a few of the members of the armed forces that he met during World War Two were gay, including one airman in particular. Britain had its share of known gay men during the 1940s and 1950s, but it seems unlikely that Jimmy knew any of their number, which included photographer Cecil Beaton, painter Francis Bacon, composer Michael Tippet, raconteur and exhibitionist Quentin Crisp, mathematician and Enigma Code breaker Alan Turing, playwright Joe Orton, actor/composer Ivor Novello, and actor/playwright and composer Noel Coward.

Jimmy Edwards must surely have been confused as to his sexuality, and equally conflicted as to how to handle it in relation to his rising celebrity status. There is no way that he could have been openly gay except possibly to a few close friends, and it is very obvious that he kept his limited gay life absolutely separate from his professional life. It seems improbable that the notoriously prudish BBC, "Auntie BBC," as it was nicknamed, would have kept an openly gay man under contract and massaged his career. Whatever else one may think of Jimmy Edwards, whatever one's opinion of him as a comedian or as a human being, he cannot and should not be criticized for living as he did.

After his demise, there were stories claiming that many in the business knew that he was gay. Actress Barbara Windsor supposedly nicknamed him "Tommy Two Ways," but, in reality, not only did she not know him but she never referred to him in that fashion.[11] Actor Melvyn Hayes, who worked with Jimmy on *Whack-O!*, *The Seven Faces of Jim* and *Sir Yellow* tells me that "Like the rest of the world, I had no idea that Jimmy was a homosexual."[12] June Whitfield, who had been a friend of the comedian for decades and tried to shield him from media attention after he had been "outed," would still sound surprised years later when the subject came up, insisting, "We didn't know he was gay!" As she told me, "I am perhaps rather unobservant but it didn't occur to me that Jim was 'gay' as you say, he preferred to keep that part of his life under wraps…He had girl friends and did get married and loved his life on the Polo field but ended up in Perth with Philip [Aylemore]. He must have had a good deal of turmoil in his life."[13] Some sources claim that it was in the Wimbledon home of

June Whitfield and her husband Tim that Jimmy Edwards sought refuge after he was "outed" — certainly he always spoke fondly of the couple — but she assures me he never stayed with her.[14]

Mark Wynter, who was appearing with Jimmy in *Jack and the Beanstalk* shortly after the comedian was outed, tells me that "Gender was never a topic of conversation or indeed mentioned." Wynter is also quick to defend Jimmy's reputation against anything I might write, adding, "All I can say is his larger than life character was loved by adults & children & his skill on the Trombone was masterful."[15] The relevance of that comment to Jimmy's being gay is unclear.

Jimmy, the confirmed bachelor, made his first attempt at living a "normal" life on October 16, 1953, when he announced his engagement to twenty-one-year old Michelle Carew-Gibbs of Cornfield, Sussex. The engagement ended, by mutual consent, on February 2, 1954. "I gave the ring back to Jimmy in the dressing room at the Adelphi," said Miss Gibbs. "There is nothing more to say." But there was, as less than a few hours later, the engagement was back on, only to be ended again in April 1954. The press remained singularly un-intrigued as to the on-again, off-again engagement. June Whifield does provide a suggestion as to why the proposed marriage never took place; Jimmy and Michelle were out riding together, when her horse threw her into a pond. "What shall I do," she yelled at her husband-to-be. "Throw out the ring," he replied.[16]

In an early 1958 interview, Jimmy Edwards insisted that he wanted to get married:

"It may surprise you, but I feel very lonely at times. I hate my own company, always have, and often in the morning, especially in the morning, I feel on extremely bad terms with myself....

"Whole slabs of my life don't need a woman at all. My TV work, for instance, the last thing any of the team would want would be to have my missus hanging round the studios, or putting in an appearance — and her oar — at all our script conferences. Then there's the farm, and my passion for hunting and polo. There's no place for a woman there either, really.

"As for home comforts, and feeding the brute, well, my brother's done it for me, and got married now, and my sister-in-law looks after us both splendidly....

"All the same, I am still looking....

"But it's not something you can arrange, is it, like crossing cattle or looking up a pedigree? The trouble is, I'm stamped for ever as a comic. I know, I'm inclined to lark about in public, at parties....And who wants to be married to a funny man, a gag merchant."[17]

These words were spoken to Godfrey Winn, a popular journalist and advice columnist of the day who was rather obviously gay. Yet, Winn, himself, felt the need to hide his sexuality by writing that marriage and a woman mattered most of all during one's time on earth, adding, "Yes, I say that as a bachelor myself."

On November 5, 1958, Jimmy was finally cajoled into marriage, with thirty-three-year-old Valerie Kathleen Constance Seymour. Since 1953,

Mr. and Mrs. Jimmy Edwards. 1958.

the bride had been a British Overseas Airways (BOAC) receptionist at London Airport, taking care of V.I.P. passengers. "She is much better-looking in real life than in many of her pictures," it was reported. "She has a lovely, clear magnolia skin, beautiful dark eyes, and one of those mobile mouths that is always on the verge of breaking into laughter."[18]

It was a mix of friendship and romance. Both loved horses. They enjoyed the company of two dogs, Teddy and Toby. Both enjoyed country life, and both were fond of the ridiculous. And a ridiculous marriage it was. Jimmy's sister, Libby, pointed out that "He wasn't madly in love with her or anything like that."[19] To Valerie, "My first impression of him was that he was courteous and very kindly." When Valerie's father told her before the marriage that "He's queer," Valerie responded, "No, he's not. He's just in show business."[20]

The wedding took place at Crowborough, Sussex, Registry Officer, with some six relatives and friends in attendance. One day after the wedding, and one day too late, Jimmy confessed to his bride that "he was a homosexual trying to reform."[21] A few days later, the new bride, whose reaction to Jimmy's confession is unrecorded, was attending a meeting of the Old Surrey and Barstow Hunt at Fletching — obviously, at least for now, the dutiful wife. Valerie must have put up with a great deal, aside from her husband's sexual orientation. The daughter of a friend of Valerie's recalls the beginning of a telephone conversation when her mother called the Edwards residence:

> JIMMY EDWARDS: Yes.
> BETTY JOHNSON: Oh, hello Jimmy, it's Betty here. How are you? Is Valerie there?
> JIMMY EDWARDS: Hang on. *(He puts the receiver down and walks to the foot of the stairs.)*
> JIMMY EDWARDS: *(yelling upstairs)* Val, it's that Betty fucking Johnson for you. Don't be too long gassing, I have to go out soon.
> JIMMY EDWARDS: *(picking up the phone)* She's just coming.[22]

Initially, Jimmy and Valerie lived, not at Atheralls Farm, but at Alchornes Cottage on Mark Street/Bell Lane in Fletching. Then, in 1963, Jimmy and his bride purchased a home, Upper Sorrells, in the West Sussex village of Fittleworth. The property boasted six bedrooms, four bathrooms, and four-teen-and-a-half acres of land, with views over the South Downs. The couple occupied the house together through 1966-1967, after which Valerie lived there alone. It was sold in August 1969 for thirty-six thousand pounds.[23]

Godfrey Winn again entered Jimmy's life, writing of supper with the happy couple in the popular British periodical, *Woman's Weekly*. "Despite all the prophets who declared him to be an entrenched bachelor, their partnership is a gay and triumphat success," reported Winn, with a curious use of words.[24] He noted that Valerie looked after Jimmy superbly, that she never disagreed with him and that he never took her advice:

"A man must do what he feels is right for him, and the wife who tries to stop him, or alter him too much, is asking for trouble."[25]

Undoubtedly, the center of Jimmy's life in Fittleworth was the Swan Inn, dating back to the 1300s. Here, in 1924, it is claimed was founded the Ancient Order of Froth Blowers, "to foster the noble art of and gentle and healthy pastime of froth blowing amongst Gentleman of Leisure and Ex-Soldiers," a charitable organization which ceased its froth blowing in 1931.

After what he claimed was much self-analysis, Jimmy parted from his wife in 1969, after ten years of marriage, and in public even linked the break-up of the marriage to a decision to move away from his image as a "brass-blowing buffoon" and concentrate on acting in comedy character roles. Nephew Roy Pennington is of the opinion that the marriage was never consummated.

Often Jimmy would leave the house for days at a time without explanation. Valerie insisted that he didn't have boyfriends *per se*, admitting "I didn't bother my head with it….As far as I know, during our marriage he tried to stay straight."[26] Jimmy being Jimmy, he didn't have the courage to ask for a divorce face to face with Valerie, but rather wrote her while on tour in Australia:

"My darling, I want our marriage to end, so if you could leave the house I'd be very grateful, and we'll get a divorce when I return."[27]

Valerie, or Val as she was known, continued to use the name "Edwards" until her death on November 16, 2007.

The one woman most closely associated with Edwards, not as a wife but as a "beard," was Joan Turner (1922-2009), who began her career as an entertainer while still a teenager. By the 1960s, she had become a major star, noted equally for her comedic and her vocal skills; as one British newspaper had it, she had the voice of an angel and the wit of a devil. She was also an alcoholic, whose drinking led to her being fired from all manner of shows, including a revival of the musical *Oliver!* and the television soap opera *Brookside*. For many years, she lived illegally in Southern California, according to the *Sunday Mirror* (March 11, 2001), "among the winos, drug addicts and down-and-outs in Beverly Hills, Los Angeles… dressed in charity shop clothes and surrounded by her worldly possessions — with barely a penny to her name." She died in Britain, basically unloved and unwanted, despite supposed love affairs with Tony Hancock, Peter Sellers, Terry-Thomas, and Jimmy Edwards.

Her humor was vulgar in extreme and she had little concept of the need to limit a performance on stage. With Joan, it was always a matter of audiences wanting less, not more. I personally recall seeing her in Los Angeles at the Variety Arts Center. One of her jokes involved a potential rape. She produced a gun to use if she was attacked and, out of her bag, if she was not raped, she pulled a dildo. After the curtain had come down after a long, long evening, she re-appeared on stage with a broom, sweeping up the dust and dirt. No amount of sweeping would remove the latter from her act.

Joan Turner had appeared with Jimmy, along with Tony Hancock, in the Blackpool presentation of *The Talk of the Town* in 1954, at which time she was married to a Lincolnshire solicitor and billed as "The Girl of a Thousand Voices." *The Stage* (July 29, 1954) reported that she sang one song, "One Fine Day," and she "also has a fair sense of humor." Two of the show's three sketches featured Jimmy and Tony Hancock, but Joan Turner joined Jimmy for the last sketch in the Second Act, "Conversation Piece."

On October 11, 1973, *The Stage* made it official, announcing that Jimmy Edwards and Joan Turner were engaged; "They hope to marry at Christmas — contracts permitting." At a party at London's Wig and Penn Club, Jimmy presented his fiancée with an aquamarine engagement ring. "Jimmy asked me to marry him 33 months ago," said Joan, "but I took a long time making up my mind."[28] Jimmy responded, "We are two people washed up by life…two cast-offs getting together. We will spend our honeymoon on a health farm. We are both overweight."[29] Comedian Joe Baker was to be the best man, actress Jean Kent would be matron-of-honor, and McDonald Hobley would serve as chief usher.

Joan Turner; as The Guardian *(October 23, 1992) reported, "Joan has always been heavily into boas."*

A month later, Joan and Jim appeared as a double act of that name at the Catholic Stage Guild Ball, held at London's Dorchester Hotel.

According to Barry Cryer, "Jimmy and Joan Turner had got pissed over lunch and Jimmy announced their engagement as a joke. But Joan took it seriously."[30]

The first reference to the comedian's sharing accommodation with a male (outside of his service in the R.A.F.) appears in his autobiography, *Take It from Me,* in which he mentions a young man named Derek Moore, "who had recently joined me as a full-time secretary." "Secretary" is a euphemism used by many well-known gay men and women to describe a domestic partner back in the day. Whether Derek Moore was really nothing more than a secretary is unknown. In 1951, while Jimmy was appearing during the summer months in Blackpool, Derek Moore shared a flat with him in nearby Lytham, and the two men apparently worked on Jimmy's autobiography. Prior to the Blackpool engagement, Moore has been with him on holiday in the South of France. When the comedian was elected rector of Aberdeen University, Moore also accompanied him to Scotland. The relationship between the two men may very well have been nothing more than a professional one, and mentioning Derek Moore some three times in the autobiography may, similarly, have been nothing more than thanking him for his collaboration. Only Jimmy and Derek Moore know the truth.

Jimmy's public life as a heterosexual came to an end on February 28, 1979, when gossip columnist William Hickey, in reality a pseudonym used by a variety of journalists, published a piece in the *Daily Express*, in which Australian female impersonator, Raymon Douglas, announced that he had shared Jimmy's life for thirteen years. Douglas was described as a Nijinski-hipped, six foot, two inches, thirty-one year old, boyishly handsome, with a penchant for jewelry including a necklace, earrings and bracelets.

The two men had met while Douglas was appearing in a Sydney, Australia, nightclub called "Les Girls." The couple was certainly together as early as 1975. "They met after the show, became friends, and subsequently travelled round the world together — and even dropped in on Mustique when Jimmy was giving a 'royal command' by Princess Margaret to entertain at a party there."[31]

Douglas was married but separated from wife, Natasha, and he and Jimmy were co-habiting in the latter's London flat.

That same day, Douglas also told his story to the London *Evening News*, explaining that Jimmy had seen his potential in becoming a star — he had been trained as a ballet dancer — and wanted him to come to England. "Jimmy is my guardian, although we never went through the formalities, he looks after me and is like my brother, my father and my son….I think it is an intriguing partnership. Lots of people have tried to break up the nice friendship we have."

Douglas was not the only female impersonator with whom Jimmy was close. While there is no suggestion of a relationship, he did enjoy the company of Britain's best known female impersonator, Danny La Rue, and could often be found both in the audience and in La Rue's dressing room while he was appearing on the London stage.

When confronted in Birmingham, where he was appearing in pantomime, Jimmy was naturally reluctant to discuss the relationship. He was obviously upset and somewhat confused as to how to respond. "Was he dressed up in all that gear?" he asked, presumably referring to female attire. "This is all very embarrassing for me."[32]

In a follow-up, brief piece in the March 4, 1979 edition of the *Sunday Express*, an unidentified journalist wrote, first suggesting that the *Daily Express* was the paper of world choice:

"The whole world now knows that comedian Jimmy Edwards, the great moustached symbol of masculinity, shares a flat with a young man who wears a kaftan, a gold stud in his left ear, a gold chain around his right ankle, pancake make-up and, for all I know, a whiff of Chanel No. 5 behind his ears.

"Poor old Jimmy.

"Yet I am prepared to forgive him much.

"Not just because he is a man who has brought enormous pleasure to millions. Not just because he has presented always a public image of dignity and discretion. But most of all because he happens to have the guts to have been a war-time R.A.F. pilot and to have won a D.F.C.

"But if he has to have a boy friend, might I suggest he picks one who not only wears a chain around his ankle but also has a piece of Elastoplast [a Band Aid] over his stupid big mouth."

The journalist might also have suggested similar restraint from the former Mrs. Edwards, of whom Jimmy was very fond, who, after revealing the post-wedding night confession, added, "we tried to make a go of it for 11 years, but it was impossible." As Jimmy himself said at the time, "I haven't 'come out. They've unbolted the door and kicked me through it." In a response to Valerie, he added, "I would just prefer my wife to use the word bisexual, that's all, if she's going to try to put a label on it."[33]

His "coming out" concerned Jimmy primarily in that his upper class, hunting, shooting and fishing brigade, might shun him. It did not happen in that his semi-aristocratic friends had not the least interest in Jimmy's private life. Indeed, the old boys with whom he would hunt did not understand what all the fuss was about; "We all did that in India," they exclaimed. The general public was equally unconcerned. As Frank Muir has written "People couldn't believe, or didn't want to believe, that Pa Glum was gay."[34]

Also basically uninterested in Jimmy's sexuality were members of the Savile Club, founded in Mayfair in 1868 by writers and artists, still going strong today, and very exclusive. Jimmy was a member and would often be found there playing snooker (or billiards) with fellow member, Ralph Richardson, who would arrive at the Club on his motorcycle. Michael Parkinson recalled playing snooker with a very drunken Jimmy Edwards, who decided to execute one shot by lifting one leg onto the table. He then fell asleep stretched out across the green baize of the table, only to be lifted off by two elderly servants who carried him from the room. "Don't worry Sir, we know what to do," one of them told Parkinson.[35]

Concurrrent with his "outing," beginning December 22, 1978, Jimmy had been playing in the Triumph Theatre Productions' pantomime, *Jack and the Beanstalk*, with Arthur Askey, Leslie Crowther and Mark Wynter, at the Alexandra Theatre, Birmingham.[36] Leslie Crowther found Jimmy crying in his dressing room; "There are women and children out there," he sobbed, refusing to go on stage. Crowther comforted him and persuaded

Jimmy to make his entrance. The reaction to the comedian's appearance on stage differed not at all from when he was assumed to be straight than when he was outed as gay — except that now he received an ovation. "People didn't know or didn't care," says Barry Cryer.[37]

The response to Jimmy's first stage appearance after the outing is reminiscent of the audience response to John Gielgud after his October 1953 arrest and conviction for importuning in a public lavatory. He was paralyzed with fear at going on stage in *A Day by the Sea*, but co-star Sybil Thorndike led him on, whispering, "They won't boo me!" Rather the opposite happened, and Gielgud received a standing ovation.

Jimmy was a member of the Lord's Taverners, a club established in 1950 at the Lord's Cricket Ground in London by a group of cricketing actors, with the intention of raising funds for cricket-related charities. After his "outing," Jimmy had been invited to speak at one of the club's lunches. He kept a very low profile, remaining quiet and subdued, but as people came up to him in friendship and support, he blossomed, and, as Barry Cryer remembers, "He was a riot when he spoke; he really came to life."[38]

It might well be that Edwards was concerned that his name might somehow be linked to another comedian, Wilfred Brambell, who like Jimmy had been married albeit briefly, and, like Arthur Howard, had been arrest for importuning in a public lavatory in the Shepherd's Bush area of London in November 1962. He was also an alcoholic, and like Jimmy, Brambell had a young man whom he brought to London as his "valet." Brambell had gained fame for his performance, with Harry H. Corbett, in the popular sitcom, *Steptoe and Son*, which was broadcast on the BBC from 1962-1965 and 1970-1974. Brambell was a far from attractive-looking individual, both in the series and in real life, and his depiction as a rag-and-bone man did not exactly help his image. He was, in the words of *The Guardian* (August 18, 2002), "a cheeky and dirty old man." And there were rumors that, like Jimmy Savile, Brambell had abused twelve- and thirteen-year-old boys.

Perhaps the only real casualty from Jimmy's "outing" was the boyfriend, who disappeared from the scene. He was replaced four years later, if not earlier, by another Australian, this time in his late twenties, the handsome, blonde-haired Philip Aylemore, Jimmy's "chum," as he was described, who had the look of a surfer. Perhaps Jimmy was in a relationship with Philip while still living with Raymon; Melvyn Hayes, who appeared with the comedian in *Sir Yellow* in 1973, recalls that "On one occasion I did see Jimmy with a — if my memory serves me right — blonde young man.

After a day's filming the young man was waiting for Jimmy in his dress-ing/hotel room."[39] The couple remained together until the comedian's death, although friends recall "they certainly had tiffs."[40] At the same time, niece Anne Gravett insists, "he and Jimmy had a long standing, loving relationship."[41]

Many in Jimmy's home village of Fletching though of Philip as a recluse in that he was seldom seen, but at the same time, Fletching, with a couple of pubs and a village shop, offered little to engage a young Australian. He did enjoy the English summers and he also enjoyed the company of Anne Gravett and her first husband, visting their home in Brighton and touring the local countryside with them.

Perhaps Philip Aylemore saw himself, like the Matt Lucas character, Daffyd Thomas, in *Little Britain* (2003-2006) as "The Only Gay in the Village." However, unlike Daffyd Thomas, he might be perceived by many as closeted as much as was Jimmy during most of his life.

The comedian took Philip off to Gambia for a three-week holiday in March 1983. "He'll be sunbathing and surfing — the things a young man of his age does. I'll be on a shady verandah writing my book [*Six of the Best*]."[42] Certainly, poor Philip quickly discovered that Jimmy was not too generous when it came to his own money. Philip enjoyed what British Caledonian had to offer in economy, while Jimmy sat up front in first class. Such an arrangement may not necessarily have been evidence of Jimmy's meanness; his sister Libby was married to an airline employee and she would arrange first or business class travel for her brother, but was perhaps not able to obtain the same perks for Aylemore.

The story does tend to suggest that nephew Roy Pennington's view of the Edwards-Aylemore relationship has perhaps some truth to it. Pennington saw Philip Aylemore as a similar to a batman in the military, a private soldier assigned to a commissioned officer as a personal servant. Philip Aylemore was there to take care of Jimmy, still perhaps remember-ing with affection his war career, and needing the company of a younger man willing and able to provide all manner of creature comforts.

Did the effort to cover up his homosexuality influence his alcohol consumption? Many psychologists might argue in favor of that argu-ment. After all, it is an accepted premise that hatred expressed against homosexual men by others, or the threat at such animosity, led to many men embracing alcohol or drugs; from a psychoanalytical viewpoint, latent homosexuality is regarded as a cause of alcoholism. Jimmy himself pointed out that he was no different to many other entertainers who enjoyed a drink, or two, or three. He explained that thanks to alcohol a basically shy young man turned into the "roaring, red-faced buffoon who…blasted on the trombone."[43] By 1968, he claimed to have drunk some 200 bottles of whiskey since the start of his professional career. "The whisky has sustained me…Or to put it another way, it has quelled the desire not to continue."[44] "I don't drink normally," he maintained, "I drink abnormally."[45] An advertisement read "Drink Canada Dry," and while Jimmy was there during World War Two, he would comment, "I did my best."

Jimmy's mother Margaret also had an issue with alcohol, and, therefore, his alcoholism may have been hereditary, although there was absolutely no other family member so affected. Margaret Edwards was also addicted to "Mother's Little Helper," as the 1966 Rolling Stones song referred to anti-anxiety drugs, better identified today as either valium or diazepam.[46]

Alcohol did perhaps help Jimmy to lose some or most of his inhibitions and become something of an exhibitionist. British writer and broadcaster Gyles Brandreth recalled a 1980 visit to Fletching, being picked up by Jimmy at Haywards Heath and driven to the village at breakneck speed. He stopped en route at a pub "for a refresher," consisting of a pint of beer and a large vodka. When he arrived at Fletching, he opened a carton of orange juice and a bottle of champagne, poured the two into a large jug, and then decanted half into a pint pot. Jimmy had a gin and tonic to set himself up for preparing lunch, consisting of two large steaks which caught fire repeatedly and a salad of lettuce and tomato. Two bottles of claret were opened to drink with the meal. The come the interesting part:

"After lunch, he went off to find the brandy, telling me, as he went, about his pride and joy: his Swedish hot tub, newly installed. When he returned he was stark naked. 'Are you going to join me?' he asked. I declined. He slapped his huge belly with both hands, went away and got dressed."[47]

Looking back, Gyles Brandreth comments,

"It was certainly an invitation to join him in the tub — but it was not predatory. I declined and he accepted that with equanimity.

"He was a splendid character — and very entertaining. His need for alcohol was alarming. His overture to me was typical, I think, in my limited experience (e.g. with Frankie Howerd) the overture was often to someone who clearly wasn't going to respond — often to married people, like me."[48]

Alcohol consumption and Jimmy Edwards were synonymous. In 1970, when the London newspaper, the *Evening Standard* bestowed the title of Pub of the Year, Jimmy was the obvious choice to make a guest appearance at the location. When, in 1954, character comedian Ronald Shiner became landlord of the Blackboys Inn in Uckfield, it was Jimmy Edwards who was invited to be filmed there by Pathé News.

One academic encountered Jimmy at an awards dinner: "He was drunk and was noisily demanding more drink. I think drink rather than gayness may have restricted his job opportunities later."[49] At the same time, those who were close to him all insist that Edwards never turned nasty no matter the amount of alcohol he might have consumed. Alcohol gave Jimmy the delusion of happiness, and, as he often admitted, that was all he needed.

Alcohol served as a cure for most, if not all of Jimmy's ills. In November 1979, when out fox hunting, his horse stumbled while trying to jump a hedge and fell on him. Both he and the horse might have been seriously injured, but the latter was unhurt, while Jimmy suffered bruises and some pain. It was all fixed up by the local doctor and a fortifying snort of brandy. Of course for the man who famously held his bulging stomach and said, "It's only puppy fat. I had a puppy for lunch," alcohol was not helpful in the dieting process, which Jimmy undertook on a number of occasions.

Colleagues have pointed out that Jimmy's performance might suffer just as much from too little alcohol before the show as too much. He knew how to maintain an appropriate balance. June Whitfield recalls that at one recording of *Take It from Here*, he arrived from a lunch with broadcaster and journalist Wynford Vaughan Thomas. The pair had begun the meal with vodka, moved on to pink champagne, followed by claret, and concluding with port and brandy.[50] When Jimmy arrived at the studio he dismissed the script as not making sense and announced the need for a pint at the pub. On his return, five minutes before recording was scheduled to commence, he went before the microphone and his performance was flawless.

While filming *Sir Yellow* in May 1973, he threatened to cut off the hand of anyone who tried to get a drink in advance of him during the lunch break at a local Yorkshire pub. After a couple of glasses of Campari at the bar, he moved on to champagne to accompany his lunch. Little wonder that Alan Edwards' wife, Betty, declared that he has the constitution of an ox.[51]

Veteran talk show host Michael Parkinson recalled Jimmy's being a guest on a three-hour long, morning radio show at the BBC:

"As we chatted away sipping cups of coffee he produced a large and battered hip flask and poured a hefty slug into both our drinks.

"When we had emptied the first hip flask he produced another.

"By the time we arrived at the end of the programme it was a toss up who looked after who.

"We lurched to a club for lunch during which we drank enough wine to decide upon a game of snooker for a large sum of money."[52]

While it might seem that Jimmy was the subject of alcohol abuse, he was also very much aware that too much would impede his ability to perform. Recalling his days as an RAF flyer, he told a friend, "It's rather like a red light on the dashboard — you have to realise when you've had enough, otherwise it affects your work adversely."[53]

For the last couple of years of his life, Jimmy was severely to reduce his intake of alcohol. Aside from the obvious alcohol-related medical issues, there was also a balance issue, perhaps because of hip problems. One newspaper even published a story as to "Why tipple will make Jim topple."[54]

1. Ian McKellen official home page, *www.mckellen.com/life/per.htm.*

2. June Whitfield to Anthony Slide, e-mail dated February 8, 2017.

3. Jimmy Edwards, *Six of the Best*, p. 135.

4. Glenn Mitchell to Anthony Slide, e-mail dated January 24, 2017.

5. *gaybirminghamremembered.co.uk/*

6. Anthony Slide interview with Roy Pennington, April 10, 2017.

7. Anne Gravett to Anthony Slide, e-mail dated April 10, 2017.

8. Anthony Slide interview with Barry Dickens, April 21, 2017.

9. All family quotes from Ronni Davis, producer, and Nigel Farrell, presenter, *Wake Up in the Back: The Life of Jimmy Edwards.*

10. In November 1968, John Gielgud sent Jimmy a copy of his book, *Stage Directions*, inscribed "Dear Jimmy Edwards — the best connection — affectionately John Gielgud."

11. Barbara Windsor's agent, Barry Burnett to Anthony Slide, e-mail dated April 4, 2016.

12. Melvyn Hayes to Anthony Slide, e-mail dated August 3, 2016.

13. June Whitfield to Anthony Slide, e-mail dated February 8, 2017.

14. Ibid.

15. Mark Wynter to Anthony Slide, e-mail dated January 17, 2017.

16. June Whitfield, *…And June Whitfield*, p. 144.

17. Godfrey Winn, "Life Is So Full, and Yet…,"p. 8.

18. Godfrey Winn, "Supper with Mr. and Mrs. Jimmy Edwards," p. 20.

19. Ronni Davis, producer, and Nigel Farrell, presenter, *Wake Up at the Back: The Life of Jimmy Edwards*.

20. Ibid.

21. Quoted in *The Sun*, September 7, 1988.

22. *theafterword.co.uk/* (accessed March 2017).

23. As reported in *The Guardian*, August 14, 1969, p. 6.

24. Godfrey Winn, "Supper with Mr. and Mrs. Jimmy Edwards, p. 19.

25. Ibid, p. 21.

26. Ronnie Davis, producer, and Nigel Farrell, presenter, *Wake Up at the Back: The Life of Jimmy Edwards*.

27. Ibid.

28. Judith Simons, "Whacko! Jimmy and Joan Name the Day."

29. Ibid.

30. Anthony Slide interview with Barry Cryer, February 6, 2017.

31. William Hickey, "My Life with Jimmy Edwards by Drag Man Raymon."

32. Ibid.

33. "What Jimmy Edwards Told Me on the Second Day of Our Honeymoon," p. 1.

34. Frank Muir, *A Kentish Lad*, p. 247.

35. Michael Parkinson, "Moments of Magic with Two Real Stars."

36. It was reported by *The Stage* (December 21, 1978) that the production had attracted the biggest box office advance in the theatre's history.

37. Anthony Slide interview with Barry Cryer, February 6, 2017.

38. Ibid.

39. Melvyn Hayes to Anthony Slide, e-mail dated August 3, 2016.

40. Michael Pointon to Anthony Slide, e-mail dated January 27, 2017.

41. Anne Gravett to Anthony Slide, e-mail dated April 11, 2017.

42. "Big Jim Takes a Break — With His Young Chum Phillip."

43. Quoted in Michael Dynan, "Variety's the Word," p. 11.

44. Peter Dacre, "It's Back to the Old Tuba Again for Jimmy Edwards."

45. June Whitfield, *…And June Whitfield*, p. 99.

46. Anthony Slide interview with Roy Pennington, April 10, 2017.

47. Gyles Brandreth, *Brief Encounters: Meetings with Remarkable People*, October 8, 1980.

48. Gyles Brandreth to Anthony Slide, e-mail dated March 27, 2017.

49. Professor Jeffrey Richards, Lancaster University, to Anthony Slide, April 14, 2016.

50. June Whitfield, *...And June Whitfield*, p. 99.

51. Ronni Davis, producer, and Nigel Farrell presenter, *Wake Up at the Back: The Life of Jimmy Edwards.*

52. Michael Parkinson, "Moments of Magic with Two Real Stars."

53. Michael Pointon to Anthony Slide, e-mail dated January 25, 2017.

54. Glenn Mitchell to Anthony Slide, e-mail dated January 23, 2017.

CHAPTER TEN

The Perfect English Gentleman

Away from the world of entertainment, but with many aspects of his personal life under its influence, Jimmy Edwards was very much a gentleman, not necessarily of the old school in that humor would often play a part in his activities, but nevertheless a fine example to us all as to how a gentleman should behave in the 1900s prior to the 1960s and the advent of a new generation, influenced by drugs, promiscuity and, of course, the Beatles. He drove a station wagon, and wore a tweed suit described as suitable either for the country or the town. His earnings as an entertainer were not tremendous, but at the same time they were more than enough for a comfortable life style. In the 1950s and 1960s, he was earning on average 30,000 pounds a year (the equivalent today of 462,000 pounds). In the late 1960s, his income had dropped to an average of 20,000 pounds a year (the equivalent today of 308,000 pounds).

A Country Gentleman at Home

Jimmy Edwards lived the life of a country squire, a life that often seemed to be interrupted by the necessity to take the train to London or further afield to entertain the masses. He might have acquired a manor house in order to pursue the image he sought in private life, but instead he decided to become a farmer — not exactly a gentleman farmer but a part-time farmer willing to get his hands dirty if necessary. With his family, he had rambled through Richmond Park, relatively close to Barnes, and while at Cambridge, he had spent the long summer vacation at Rolf Gardiner's farming camp in Dorset. Indeed, Jimmy was out in the field picking potatoes on September 3, 1939, when he was told that war had been declared. "Perhaps I like the country most of all because I can get away from everybody else," he wrote. "Alone in a large wood with a gun or even without a gun, I feel happy."[1]

What was apparently the first home of his own, into which he moved in May 1950, was an old and small white cottage, dating back to the 1600s, called Court House Close, and located in the Sussex village of Rottingdean. Why Jimmy was to choose the county of Sussex as his home for much of his later life is unknown, although his nephews are of the opinion that it was within easy reach of both the family home in Barnes and the BBC studios at Shepherds Bush. Jimmy claimed to have no ability in regard to cooking in his new abode, and this is perhaps confirmed by a recipe for "Crunch Cos Lettuce and Cabbage Lettuce Salad," that he contributed to *The Complete Book of Salads*, compiled by Bebe Daniels and Jill Allgood in 1952.[2] A typical daily routine at the cottage was described by one reporter, beginning with two soft-boiled brown eggs:

"Everything in that cottage is giant-sized, from the large brown teapot ('can't bear silly little teapots or cups')….After breakfast, while I washed up, Jimmy went aloft to make the bed and straighten the bedroom….After a quick flick round with a wheezy carpet-sweeper, a mighty poof to get the dust off the television and radio sets, he put on his riding boots…."[3]

At which point, Jimmy took the reporter to meet his two horses, Doodles and Paddy, stabled close by. On most days, he would take lunch at a local pub, owned by a friend from the R.A.F., while on Tuesdays, ready to rehearse *Take It from Here*, he would drive to Brighton and take the 1:25 P.M. train, the "Brighton Belle," to London.

It seems an ideal life for a confirmed bachelor who does not need the companionship of women, but as the reporter noted, "Though a bachelor, Jimmy Edwards is not agin us women. 'I am still weighing up the pros and cons of marriage.'"[4] Also noted, perhaps in an effort to dispel any rumors as to Jimmy's sexuality, he does not like poodles.

The idea to take up farming dated back to the late 1940s. Jimmy realized that his career would prevent full-time activity in the field (both literally and figuratively), and so, to join him, he persuaded brother Alan, who had more than a passing interest in farming in that at the beginning of World War Two, he had worked as farm manager in Wales at Tynewydd Farm, Mgon Mellons, Monmouthshire. In 1944, it was reported, "he looks forward to simple country life in a post-war world."[5] Alan was apparently more than happy to give up his job with the Ministry of Transport, and take a refresher correspondence course on the subject, followed by a year working on three separate farms. Jimmy and Alan were closer than most brothers throughout their entire lives, and even before the joint farming venture, Alan had served as Jimmy's manager beginning in the 1940s.

In 1950, Jimmy became the tenant of Atheralls Farm, its three-storey farmhouse and 140 acres of land in the village of Fletching, East Sussex, thirty-six miles south of London. Fletching has two claims to fame thanks to two of its most prominent residents. The first is Jimmy Edwards,

and the second is the Piltdown Man, discovered in 1912 and hailed as the missing link between humans and apes, but subsequently exposed decades later as a forgery.

A highly picturesque village, with a population of approximately 1,000, Fletching derives its name, French in origin, either from the feathers used on arrows to stabilize them while in flight — bows and arrows were produced here in the Middle Ages — or from a 5th Century family of invaders named "Flecci." The Fletching Bonfire Society hosts fireworks and a bonfire in honor of Guy Fawkes Night, as close as possible to November 5, and both Jimmy and Alan would play the trombone with the Fletching Bonfire Society Band.[6] The churchyard in Fletching, where Jimmy Edwards is buried, is also the resting place of Edward Gibbon, the author of *The History of the Decline and Fall of the Roman Empire*.

Jimmy and Alan took over the herd of milking cattle at Atheralls Farm, but all proved to be "reactors," carriers of T.B., and all were disposed of. To replace them, Jimmy purchased a new herd of Ayrshire heifers from

Scotland. Their arrival had all the comedy-drama that might be found in a motion picture:

"The station for Fletching is Sheffield Park, and one day Jimmy had a phone call to say the heifers had arrived. 'Right, we'll nip up and get them with the horse-box,' said Jimmy. 'T'will be a bit of a journey,' replied the caller, with a strong North Country accent, 'I'm speaking from Sheffield in Yorkshire.'

Not only had they arrived at the wrong Sheffield, but for some obscure reasons had reached the *abattoir* there. Luckily for Jimmy the *abattoir* manager realised that good Ayrshire heiffers were not intended for his department and had set to work to contact the rightful owner."[7]

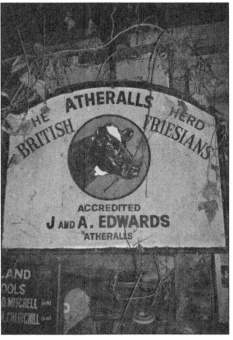

While the two brothers handled the day-to-day operation of the farm, their mother came down from London on a regular basis to attend to the garden, in which the two men had little interest. "For a bachelor household, it is extremely cosy, where you are made to feel at home at once," wrote a visiting reporter, "where Alan sits and smiles as he tells Jimmy to carve the joint for a change and Jimmy struggles, saying, 'You'll have to have chunks.'"[8]

Atheralls Farm, along with several others in the area, was owned by Arthur Gilstrap Soames, and when he died, his nephew, Arthur Granville Soames,[9] inherited the estate and, in the summer of 1952, sold off the various properties, including Atheralls Farm, to their tenants.

In December 1953, Jimmy acquired a neighboring farm, East Park, with 117 acres, used for arable crops and the raising of beef cattle, for 6,600 pounds. He also purchased a further seventeen acres of land at Atheralls Farm for a mere 650 pounds and a semi-detached, half-timbered house opposite Fletching Church for 1,250 pounds (presumably as an investment). At East Park, Jimmy kept his two hunters, King of Diamonds and Robbers, horses bred for fox hunting with their ability easily to take a jump and to gallop with a pack of other horses.[10] By this time, he also had a number of large, white pedigree pigs at Atheralls. Courtesy of the chief electrician at the Adelphi Theatre, he also acquired a cocker spaniel by the name of Susie.

The sign indicating Jimmy's farming empire read, "J and A Edwards accredited British Friesians," a reference not to Friesian horses as one

Alan and Jimmy Edwards, farmers.

might expect but to a breed of black-and-white cattle with a high milk yield (and known in the U.S. as Holstein).

On the surface at least, Atheralls Farm might seem to be managed by Jimmy, but, in reality, it was brother Alan who was in total charge of running the farm. Jimmy was not always reliable, and once put gasoline instead of diesel fuel in the new tractor, one of the first in the phase-out of the horses that had been doing the work. As Alan described his brother's work at the farm, "He liked to make himself responsible for the pest control, shooing anything that came in sight."[11]

More land was added to Atheralls with the purchase of Fliteridge Farm, Down Street Farm, Knabbs Farm, and Holmesdale Farm. Atheralls, Fliteridge and Holmesdale each had its own herd of dairy cattle, each with its own herdsman. Seven additional workers were on staff full-time to handle the arable farming, oats, barley, wheat, maize, used for cattle fodder, and all requiring ploughing, sowing, harrowing, and rolling.[12] In addition, pig man Jack Beech looked after the pigs at Atheralls and East Park, and there was a full-time groom for the horses, Jean Steele, as well as a maintenance fitter in the workshop.

Life at Atheralls Farm was pleasant and, thanks to Alan, business-like. However, to nephew Roy Pennington, a visit to the farm was what a

ATHERALLS FARM   FLETCHING

An aerial view of Atheralls Farm.

visit to the fictional Cold Comfort Farm might have resembled.[13] Set in Sussex, Stella Gibbons classic novel, first published in 1932, is peopled with ignorant and emotionally-troubled individuals, including Aunt Ada Doom with her constant references to "something nasty in the woodshed." That "something" at Atheralls Farm was surely Jimmy's homosexuality well hidden in the closet.

Jimmy spent much of the rest of his life at Atheralls Farm,[14] boasting that within one hour of the end of a stage performance in London he could be back at the farm, breathing good Sussex air. Here, he was very much the country gentleman, the lord of the manor in everything but name. He would host the annual Fletching Horse Show and Gymkhana at the farm from August 1951 onwards. Celebrities would happily oblige with their presence; as, for example, in August 1953, when Terry-Thomas, John Mills and his wife, bandleader Jack Hylton, and Jerry Desmonde participated in a one-mile theatrical challenge race in aid of the Fletching branch of the British Legion. As a one-off, Jimmy and Alan organized an inter-farm cricket match; cricket remains popular in Fletching and the current owner of Atheralls Farm tells me that he plays cricket for the Giffin Inn but is also captain of the Rose and Crown team playing against them. It seems the type of arrangement of which Jimmy might approve, particularly with both sides closely linked to alcohol consumption.

Many evenings, Jimmy could be found "holding up the bar" at his local pub of choice, the Rose and Crown,[15] a choice shared with most in the village. There he would talk on any subject except his career. If anyone might approach him about show business, Jimmy would turn his back on the offending individual. In many respects, his attitude was similar to that of legendary American novelist J.D. Salinger, who despite being regarded as a recluse would socialize with locals in his New Hampshire village, but walk away if anyone had the audacity to ask about his writing.

Farming and show business might cross paths as when, for example, Jimmy received a letter from a television viewer in Brighton: "I've enjoyed your shows on the telly…and now last week, I enjoyed a piece of your beef, too. It was extremely tender." As Jimmy responded, "It's lucky she didn't write and say that the weekend joint was as tough and as stale as my jokes. Now, *that* would have been the worst of both worlds!"[16]

In 1955, in Chelsea, Alan Edwards eventually married a local girl, Betty Dobson, whose parents, Joe and Vera, ran one of the local pubs, The Griffin Inn.[17] It was Betty's second marriage — she had previously been the wife of Reginald Baulu — and she was to die young, at the age of forty-seven, in June 1972. The couple had one daughter, Anne, and Betty had a son from her previous marriage.

Other comedians who have lived in Sussex include George Robey, Max Miller, Spike Milligan, and Sandy Powell. At the end of his autobiography, *Take It from Me*, Jimmy quotes the words of Rudyard Kipling, who from 1897 until his death had lived in Rottingdean, Sussex:

> *God gives all men all earth to love,*
> *But since Man's heart is small,*
> *Ordains for each one spot shall prove*
> *Beloved over all.*
> *Each to his choice, and I rejoice*
> *The lot has fallen to me*
> *In a fair ground — in a fair ground —*
> *Yea, Sussex by the sea!*[18]

Fox Hunting

Like a certain class of country gentleman, so aptly described by Oscar Wilde in *A Woman on No Importance* as "the unspeakable in full pursuit of the uneatable," Jimmy was an avid supporter of fox hunting, and would run with the hounds whenever possible. Early in his career, he announced that his hobbies were brass bands and riding to hounds.[19] However, while he had no objection to be photographed with the former, he would always urge photographs not to capture the image of his getting on a horse; "I look awful — most undignified."[20] Today, many would point out it is not the getting on the horse but rather the combination of the two of them in pursuit of a harmless fox that is truly undignified. Certainly, Jimmy would not have cared what the public thought of his behavior in the field; he had more than a taste for public controversy.

Jimmy Edwards with Terry-Thomas participating in the Old Surrey & Burstow Hunt.

Speaking before 500 supporters of the Southdown Hunt in Ringmer, East Sussex, in 1951, he reported that he had been hunting for eighteen months and he had enjoyed every minute of the experience. He had recently seen a fox killed for the first time, which evoked laughter from his audience, and commented that when he first saw the fox he was uncertain as to what to say. Should he shout, "There it is," or should the response be "I taut I taw a puddy tat." If necessary, Jimmy assured his audience he would be "the first to take up the cudgels against those who tried to stop fox hunting."[21] Jimmy, riding a horse named Bandit, appears to have been a regular member of the Southdown Hunt which remains active to the present and is now known as the Southdown & Eridge Hunt. From 1972-1974 and from 1979-1981, he was Joint Master of the Old Surrey & Burstow Hunt;[22] Terry-Thomas was also a member. The comedian was also featured in a 1960 volume, *In Praise of Hunting: A Symposium*, published by Hollis & Carter.

On February 17, 1954, he was in Melton, running with the Belvoir Hunt. Later that same day, he attended the Belvoir Hunt Farmers' Ball, and borrowed a trombone from one of the members of the band to liven the performance. He also auctioned a pig and a case of whiskey, asking,

Acting as umpire of a women's polo match at Richmond in 1972.

"What am I bid? Speak up, you clots!" Later the same year, on March 19, he was at the Beaufort Hunt Farmers' Ball in Chippenham, Wiltshire, playing his trombone as he led the conga.

It was often convenient to combine fox hunting with his professional life, as in October 1969 when he rode with the local hunt, the Harriers, while appearing in cabaret at Webbington Country Club in Axbridge, Somerset. In 1958, he proudly noted that, "Last winter, I played a cinema in Shrewsbury, and hunted in Shropshire, and last summer, I was billed in Cheltenham by night and played polo by day in Cirencester."[23] When offered a date by his agent, the first question that Jimmy would ask concerned what the hunting might be like in that area.

If Edwards' enjoyment of fox hunting may be offensive to many, including this writer, his pleasure at the killing of a deer is even more so. In September 1958, the League Against Cruel Sports protested at the ritual of "blooding," at which new members of the hunt have the hot blood of the prey smeared over their faces. It was not the blood of a fox that aroused the League's ire, but that of a stag, which was chased by hounds, wounded by a gun shot and then eventually killed with another shot at a meeting of the Somerset-based Quantock stag hounds.[24] Jimmy and a boy and girl were subsequently smeared with the stag's blood. Edwards was quick to defend the hunt and the practice of "blooding":

"So far as I am concerned, I went to the hunt because I am a member of the British Field Sports Society. I support all forms of hunting. As I happened to be in the neighborhood I went stag hunting. I saw nothing cruel. 'Blooding' is a ceremony with some tradition and history behind it, to which I submitted because it was the first time I had been out staghunting. I saw nobody who did not thoroughly enjoy the day. I think it gave pleasure to the local people to see me 'blooded.'"[25]

When not killing foxes or deer, Jimmy was quite happy to take his gun and aim it at troublesome birds. Comedian Cyril Fletcher, who lived close by, would call upon Jimmy to bring his shotgun and aim at rooks who had built their nests too close to his house. As Fletcher wrote,

"Actually he only had to put his heavily moustachioed face round the door for the rooks, who are either over-intelligent, intuitive or psychic, to take to the wing and disappear!"[26]

Rector of Aberdeen University

As witness Jimmy Edwards' background as a Cambridge graduate, his wartime career and his place as a distinguished gentleman, it should be no surprise that he was elected rector of Aberdeen University. Well, perhaps it is somewhat surprising to many unfamiliar with the position of rector at this Northern Scottish university. The rector at Aberdeen was elected by the students and served a three-year term as their representative in the University Court. Aberdeen University — not the only Scottish university to boast of a rector — has had a curious group of individuals elected to the position, ranging from Maggie Chapman, the leader of the Scottish Green Party in more recent times, and Winston Churchill during World War One to broadcaster and conservationist Peter Scott in the early 1960s, Scottish character actor Iain Cuthbertson in the 1970s and, of course, Jimmy Edwards.

Jimmy learned of the students' interest in the summer of 1951, and was somewhat surprised to discover that he was also being asked to "compete" for a similar position at Edinburgh University, to replace the retiring rector, comedy actor Alastair Sim. As Aberdeen asked first, Jimmy agreed to allow the students there to put his name forward for consideration in the October election. There were four nominees: Jimmy, two World War Two leaders, Lord Lovat and Captain Farquhason, and Paul Robeson. Jimmy's manifesto declared him to be,

"a man of unquestionable initiative and courage...[a] farmer who spends time, despite his other commitments, tending his dairy herd of Ayrshire cattle. Lastly, we give you Jimmy Edwards, a man of character, wit and out-standing personality — a man who in our opinion and, we hope in yours, is eminently suited to become the new Rector of Aberdeen University."[27]

Jimmy himself was not permitted to participate in his own campaign, which was subject to a certain amount of frivolity with the leader of Jimmy's supporters being held prisoner by the supporters of Lord Lovat, who came in second. Despite the criminal efforts of the opposition, Jimmy was elected Rector by 430 votes from the 1,008 students who participated. Paul Robeson received a mere 104 votes. Even after the election was won fair and square, there were issues as to Jimmy's being installed, with the university administration concerned that the event might descend into hooliganism, as had happened at the recent election of the rector at Glasgow University.

It was not until January 1953 that the university agreed to go ahead with the installation, and Jimmy made the journey of twelve hours by night train from London to Aberdeen, arriving two days before the cere-mony, which took place on January 25, 1952. At the ceremony in Mitchell Hall before an audience of more than 1,000 students and faculty,[28] and with considerable rowdiness, the comedian spoke of the influence of radio, noting his concern that mass listening had the potential to effect the younger generation. He continued that

"Although there were certain programmes at seemingly appropriate times of the day which were directed specifically towards children, it was far too easy for them to eavesdrop on less suitable material at any hour of the day or night.

"Unless a child was blessed with parents who were intelligent and strict enough to regulate its listening, what was there to prevent it being sub-jected to all kinds of dangerous influences?

"But as you know, an even greater menace is lurking across the border. Preparing to insinuate its way into your lives is the tangible terror of television.

"The television screen has a hypnotic effect — there is a horrible fas-cination about it — and as you sit there with the curtains drawn and the light switched out you need a very strong will not to remain until the evening's programme is over. In fact it has been said that television is rapidly taking the place of entertainment.

"Television would find its own level in the scheme of things, and there would always be room for radio.

"But the greatest danger from these vehicles of mass entertainment, radio, television and films, is that they prevent people from entertaining themselves, and when these three media are added to the already manifold distractions of University life, the dangers are obvious."[29]

It was a speech of which certainly any Conservative politician of the period might be proud, and it is somewhat surprising that the students of Aberdeen University did not rebel against its somewhat censorial quality and demand a recount in their election of Rector. They didn't, and, in fact, when Jimmy returned to London the next day, there were forty of their number, in evening gowns and dinner jackets on the station platform waiting to see him off.

He made a number of visits to Aberdeen during his tenure as Rector. Most notably, on April 22, 1954, he was there in part to participate in a favorite hobby, flying in a Chipmunk training aircraft of the Aberdeen University Air Squadron. The plane took off from Dyce Airport, just outside of Aberdeen, and Jimmy had hoped to parachute from the plane to Union Street and collect money for various charities. Permission for the stunt was refused.

The previous day, Jimmy had been in the Mitchell Hall of Marischal College to debate Robert Boothby on the motion that "This house does not believe in the importance of being earnest." Jimmy spoke in support, while Boothby opposed. Robert Boothby (1900-1986) had been Conservative M.P. for East Aberdeenshire until giving up his seat when he became a peer. He was openly bisexual, enjoying affairs with London gangsters, but was also defiantly heterosexual, fathering a number of illegitimate children and having an affair with the wife of Prime Minister Harold Macmillan.

More than 1,000 students turned up for the debate in which Jimmy spent much of his time recalling his previous address upon election as rector:

"On that day I was charged with emotion — I was charged with something anyway — but I daresay many of you are too young to remember it. I shall never forget it. It was a time of signal honour which I appreciated very much at the time.

"Then I got into the mood of the thing. I pulled myself up suddenly with a jerk — you know him, Bentley is the name.

"Bentley is not nearly so old. Of course, he was still on the radio when Mrs. Dale was on her honeymoon [a reference to a popular daily BBC radio soap, *Mrs. Dale's Diary*, which ran from 1948-1969].

"Bentley is the only man alive today whose Balaclava helmet was actually issued at Balaclava.

"There is nothing worse than the professional comedian beginning to take himself seriously. I said to myself, 'Come off it, Jim: who the hell do you think you are?'"

Boothby agreed with much the rector had to say and spoke out against a forthcoming television bill that would place restrictions on what might be broadcast, far more than those already in place from the BBC management.

"I don't think you are going to get very lively entertainment on TV, either from the rector of myself or anyone else.

"Be earnest on appropriate occasions — and by no means earnest all the time."

As Jimmy Edwards' term as rector grew to a close at the end of 1954, he was succeeded by the First Sea Lord, Admiral Sir Rhoderick McGrigor. From the air force to the navy or from the high comedy represented by Jimmy Edwards to the high seas which were home to Sir Rhoderick. Jimmy might perhaps have admired the latter for his advocacy of aircraft carriers.

The comedian was certainly honored by his association with Aberdeen, and would proudly show visitors to his home the complete *Oxford English Dictionary*, which the University had presented to him.

Perhaps the ease of his election as Aberdeen University Rector influenced Jimmy's decision to campaign for election to a more serious position, not in Scotland but in England, and closer to home.

A Conservative Politician

"I am considering entering politics and becoming the Grand Old Man of the Conservative Party," Jimmy told Dick Bentley on an episode of *Take It from Here*. "Watch it," responded Dick Bentley. "Politics is a dirty business." To which Jimmy replied, "Then I'll be the Dirty Old man of the Conservative Party." In 1954, while appearing in *The Talk of the Town*, he appeared in a sketch titled "Votes for Jim," wherein he discussed the principles of "Jimmunism."

Eventually, life imitated art when Jimmy decided to become a member of parliament. In 1964, he stood in the General Election as the Conservative candidate for the London borough of Paddington North. "We are in favour of people like Jimmy Edwards standing for Parliament," opined the entertainment newspaper, *The Stage* (August 15, 1963), "because we know their behavior during the contest will reflect nothing but dignity on their profession." In reality, he was more a distraction than a viable candidate, with constituents yelling at him as he was canvassing for votes to "give us the trombone and go home."

The only negative aspect of Jimmy's candidature was that in the interest of fairness and balance, the BBC had to stop broadcasting *Take It from Here* during the election campaign. It ignored a suggestion from writers Frank Muir and Denis Norden that the obvious solution was to commission a thirty-minute comedy series starring the Labor Party candidate. Denis Norden reported that the BBC did not respond.[30]

The previous year, in May 1963, Jimmy welcomed Conservative Prime Minister, Harold Macmillan, to the Variety Club of Great Britain lunch at London's Dorchester Hotel. As a good Conservative, he must have been proud to participate in the BBC's 90th birthday tribute to Winston Churchill, *Ninety Years On*, broadcast in November 1964. Introduced by Noel Coward and written by Terrence Rattigan (both gay), the program celebrated not only the prime minister's birthday but also the music and stars that he might have seen through the years. Jimmy appeared as George Laybourne, and others in the cast included Cicely Courtneidge (as male impersonator Vesta Tilley), Alma Cogan (as Florrie Forde), Margot Fonteyn (as Anna Pavlova), and Ted Ray (as Will Hay).

Reported conversations at lunches and dinners of friends often featured a typically Conservative comment from Jimmy. At the home of Biddy and Alan Fletcher, he was introduced to a fellow guest, of whom he asked his occupation.

"I'm a student," he said.

"How old are you, then?" said Jim.

"I'm thirty-two."

"What? You mean you're thirty-two and you've never done a day's work in your life." Jim refilled his glass and mumbled into it. "And I'm paying for it."[31]

Jimmy Edwards might have espoused middle-class and Conservative values, but he was always supportive of his fellow performers and of live theatre when it mattered most. In 1956, Jimmy headed a legation to the House of Commons, lobbying politicians to remove the tax on theatre seats. He was chairman of the Variety Artistes Foundation, and he actively promoted the merger with the union Actors' Equity. He was less supportive of Actors' Equity in 1976, when a visit by him and Eric Sykes to Rhodesia (now Zimbabwe) to present *Big Bad Mouse* and to entertain Rhodesian troops was heavily criticized. Actors' Equity had already denounced South Africa's apartheid policy, and white-run Rhodesia had been included in an advisory ruling that members not work in either country. Up to the Edwards/Sykes visit, members had been allowed to follow their conscience — apparently Jimmy's conscience was sufficiently right-wing to permit this implied support for the Rhodesian all-white government and its troops — but following the visit, Actors' Equity had under consideration and instruction that its members *not* work "live" in either country. Indeed, both Sykes and Edwards were censured at the annual general meeting of Actors' Equity in April 1976.[32]

Obviously, neither Jimmy nor Eric Sykes felt any embarrassment at their Rhodesian experience. Eric Sykes writes with pleasure of the country and meeting premier Ian Smith, who had defied the British government in refusing to share power with the Black majority. Eric Sykes actually describes himself as "a born-again Rhodesian.[33] From what Sykes writes, it is very obvious that neither he nor Edwards had any respect for British Prime Minister Harold Wilson. One repercussion from the Rhodesian episode was a student demonstration outside the Coventry Hippodrome where the two were playing in *Big Bad Mouse*. "It was a pretty cold night and I assumed that the heating had failed in their university and that this protest was as good a way as any to ward off hypothermia."[34]

While Jimmy did not personally experience the fight for African independence in either South Africa or Rhodesia, he did learn first-hand of the fight for independence from Britain that was taking place on the island of Cyprus when, in April 1956, two bombs were thrown at the jeep in which he and his concert party were traveling. (Prior to coming to Cyprus, the group had performed twelve shows for British troops in Kenya, with proceeds going to the Sailors', Soldiers' and Airmen's Families Association.)

The Passing Years

With the passing years, Jimmy Edwards changed little. The temperament remained much the same, and while the whiskers and the hair might have become grey and the moustache turned white, the face may have looked a little fatter perhaps, but the upper body did not grow outrageously in size. Perhaps the only appreciable difference was that the moustache and sideburns seem to have become one. There was no lack of enthusiasm for life, and Jimmy was always available, and calls for his services remained relatively strong. Yet, he seems not to have craved the limelight that his standing in the entertainment community might have offered, preferring to spend long periods of time on the farm, with evenings boozing at the local pub.

At the same time, he did need to work and he did need to watch his weight. He started to drink pink gins, made with gin and angostura bitters, claiming it was better for the waistline. In 1967 and 1968, he was forced to admit that he had spent more money than he had earned. A May 1968 vacation in Bermuda could only be available to him if he agreed to perform two weeks in cabaret there in return for air fare and accommodation. As he pointed out, he liked to sit in the sun in Bermuda, and so the engagement was no real chore. Jimmy loved to travel and he did not travel light, generally taking fifteen pieces of luggage, including all his musical instruments, polo boots and helmet. Clothes were of lesser concern, often consisting in warm climate of khaki Bermuda shorts and a long, matching jacket, what he described as his "Safari Suit":

"I don't choose clothes…I don't care about clothes. They're a bore, but you have to wear them, don't you. After all, can you imagine me in the nude? I'd look ghastly!"[35]

The 30,000 pounds a year he had been earning at the height of his fame might now be closer to 20,000 pounds, but that was still around a quarter-of-a-million pounds by today's standards. It might have been more than enough for most people in and out of show business, but Jimmy had expensive hobbies, including three polo ponies and two horses for fox hunting. He still had the farm, and, as early as 1970, he also had a 14th floor flat near Victoria Station in London, overlooking Buckingham Palace and Westminster, to which non-gay friends were not invited.

It is unclear as to whether Jimmy ever really learned or wished to slow down. When work was available, he was also available. He would do just about anything he was asked, decade after decade. Aside from summer seasons at pier theatres and the like and the Christmas pantomimes, he might be found opening a branch of the W.H. Smith bookshop on the High Street in Lewes in July 1952 or crowning the Carnival Queen at the Odeon Cinema, Southend (where he was starring in *Let's Make a Night of It* at The Cliff's Pavilion) in June 1965.

Workers at Atheralls Farm were all familiar with Philip Aylemore, and his relationship with Jimmy was no secret, yet they were never aware of his actually living there but rather as a frequent visitor. He is the only identified young male to have visited the farm. At the same time, Philip

Aylemore did not get involved with the village at all.[36] However, once Jimmy had consolidated his relationship with Philip Aylemore, the two men lived in Fletching, not at Atheralls but at Riven Oak, a property now known as Raven Oak, across an adjacent field, and on land, from the former. Here, at the three-bedroom home built in 1973, guests were invited for summer barbecues, with access to an outdoor Jacuzzi, and with

Jimmy Edwards, 1975.

Jimmy's offering brandy while explaining, "It's only pouring cognac — you have to put your hand over the label!"[37]

"I wasn't born into the landed gentry, you know," he told a reporter, "I fell into it, and to keep it up I need to continue to earn a good income."[38]

After *Big Bad Mouse*, Jimmy decided to change the approach to his career, wanting to concentrate more on being a character comedian than a stand-up comic, a boisterous buffoon. But the problem was a lack of opportunity and the need for a steady income, and so he decided to dust off the trombone and work the clubs. "What I need, of course, is a television series. But the truth is I'm a lazy person. I tend to sit in a world of my own — and have done for years — waiting for something to turn up. If I had more push I would be banging on doors asking 'What about it?'"[39]

One friend, Michael Pointon recalls Jimmy's professional activities in the 1980s:

"I have worked in documentaries for many years, mainly for BBC radio, and wrote *The Life of Jim* series for and with Jimmy Edwards in the early 80s, which went out on Radio 2....Jim would come to my Wimbledon flat and we'd sit and tape our conversations which I then fashioned into scripts, allowing for inserted recorded extracts. Since Jim was touring we decided to record some of the shows, produced by Ron McDonnell, at Pebble Mill in Birmingham near Birmingham Hippodrome where Jim and Roy [Hudd] were appearing [in *Oliver!*]. They finished on the Saturday and we recorded on the Sunday. I'd written one of the fifteen-minute shows so that Jim would speak of working with [Tony] Hancock in *London Laughs* and it brought out the contrast between their styles, Jim's fearless improvising versus Tony's sticking to his lines and being thrown by any digression from the script. On reading it before we recorded Jim said to me, 'There's not so much about me in that one is there?' (The other shows allowed more space for personal asides, etc.) Ron and I just said, 'Just see how it goes, Jim,' and it went down so well that afterwards Jim remarked on this. So I ventured to say, 'That's because it wasn't just about you this time!' He smiled…After the show Jim said he'd heard that one of his favorite contemporaries, Les Dawson, was appearing at a Birmingham night club. I rang the club and Jim, Ron and I went that evening. I'd already worked with Les when I'd written the first radio documentary on one of his heroes, W.C. Fields, a few years earlier so I fixed up a visit backstage afterwards and they got on very well."[40]

As Michael Pointon also recalls,

"I am also a jazz musician and had previously met Jimmy via David Mills, a pal of mine, a drummer who had led the Temperance Seven and for whom Jim was best man at, as he put it, 'one of his weddings.' By that time Dave lived in Bahrain and was also a broadcaster on local radio. He then ran a touring jazz band called the British All Stars, bringing over well-known musicians from the UK and Jimmy toured the Gulf with us as guest star twice, to the delight of the ex-pats. Although we had spoken briefly on the phone once before it was during these tours I got to know Jim well and when we returned to England he often invited me to his place in Sussex, where Philip was usually in residence. I felt that it was more a question in Jim's case of just having someone there. During this time Jimmy appeared in a BBC TV series called *Spotlight On…*where comedians reminisced about their careers and he invited our band to take part and was featured on the trombone. The show was recorded in a theatre in Eastbourne."[41]

"I compiled the BBC Radio tribute to Jim after he died and one of my most treasured memories from one of our Middle East tours is of him happily floating in a swimming pool embracing a jeroboam of champagne (he drained many of the 5-star hotels in which we appeared of their champagne resources!)."[42]

The End

In the final years of his life, Jimmy spent more and more time in Australia, in company with Phillip Aylmore, and eventually acquired a home in Perth, Western Australia, a city with sandy beaches, hot, dry summers and mild winters, located on the Indian Ocean in one of the most gay-friendly countries in the world. His Tibetan/Jack Rabbit dog, Rubu, meaning "moustache" in Swahili, was taken care of by June Whitfield and her husband, Tim, whenever Jimmy went away, and he was eventually persuaded that they should keep him. So there was one less tie holding him to England.

Life in Fletching had changed drastically for Jimmy since his divorce from Val. He leased Atheralls Farm from National Westminster (NatWest) Bank, after selling it to the bank following his divorce. In 1984, Jimmy and brother Alan decided to retire from farming and advised NatWest Bank that they would not be renewing the lease. That same year, the property, now consisting of Atheralls Farm, East Park Farm, Fliteridge Farm (with 100 acres) and Holmesdale Farm (with 100 acres), was sold to Atheralls Farms Ltd., a subsidiary of Hollings Holdings Ltd., owned by David Hollings, his father and his younger brother. Alan retired to Dorset with his second wife, Helen. "The village fell apart when Alan left," states one long-time resident, Barry Dickens.[43]

In all probability, Alan himself was far from happy at the move. When he and Jimmy gave up the tenancy of Atheralls Farm, he wrote to the farm staff:

"Most of you will at least have a roof over your heads in Fletching, which is more than I will be able to say."

It was while in Perth, on February 7, 1986, that Jimmy prepared his last will, appointing Michael Charles Downs of London as his solicitor, brother Alan as his executor, and leaving the bulk of his estate to Philip Maxwell Aylemore, with the exception of 1,000 pounds to Fletching neighbor Tanya Appleby.[44] The value of Jimmy's estate was not overly sizeable, amounting to 241,586 pounds, the equivalent today of 766,000 pounds.

In June 1986, he found time while in Perth to hunt with the Western Australian Hunt Club. He had become a part of Western Australian society, and it is obvious that his connections with Perth extended back into the previous decade; on November 5, 1974, he had been invited to draw the numbers of the Western Australia Lottery.

One of Jimmy's last stage appearances, if not his last, took place in Perth, when in October and November 1986 he played an eccentric aristocrat fighting the building of a bypass through his property in William Douglas Home's black comedy, *Lloyd George Knew My Father*. Directed by Edgar Metcalfe, the play was presented at the Regal Theatre, Perth, and then at the Queen's Park Theatre, Geraldton, north of Perth, in December 1986.

Jimmy's last arrived in Australia on December 18, 1987. His final departure from the continent of which he had grown so fond is not recorded by what appears to be a somewhat lax Australian immigration service.[45]

Jimmy Edwards certainly seemed to feel more liberated in Australia. It was as if he no longer needed to live a life restricted by the customs and conventions of the upper middle class society to which he had clung for most of his life. He had avoided, at least in public, the use of four-letter words, but here in Australia he would embrace the language of the gutter. As *The Guardian* reported, "the ratio of funny to filthy got rather out of hand."[46] This is no more apparent than in a two-act, unproduced and unpublished play which he wrote titled *Come-Back, Come-Back*, set in Sydney, Australia, and concerning a theatrical agent and his girlfriend whom he books on *The David Frost Show* as the worst entertainer in the country. Typical of the text is a joke concerning a fellow who falls asleep while sunbathing in the nude and gets a "sunburned cock." In the middle of the night, it begins to itch; he goes to the refrigerator, finds a glass of milk, and "sticks his pecker" in the glass. At this point his wife appears and says, "I wondered how you re-loaded that thing, darling."

Here is a new, and not altogether attractive Jimmy Edwards. However, it must be acknowledged that the "pecker" joke was not new, but used by Jimmy when he toured the Middle East performing for ex-pats. During his act, he would turn to the members of the band and ask if the audience was ready for the "pecker" joke. There is certainly a suggestion of childish glee at the use of a "naughty" word, as for example with Jimmy's reference to the Archbishop of Canterbury, Robert Runcie, as "Cuntsy Runcie."[47]

Returning from a trip to Australia in the spring of 1988, Jimmy became ill, not surprisingly in view of his alcohol intake, with liver problems. "He had some liver problems and had a weak chest for years," brother Alan told *The Guardian* (July 9, 1988). Jimmy was admitted to the private Cromwell Hospital, which had opened in South Kensington in 1981. Jazz musician and documentary producer Michael Pointon, a longtime friend, visited him there: "he looked up from his bed, smiling ruefully, and said 'Self-inflicted.'"

Sister Libby was a frequent visitor to his bedside, and also took care of providing him with clean sleeping attire. She fumed whenever Philip Aylemore came to visit, sarcastically commenting that his performance at Jimmy's bedside was worthy of an Academy Award. She was aware of Jimmy's will, and complained bitterly to Alan that it was so unfair in view of all he had done for his brother.

On July 8, 1988, Jimmy died of bronchial pneumonia.[48] The death was widely covered in the British press, most of which managed to ignore his homosexuality.

The Independent (July 11, 1988) wrote,

"The mere remembrance of Jimmy Edwards in full cry brings a smile. He seemed to be a naturally funny man, and who could no more help responding to an audience — even if it was a couple of waiters and a newspaper man — than he could breathing."

To *The Times* (July 9, 1988), he "was not merely a peculiarly British comedian but an authentic English character in a line stretching back to Surtees' Jorrocks and Tristram Shandy's Uncle Toby. He was also part of a unique generation of comics."

His relative lack of fame in the United States is evidenced by the obituary in *Variety* (July 13, 1988), which is five short paragraphs in length, filling less than half a column.

There were what might be described as the usual tributes. As quoted in *The Sun* (July 9, 1988), Frank Muir said, "He was a tremendously warm person, very honest and very funny....Jimmy was a gentleman and a player."

In the *Sunday Express* (July 10, 1988), there was a tribute from comedic character actor Derek Nimmo, who had appeared with Jimmy in *More Faces of Jim* and *The World of Wodehouse: Blandings Castle*, and who was one of the original panelists on the BBC Radio 4 program *Just a Minute* (first broadcast 1967), on which Jimmy was originally intended to be the chairman, but was replaced after the first episode by Nicholas Parsons:[49] "Jimmy was nothing like the man the public saw on television or in the theatre. He was intensely shy and scholarly but great company." Michael Bentine, another Windmill graduate, said, "He was a special kind of Englishman... he was larger than life, a real shooting, fishing and quaffing-of-ale man. At the same time he was very intelligent and scholarly." Jimmy's agent for the past fifteen years, Peter Charlesworth was quoted, "He was a much better actor than he was given credit for. He was a lovely human being and a great professional."

The funeral took place at the Church of St. Andrew and St. Mary the Virgin[50] in Fletching on July 15, 1988. Denis Norden, Harry Secombe, Cardew Robinson, Eric Sykes, Barry Cryer, Joan Turner, and Frank Muir were there, with the last paying tribute, "I only hope there is a bottle of whiskey nearby, a horse and some people to listen to him." The service began with the hymn, "The King of Love My Shepherd Is," followed by a reading from Romans, Chapter Eight — "If God Be For Us, Who Can Be Against Us?" — followed by the hymns, "Rock of Ages, Cleft for Me" and "The Day Thou Gavest, Lord Is Ended." An R.A.F. trumpeter played "The Last Post" over the gravesite. Not present was Philip Aylemore, whom the family did not invite. "I think the family did close ranks and ask Philip not to attend. Perhaps he felt it best to stay away in case the media picked up on him."[51]

Joan Turner gave the impression that she was the grieving widow, wearing a black veil. At the pub after the funeral, she clutched a bottle of champagne and one glass; "she wasn't sharing it with anybody," recalls Barry Cryer.[52]

Jimmy's gravestone is a simple one, with the wording, "In Memory of James Keith O'Neill Edwards/D.F.C. M.A. M.E.B/"Professor Jimmy"/1920-1988/of Atheralls Farm/per risum ad honorem [Through Laughter to Honor]. Brother Alan had some other ideas as to appropriate comments, including "Gone to Earth...Tally-Ho" and "per risibilitarium ad astrum" [By Laughter to a Star].

After Jimmy's death, there was no major memorial announced. The closest prominent city to the comedian's home is Brighton, ironically also renowned as a gay resort on Britain's South coast, and it is Brighton which paid tribute to him in most unusual fashion. In March 2009, a double-decker bus in the Brighton & Hove fleet was named "Jimmy Edwards." Initially, the bus[53] serviced the No. 12 route from Brighton Station, through Rottingdean, Saltdean, Peacehaven, Newhaven, Seaford, to Eastbourne. In August 2012, the "Jimmy Edwards," now repainted but

the same vehicle, serviced the No. 49 route from Portslade, through Hove and Brighton, to East Moulescomb.

"I don't think Uncle Jimmy would be particularly happy to have a bus named after him," noted nephew Roy Pennington.[54]

Some years later, at BBC Television Centre, twenty-four memorial plaques were erected by the BBC and the Heritage Foundation, each with clapping hands and the name of the honoree. One of those plaques, quite rightly honored Jimmy Edwards.

In 1996, the British Comedy Society (which began life with the delightful title of the Dead Comics Society) commissioned Keith Turley to paint a portrait of Jimmy in full polo-playing attire. The painting was auctioned for charity at the Richmond-based Ham Polo Club (also known as the London Polo Club), of which Jimmy had been a member. The British Comedy Society is dedicated to preserving and fostering the tradition of British comedy, primarily through the placement of appropriate blue plaques at the former homes of the comedians. Sadly, there has been no blue plaque for Jimmy either at his birthplace in Barnes or Atheralls Farm.

The comedy of Jimmy Edwards was always unpretentious and undemanding of its audience. Perhaps appropriately, *Take It from Here* would conclude with the song, "Just One of Those Things." With it last words seeming most appropriate as a farewell to a great comedian:

"So goodbye, dear, and Amen

"Here's hoping we'll meet now and then

"It was great fun

"But it was just one of those things."

One might also conclude with words from Jimmy's 1974 recording of "Was It Something I Said," He sang of "An empty glass. An empty space. I really miss your smiling face." A perfect epitaph for an individual who loved his alcohol, loved a good joke, always did the best that he could, sometimes at great personal danger to himself, and should be missed far more than in reality he is.

---

1. Jimmy Edwards, *Take It from Me*, p. 199.

2. *The Complete Book of Salads, including Favorite Recipes of American and British Personalities and Stars*, published in the U.S. by Prentice-Hall. American contributors included Humphrey Bogart, Bing Crosby, Jimmy Durante, Betty Grable, and Tyrone Power.

3. Gwen Robyns, "The Genial Squire of Court House Close."

4. Ibid.

5. "Good Luck…and Thanks a Lot," p. 12.

6. I had the good fortune to attend the Bonfire Society celebration on Saturday, October 29, 2017, and it was quite an impressive event, culminating in a massive bonfire and a fireworks display that would put to shame those on offer in most big cities. The evening begins with a torchlight procession through the village, with more than 100 participants in a parade that resembles both a Nazi rally and the villagers marching on Frankenstein's castle. It also seems a good excuse for what is described in England as a "booze-up."

7. "Jimmy Edwards — Farmer," p. 647.

8. Ibid, p. 649.

9. His sister, Olave, married Robert Baden-Powell, founder of the worldwide Boy Scouts and Girl Guides movement. The Soames family, and its predecessor, the Earl of Sheffield, would gift "the living" at Fletching to an appropriate clergyman, thereby controlling who was the local vicar.

10. The first horse he had acquired, in 1951, was named Matchless.

11. Ronni Davis, producer, and Nigel Farrell, presenter, *Wake Up at the Back: The Life of Jimmy Edwards*.

12. For the record, they were foreman Ken Robson, Jim Bradford (whose twin brother Henry was one of the herdsmen), Harry Watson, Peter Stevens, Bob Kemp, and Jonathan Mepham.

13. Roy Pennington to Anthony Slide, e-mail dated April 19, 2017.

14. On December 27, 1955, the BBC television program, *At Home*, presented by Berkeley Smith, featured Jimmy at Atheralls Farm.

15. The Rose and Crown pub, on the High Street, dates back to 1150.

16. Godfrey Winn, "Life Is So Full, and Yet…," p. 7.

17. Joe and Vera Dobson were succeeded as landlords of the Griffin Inn by the Pughe-Morgans, whose son is Piers Morgan. The latter is one of the most notorious British journalists/broadcasters to have gained some fame in the United States. He is usually referred to by the British satirical magazine, *Private Eye*, as "Piers Moron." After being told to "fuck off" by Australian comedian, Jim Jefferies, on *Real Time with Bill Maher*, novelist J.K. Rowling tweeted, "Yes, watching Piers Morgan being told to fuck off on live TV is exactly as satisfying as I'd always imagined."

18. The last verse of Kipling's 1902 poem, "Sussex."

19. R.B. Marriott, "Quintessence of British Variety," p. 9.

20. "'Take It from Here,' Said Jimmy Edwards, p. 1.

21. "Comedian's Tilts at Hunting Terms," p. 7.

22. Founded in 1915, it is now the Old Surrey, Burstow & West Kent Hunt.

23. Godfrey Winn, "Life I So Full, and Yet…," p. 6.

24. Founded in 1902, the Quantock Stag Hounds are still active; they have been accused of illegal hunting on a number of occasions.

25. "Jimmy Edwards Blooded," p. 1.

26. Cyril Fletcher, *Nice One Cyril*, p. 66. Both "Fletcher" and "Fletching," Jimmy's village, have the same name derivation, that of the feathers on an arrow.

27. Jimmy Edwards, *Take It from Me*, p. 191.

28. A Fox Movietone cameraman was outside the Hall, and the news company's commentator reported that the comedian would be delivering "some striking remarks on the subject of entertainment."

29. "The Tangible Terror of Television," p. 1.

30. Denis Norden, *Clips from a Life*, p. 115.

31. June Whitfield, *...And June Whitfield*, p. 143.

32. For what appears to have been nothing more than a technicality, Edwards resigned from Equity in February 1962 after the Variety Artistes' Federation, of which he was chairman, reached an agreement with the independent television companies in a dispute over fees, to which Equity was not a partner. He rejoined Equity in June 1962.

33. Eric Sykes, *If I Don't Write It, Nobody Else Will*, p. 411.

34. Ibid, p. 414.

35. Undated press release re appearance on *The Des O'Connor Show* in Australia.

36. Anthony Slide interview with Barry Dickens, April 21, 2017.

37. Michael Pointon to Anthony Slide, e-mail dated January 29, 2017.

38. Peter Dacre, "It's Back to the Old Tuba Again for Jimmy Edwards."

39. Ibid.

40. Michael Pointon to Anthony Slide, e-mail dated March 29, 2017. Les Dawson was an over-weight, deadpan comedian who would sometimes appear in grotesque female attire; like Jimmy Edwards he was a heavy drinker.

41. Michael Pointon to Anthony Slide, e-mail dated January 25, 2017.

42. Michael Pointon to Anthony Slide, e-mail dated January 27, 2017.

43. Anthony Slide interview with Barry Dickens, April 21, 2017.

44. Tanya Una Appleby died on October 21, 2013, at the age of ninety-two. She and her husband, Jack, had been good friends of both Jimmy and Alan. They lived close to Fletching.

45. Australian immigration records, dating from 1981-1988, are somewhat incomplete at least as far as Jimmy is concerned. There is no evidence that he visited the continent at all in 1982 and 1983. He visited Australia on three separate occasions in 1981; he arrived in February and departed in May 1984; he arrived in November 1985 and possibly stayed until as late as June 1986. On each visit, depending on his mood apparently, he would identify himself as either a married or a divorced man.

46. "Joker in the Pack."

47. Michael Pointon to Anthony Slide, October 7, 2017.

48. At least one gay website states that he died of an AIDS-related illness, but there is absolutely no evidence to support this claim. Indeed, the confusion may have arisen in that there is a strong suggestion that Jimmy Edwards did not respond to the treatment for pneumonia because he had an autoimmune disease (AID), and AID is not AIDS (acquired immune deficiency syndrome).

49. The program was recorded on a Sunday, and Jimmy did not want to work Sundays.

50. Built in 1230, the church is unusual in that it has a dual dedication.

51. Anne Gravett to Anthony Slide, e-mail dated April 11, 2017.

52. Anthony Slide interview with Barry Cryer, February 6, 2017.

53. Built by the Scania Omnidekka company in East Lancashire, England, the bus is no longer manufactured.

54. Anthony Slide interview with Roy Pennington, April 10, 2017.

Epilogue

Philip Aylemore now lives in Australia, but "wants no part of this" book. He did take time after Jimmy's death to distribute mementoes to friends and acquaintances according to the comedian's wishes, and apparently lived for a couple of years in the town of Lewes in East Sussex. In 2010, he attended an Edwards family reunion, accompanied by his wife. One family member present described him as a typical "beer-swilling Aussie, round, jolly and very brash."

Alan Raven Edwards died in West Dorset on January 20, 1998 at the age of eighty-three. His second wife, Helen, is still alive, as is his daughter Anne Gravett, by first wife Betty, and living in East Sussex.

Atheralls Farm, consisting of a total of 350 acres, continues as a going concern under the proprietorship of David Hollings. It still has the fifteen stables in which Jimmy housed his polo ponies, and in 2016, Hollings staged a polo match partly in his memory. Contrary to what non-farmers, such as myself, might suppose, the polo ponies were kept in the stables during the summer months in order that they would look good on event days, but were turned out in the fields each winter. Jimmy's housekeeper, Gwen Soame, and his secretary stayed on at the farm beyond his death, and today there is still one employee, Jim Bradford, who has worked at Atheralls Farm since the age of fifteen in 1945.

Jimmy's grave is not particularly well cared for (and not that easy to locate). The village of Fletching has changed somewhat since he and Alan lived there, becoming more a home for the wealthy working in London and needing a residence within commuting distance of the capital. There are few villagers who remember Jimmy, but I did come across one gentleman there who recalled, as a boy, moving with his family to a house bordering on Atheralls Farm. One day, while trespassing on farm property, he was accosted by Jimmy. The boy asked, "Are you an Edwards?" Jimmy's response was furious, and laced with four-letter words, unhappy that he had not immediately been recognized. If he visited Fletching today, he would be even angrier at how he is forgotten — except by the current resident of Atheralls Farm.

The Library of Spanking Fiction (yes, there is such a site) describes Jimmy Edwards thusly: "In Great Britain at least, this charming man has become something of a gay and spanko icon. To the rest of the world, he is a more obscure figure."

The author at Jimmy Edwards' grave, 2017.

Bibliography

Alison Barnes, "The Handlebar Club," *Tit Bits*, May 8, 1954. *http://www.handlebarclub.co.uk/1954report2.htm* (accessed August 2016).

"And We Applaud," *The Sketch*, March 1, 1950, p. 205.

Annakin, Ken. *So You Wanna Be a Director?* Sheffield: Tomahawk Press, 2001.

Apps, Edwin. *Pursued by Bishops*. Bourneau, France: Durand-Peyroles, 2013.

"At Blackpool," *The Stage*, September 21, 1950, p. 3.

"B.B.C. Audiences Told When to Applaud," *The Sunday Post*, June 12, 1949, p. 1.

Banks-Smith, Nancy, "Present Imperfect," *The Guardian*, October 23, 1992, p. 29.

"Birthday Present Fit for Sir Winston," *The Stage and Television Today*, November 26, 1964, p. 11.

Black, Peter, "Jimmy Edwards," *The Guardian*, July 11, 1988, clipping in the possession of Roy Pennington.

Boothroyd, Basil, "Brush with Fame," *Punch*, July 4, 1984, p. 38.

Brandreth, Gyles. *Brief Encounters: Meetings with Remarkable People*. London: Politico's Publishing, 2001.

Brown, Dave, "*Take It from Here*," April 5, 2002, *http://web.onetel.com/~gnudawn/otr/tifh-1stlines.html* (accessed October 2016).

Busby, Roy. *British Music Hall: An Illustrated Who's Who from 1850 to the Present Day*. London: Paul Elek, 1976.

Cayenne [sic], "'Professor' Jimmy Edwards and 'Whack-O!,'" *The Library of Spanking Fiction: Wellred Weekly*, June 3, 2012, *http://www.wellredweekly.com/index.php?article=342* (accessed August 2016).

Chambers, Peter, "Show That Hopes to Beat ITMA Record," *Aberdeen Evening Express*, March 2, 1953, p. 3.

"Charles Maxwell," *The Stage*, August 20, 1998, p. 35.

"Comedian's Tilts at Hunting Terms," *Sussex Express & County Herald*, May 11, 1951, p. 7.

Cowan. Margaret, "Britain As a Market, Is Important to the U.S.," *The Stage and Television Today*, November 12, 1959, p. 7.

Cryer, Barry. *The Chronicles of Hernia*. London: Virgin Books, 2009. [First published 1998 as *You Won't Believe This But…*]

Dacre, Peter, "It's Back to the Old Tuba Again for Jimmy Edwards," *Sunday Express*, April 21, 1968, unpaged clipping in British Film Institute Library.

Davis, Ronni, producer, and Nigel Farrell, presenter. *Wake Up at the Back: The Life of Jimmy Edwards*. BBC Radio 4, June 3, 1993.

Dynan, Michael, "Variety's the Word," *The Stage*, July 9, 1998, p. 11.

Edwards, Jimmy. *Take It from Me*. London: Werner Laurie, 1953.

_____. *Six of the Best*. London: Robson Books, 1984.

"Equity Ban on Rhodesia?," *The Stage and Television Today*, April 15, 1976, p. 6.

Fisher, John. *Funny Way to Be a Hero*. London: Random House, 2013.

"The Five Faces of Jimmy Edwards," *The Stage and Television Today*, November 10, 1960, p. 9.

Fletcher, Cyril. *Nice One Cyril: Being the Odd Odessey and the Anecdotage of a Comedian*. London: Barrie & Jenkins, 1978.

Ford, Richard and Amanda Brown, "My 13 Years of Friendship with Jimmy Edwards," *Evening News*, December 28, 1979, unpaged clipping in British Film Institute Library.

"400 at Sheffield Park Estate Sale," *Sussex Express & County Herald*, December 11, 1953, p. 3.

Fraser, Liz. *Liz Frazer…And Other Characters: An Autobiography*. London: Signum Books, 2012.

Gifford, Denis. *The Golden Age of Radio: An Illustrated Companion*. London: B.T. Batsford, 1985.

Goddard, Liza. *Working with Children and Animals*. Clacton on Sea, U.K.: Apex Publishing, 2011.

"Good Luck…and Thanks a Lot," *The Mount Hope Meteor*, March 1944, pp. 11-12.

Green, James, "Early Comedy That's Light Years Ahead," *The Stage and Television Today*, October 30, 1986, p. 19.

Greenfield, George. *A Smattering of Monsters: A Kind of Memoir*. London: Little, Brown, 1995.

Halliday, Hugh A., "Arnhem and 'Jimmy' Edwards," October 15, 2002, *Royal Air Force Commands*, *http://www.rafcommands.com/archive* (accessed November 2016).

"Handlebar Club," *The Stage*, May 29, 1947, p. 3.

Harding, James. *Agate*. London: Methuen, 1986,

Hartley, James, "Blackpool's Bright Brigade," *The Stage*, July 29, 1954, p. 5.

Hewison, Robert. *Footlights!: A Hundred Years of Cambridge Comedy*. London: Methuen, 1981.

Hickey, William, "My Life with Jimmy Edwards — by Drag Man Raymon," *Daily Express*, February 28, 1979, unpaged clipping in British Film Institute Library.

Howe, B.W. *Fletching: A Brief History of the Parish and a Description of the Parish Church of St. Andrew & St. Mary the Virgin*. Privately Published, 1998.

James, David and Wilson Stephens, eds. *In Praise of Hunting: A Symposium*. London: Hollis & Carter, 1960.

"Jim Edwards to Captain Handlebar Club Eleven," *Sussex Agricultural Express*, September 4, 1953.

"Jimmy Edwards Blooded: Tradition or 'Disgusting Rite'?," *The Manchester Guardian*, September 15, 1958, p. 1.

"Jimmy Edwards Goes Aloft," [Aberdeen] *Evening Express*, April 22, 1954, p. 16.

"Joker in the Pack," *The Guardian*, July 11, 1988, clipping in the possession of Roy Pennington.

Kenworthy, Chris, "Jim Is So Glum About His Whiskers," *The Sun*, October 14, 1978, unpaged clipping in British Film Institute Library.

Lewisohn, Mark. *Radio Times Guide to TV Comedy*. London: BBC Worldwide, 1998.

Lutz, Deborah. *Pleasure Bound: Victorian Sex Rebels and the New Eroticism*. New York: W.W. Norton, 2011.

MacMillan, Archie, "Jimmy Edwards," *Equity Journal*, Christmas 1988, clipping in the possession of Roy Pennington.

Madden, Cecil. *Starlight Days*. London: Trevor Square Publications, 2007.

Marriott, R.B., "Quintessence of British Variety," *The Stage*, November 1, 1959, p. 9.

_____, "Star Spangled Parade," *The Stage*, November 6, 1952, p. 6.

McKay, Mark, "Radio: Take It from Here," *Laugh Magazine*, No. 5, 1992, *http://laughterlog.com/2009/02/.07/radio-take-it-from-here/* (accessed December 2016).

McKay, Mark, "TV: Whack-O!," *Laugh Magazine*, No. 15, 1996, *http://laughterlog.com/2009/01/04/whack-o/* (accessed August 2016).

Midwinter, Eric. *Make 'Em Laugh*. London: George Allen & Unwin, 1979.

_____, "*Take It from Here*," source unknown, pp. 7-8.

"More Faces of Jim," *Television Today*, November 1, 1962, p. 1.

Muir, Frank. *A Kentish Lad*. London: Bantam Press, 1997.

_____, "A Little Foil to Big Jimmy," *The Guardian*, July 8, 1995, p. 32.

Muir, Frank and Denis Norden. *The Glums*. London: Robson Books, 1979.

Muir, Frank and Simon Brett. *Frank Muir Presents the Best of Comedy Sketches*. London: Elm Tree Books, 1982.

"Names on the Buses, 648 Jimmy Edwards," *http://history.buses.co.uk/history/fleethist/648je.htm* (accessed August 2016).

Norden, Denis. *Clips from a Life*. London: Fourth Estate, 2008.

"Notes of the Day," *Western Daily Press*, July 10, 1947.

Parkinson, Michael, "Moments of Magic with Two Real Stars," *Daily Mirror*, July 11, 1988, unpaged clipping in British Film Institute Library.

Pearce, Lucy, "Comedians with Links to Our County," *The* [Brighton] *Argus*, May 13, 2016, *www.theargus.co.uk* (accessed March 2017).

Pedrick, Gale. "Our 'Fruitiest' Comedian," *Dublin Radio Review*, October 23, 1959, clipping in the possession of Jim Pennington.

"Play It Again Jim!," *News of the World*, March 4, 1979, p.1.

Ramsden, Greig, "On or Off a Horse, Jimmy Edwards Is No Fool," *Evening Standard*, November 28, 1959, p. 10.

Reid, Beryl. *So Much Love*. London: Hutchinson, 1984.

Richards, Dick, "A Whack-O Bang-On Type," *TV Mirror*, December 1, 1956, p. 13.

Robyns, Gwen, "The Genial Squire of Court House Close," syndicated feature article, June 16, 1950.

"Show That Hopes to Beat ITMA Record," [Aberdeen] *Evening Express*, March 2, 1955, p. 3.

Simkins, Michael, "An Actor's Life," *The Guardian*, April 24, 2002, p. A15.

Simons, Judith, "Whacko! Jimmy and Joan Name the Day," *Daily Express*, October 3, 1973, unpaged clipping in British Film Institute Library.

Smith, Gus. *Eamonn Andrews: His Life*. London: W.H. Allen/Virgin Books, 1988.

Stanley, Raymond, "London Flop Becomes Australian Success," *The Stage*, April 11, 1974, p. 24.

Sykes, Eric. *Eric Sykes' Comedy Heroes*. London: Virgin Books, 2003.

_____. *If I Don't Write It, Nobody Else Will*. London: Fourth Estate, 2005.

Take It from Here, *http://www.britishcomedy.org.uk/comedy/tifh.htm* (accessed October 2016).

"'Take It from Here, Said Jimmy Edwards," *The Grantham Journal*, February 19, 1954, p. 1.

"The Tangible Terror of TV," *Northern Daily Mail*, January 25, 1952, p. 1.

Tatchell, Peter, "Radio: Does the Team Think?," Laughterlog.com, February 23, 2009.

Taylor, Guy, "Not Good — But You Musn't Blame BBC for Trying," *The Stage and Television Today*, May 19, 1960, p. 16.

Taylor, Rod. *The Guinness Book of Sitcoms*. Enfield, United Kingdom: Guinness Publishing, 1994.

"Tessie and Jim," *The Stage and Television Today*, April 21, 1977, p. 3.

Tickner, Monica, "Jimmy Edwards — Farmer," *Sport & Country*, June 22, 1955, pp. 647-649.

Tomlinson, David. *Luckier Than Most*. London: Hodder & Stoughton, 1990.

Took, Barry. *Laughter in the Air: An Informal History of British Radio Comedy*. London: Robson Books/BBC, 1981.

_____, "Obituary: Frank Muir," *The Independent*, January 3, 1998, *www.independent.co.uk*.

Towler, James, "The Forgotten World of Musical Comedy," *The Stage and Television Today*, March 23, 1978, p. 20.

Van Damm, Sheila. *We Never Closed*. London: Robert Hale, 1967

Van Damm, Vivian. *Tonight and Every Night*. London: Stanley Paul, 1952.

"The Variety Stage," *The Stage*, February 9, 1950, pp. 3-4.

Vauncez, Sidney, "Jimmy — the Big Tash Hit," *The Stage*, August 17, 1995, p. 9.

Warden, Ian, "An Antidote to the Saccharine," *The Canberra Times*, August 1, 1981, p. 17.

Watson, Howard, "Bold as Brass: Raising the Wind with Jimmy Edwards," *http://www.4barsrest. com/articles.2003/art327.asp* (accessed August 2016).

Wearing, J.P. *The London Stage*. Metuchen, N.J.: Scarecrow Press, 1993.

"What Jimmy Edwards Told Me on the Second Day of Our Honeymoon," *News of the World*, March 4, 1979, pp.1-2.

Whelan, Andy, "Jimmy Edwards' Club Celebrates Moustache Milestone," *The* [Brighton] *Argus*, April 1, 2007, *www.theargus.co.uk/* (accessed March 2017).

Whitfield, June, *...And June Whitfield*. London: Bantam Press, 2000.

Whittaker, Herbert, "Toronto Repeats a Pleasure for Big Bad Mouse Comedian," [Toronto] *Globe and Mail*, January 30, 1974, p. 11.

"Whack-O!," *http://www.bbc.co.uk.comedy/whacko/*

Wilmut, Tony. *Tony Hancock — "Artiste"*. London: Methuen, 1978.

Winn, Godfrey, "Life Is So Full, and Yet...I Feel Very Lonely at Times," *TV Mirror*, February 8, 1958, pp. 6-8.

_____ , "Supper with Mr. and Mrs. Jimmy Edwards," *Woman's Weekly*, May 30, 1964, pp. 18-21, 52.

Wragg, Stephen. *Because I Tell a Joke or Two: Comedy, Politics and Social Differences*. London: Routledge, 1998.

Index

Aberdeen University, 172-175
Accordion Club, 53, 55
"The Acrobat," 16
Adelphi Theatre, 78
Adler, Larry, 106
Agate, James, 48
Alcoholism, 20, 157-160, 178
Allenbury's Milk Food Products, 25
An Alligator Named Daisy, 134-135
And So to Bentley, 64
Andrews, Eamonn, 88
Angel, Daniel M., 130, 131
Annakin, Ken, 136
Anoop and the Elephant, 139
Apps, Edwin, 19, 88, 93, 96, 97
Archer, Barbara, 88
Askey, Arthur, 106, 155
Atheralls Farm, 150, 165-168, 178-179, 181, 191
Atkinson, Rowan, 87
Attenborough, David, 103-104
The August Game, 104
Australia, 16, 64, 123, 127, 145, 181-182
Autumn Spectacular, 103
Aylemore, Philip, 147, 156-157, 178-179, 181, 182, 183, 184, 191

BBC, 52, 53, 58, 64, 67, 69, 76, 77, 87, 90, 92, 93, 96, 98, 100, 101, 104, 107, 147, 180, 181
Babbage, Wilfred, 68
Babes in Wood, 111
Barclay, Humphrey, 104
Baddeley, Angela, 103
Barker, Ronnie, 57, 76, 101, 103
Barnes, 25, 26, 49, 141, 163

Barry, Len, 49
Barrymore, Michael, 12
Bassey, Shirley, 79
The Bed Sitting Room, 141
Belvoir Hunt, 171
Bennett, Harold, 88, 98
Bentley, Dick, 15, 64, 67, 68, 70, 71, 73, 76, 78, 79, 96, 174-175
Beves, Donald, 33
Big Bad Mouse, 23, 120-125, 180
Black, George and Alfred, 116, 129
Blackpool, 37-39, 51, 53, 78, 115, 152, 153
Blair, Lionel, 119, 141
Blake, Patricia, 77
Bold as Brass, 102-103
Boothby, Robert, 174
Bottoms Up!, 13, 18, 19, 22, 98-100, 132
Bradford, Jim, 191
Brambell, Wilfred, 139, 156
Brandreth, Gyles, 158
Brass Bands, 29, 45, 102-103
Brendon Chase, 106
Briers, Richard, 101
British Field Sports Society, 172
Bury the Hatchet, 104
Butler, Ivan, 125
Bygraves, Max, 89

Cambridge, 29-34, 163
Cambridge Union, 31
Cambridge University Non-Party Association, 31
Canada, 39, 42, 43, 44, 53
Carew-Gibbs, Michelle, 148
The Carroll Levis Show, 53

Carstairs, John Paddy, 132

Cary, Falkland, 120, 121

Castaldini, Paul, 100

Castle, Roy, 122, 140

Catchphrases, 14-15, 70

Chaffey, Don, 137

Chaplin, Charlie, 11, 73, 143

Chester, Charlie, 104, 120

Children's Film Foundation, 139

Christmas Night with the Stars, 72, 86-87

Cinderella, 76, 111-112

Climie, David, 96, 106

Cogan, Alma, 74, 83, 176

Colonna, Jerry, 60

Combs, Pat, 105

Come-Back, Come-Back, 182

Connor, Kenneth, 119, 137-138, 143

Conservative Politics, 15, 127, 175-177

Cooper, Tommy, 11, 25, 57, 140, 141

Cope, Kenneth, 88

Coronation Stone, 69-70

Costa, Sam, 55, 129, 130

Court House Close, 164

Courtneidge, Cicely, 104

Cowan, Phyllis Keith, 25, 158

Coxall, John, 96

The Cream — As Seen by a Clot, 15

Crier, Gordon, 63

Crockett, B. Barrington, 129

Crowther, Leslie, 155

Croydon Empire, 51, 53

Cryer, Barry, 19, 49, 104, 129, 153, 156, 184

Cyprus, 177

Dad's Army, 21

Dawson, Les, 104, 180

De Grunwald, Anatole, 134

de la Mare, Walter, 27

Deayton, Angus, 87

Delfont, Bernard, 18

Dent, Alan, 48, 100

Desert Island Discs, 28-29

Desmonde, Jerry, 28, 48, 89, 168

Dickens, Barry, 181

Distinguished Flying Cross, 42

Dixon, Reginald, 53

Doctor in the House, 119

Dodd, Ken, 11, 12, 14, 25, 89, 122

Does the Team Think?, 21, 106, 107

"Don't Dilly Dally on the Way," 105

Dotrice, Roy, 96

Douglas, Raymon, 154

Down Ampney, 40, 43

Driver, Betty, 53

Duke of Edinburgh, 113

Dulley, Miranda, 44

Dunn, Clive, 105, 106

Eaton, Wallas, 68, 78, 103

Edwards, Alan, 25, 28, 29, 43, 146, 159, 164, 165, 169, 181, 182, 191

Edwards, Hugh, 28

Edwards, Jimmy, autobiography, 15-16; birth, 25; bus named after, 185-186; education, 26-29; as farmer, 164-168, 181; film career, 129-144; funeral, 184; marriage, 149-150; "outing," 154-157; politics, 15; radio career, 63-81; recording career, 76; stage career, 111-128; stands for parliament, 175-176; television career, 83-109; vulgarity, 16, 19-20, 21; war years, 37-46

Edwards, Dr. R.W.K., 25

Falstaff, Sir John, 18

"Fatal Beatings," 87

Feldman, Marty, 76

Field, Sid, 28, 48-49

Fielding, Fenella, 122

Fittleworth, 150-151

Flanagan, Bud, 11, 15

Fletcher, Cyril, 107, 172

Fletching, 150, 157, 158, 165-169

Foolish Things, 47

Footlights Dramatic Club, 31-32

Forbes, Meriel, 104

Forlong, Michael, 139

Formby, George, 12

Forsyth, Bruce, 11, 45, 51, 53

The Fossett Saga, 105

Fox Hunting, 103, 170-172, 182

Fraser, Elizabeth, 88

Freeman, Dave, 105

Frinton, Freddie, 129, 130

The Galton and Simpson Comedy, 105

Garside, John, 88

Gastleigh Manor, 66

Gentleman Jim, 106

Gently Bentley, 64
Geraldo and His Orchestra, 51
A Ghost of a Chance, 139
Gielgud, John, 156
Glendenning, Raymond, 59, 61
"The Glums," 22, 73-76
Goddard, Liza, 106
Golders Green Hippodrome, 111, 129
Gravett, Ann, 146, 157
Greene, Peter, 98
Greenwood, J.A., 16
Griffin Inn, Fletching, 169
Guest, Val, 130
Guinea Pig Club, 42

Haigh, Peter, 21, 106
Halfway Up the Tree, 117
Hancock, Tony, 11, 20, 21, 25, 51, 57, 78, 79,
    91, 93, 107, 152, 180
The Handlebar, 55, 61
The Handlebar Club, 57-62
Handley, Tommy, 69
Hare, Robertson, 104, 136
Hart, Derek, 89
Harvey, Laurence, 133, 135, 136
Hay, Will, 85
Hayes, Melvyn, 19, 96, 99-100, 147, 156
Hearne, Richard, 61, 132
Heirs on a Shoestring, 105
Helter Skelter, 132
Henderson, Dick, 11
Henderson, Dickie, 11, 45
Henderson, Mrs. Laura, 49, 50
Hickey, William, 154
Hobley, McDonald, 106
Hollings, David, 181, 191
Homan, Max, 31, 96
Homosexuality, 13, 31-32, 39, 48, 145-157
Hooper, Bill, 60
Hopkins, Dr. W., 31
Horden, Michael, 142
Howard, Alan, 90-91
Howard, Arthur, 13, 65, 89-92, 95-98, 99, 112
Howerd, Frankie, 89, 141, 158
Hulla Baloo, 117-118
Hunt, Martita, 99, 132-133
Hylton, Jack, 79, 168

I Object, 104

I'm Forever Blowing Bubbles," 16
If..., 100
Innocents in Paris, 65, 133-134
It's That Man Again, 69, 70

Jack and the Beanstalk, 111, 148, 155
Jacques, Hattie, 140, 143, 144
James, Jimmy, 11
Jason, David, 105
Jim the Great, 77
Jim the King, 77-78
"Jimmunism," 175
The Jimmy Edwards Show, 126-127
"Jimmy Edwards Sings 'Pa Glum,'" 76

The Keynotes, 67
King, Phillip, 120,121
King's College School, Wimbeldon, 28-29

La Rue, Danny, 154
Lavender, Ian, 77
League Against Cruel Sports, 171-172
Lester, Richard, 141
Lestocq, Humphrey, 61
Let's Make a Night of It, 178
Levis, Carroll, 53
The Life of Jim, 180
Lionheart, 139
"Little Red Monkey," 76-77
Lloyd George Knew My Father, 182
London Laughs, 78, 79
London Palladium, 111
Lucan, Arthur, 12
Lynn, Vera, 45, 47, 78, 89, 113

Madam Tussauds, 70
Madden, Cecil, 59, 100, 101
The Magnificent Six and ½, 139
The Maid of the Mountains, 76, 114
Make Room for Daddy, 102
The Man Who Came to Dinner, 117
"The Market Gardener," 73
Marsden, Betty, 74, 112
Marsh, Carol, 132
Maude-Roxby, Roddy, 96
Maxwell, Charles, 64, 96
Merriman, Eric, 76
Michelmore, Cliff, 89
Miller, Max, 12

Milligan, Spike, 142, 169
Mills, David, 180-181
Mr. John Jorrocks, 58, 102, 103
"Mrs. Brown," 12
Mitchell, Charlotte, 88, 137
Mitchell, Glenn, 97, 145
Mitchell, John Graham "Mitch," 88
Moodie, Douglas, 87, 92, 94
Moore, Derek, 153
More Faces of Jim, 101, 184
The Mortarboard, 27
Mostyn, Herbert, 66
Mother Goose, 111
The Mount Hope Meteor, 43
Muir, Frank, 13, 52, 59, 64, 65-66, 69, 70, 75,
   78, 79, 83, 84, 85, 87, 89, 91, 92, 94, 96, 97,
   99, 101, 107, 155, 182, 184
Murder at the Windmill, 50, 130-131
Mystery at the Burlesque, 131

Navy Mixture, 63, 64
Nearly a Nasty Accident, 137-139
Nichols, Joy, 57, 63-64, 67, 70, 72, 73, 96
Nichols, Keith, 92, 97
Ninety Years On, 176
Nixon, David, 106
Norden, Denis, 18, 64, 65-66, 70, 71, 75, 78, 79,
   83, 85, 87, 89, 91, 92, 94, 96, 99, 101, 184
Nuffield Centre, 47

O'List, Reg, 51
O'Neil, Michael, 44
O'Shea, Tessie, 125-126
Oh! Clarence, 104
Oh! Sir James!, 119-120
Old Surrey & Burstow Hunt, 170
Oliver!, 127, 180
"Operation Market Garden," 40
Orchard, Julian, 98
Owen, Bill, 129

"Pa Glum," 22, 73-75, 76, 77, 155
Paris Cinema, 69
Parkinson, Michael, 159
Pathos, 21-22
*PC 444: The Lonely Copper or I Then Became
   Suspicious*, 21
Pedrick, Gail, 16
Pennington, Roy, 146, 151, 157, 168, 186

Pertwee, Jon, 99, 129, 130
Pertwee, Michael, 99
Peterson, Wally, 72
Phillott, Gordon, 88
The Plank, 23, 140-141
Plomley, Roy, 28, 55
Pointon, Michael, 15, 19, 180, 182
Potter, Aubrey, 96
Prince of Wales Theatre, 48, 78, 122
Puss in Boots, 111

R.A.F., 37-45, 47, 53, 61, 65, 113, 138
Radio Fun, 16
RAFters Raiders, 43
Ray, Ted, 11, 16, 47, 53, 104, 107, 176
Reid, Beryl, 18, 103, 107
Revudeville, 51, 52, 53
Rhodesia, 177
Rhubarb Rhubarb!, 143
Riven Oak, Fletching, 179
Robey, George, 18, 169
Rogers, Michael, 118
Rose and Crown, Fletching, 169
Rothwell, Talbot, 78, 166
Royal Air Force Benevolent Fund, 45
Royal Family, 112-144
Royal Variety Performance, 112-113

St. Clare Preparatory School, 29-30
St. John's College, Cambridge, 29-30, 58
St. Paul's Cathedral School, 26-28
St. Trinian's Films, 85
Sanderson, Joan, 77
Saunders, Charles, 129
Savile Club, 155
Scales, Prunella, 74
The Seances, 27
Searle, Ronald, 85
Secombe, Harry, 51, 59, 127, 142, 143, 184
The Seven Faces of Jim, 19, 101
Seyler, Athene, 132, 133
Seymour, Valerie, 149-152
Shepherd, Roger, 96
Shepherd's Bush Empire, 94
Silvers, Phil, 86
Simkins, Michael, 124
Sir Yellow, 19, 159
Six More Faces of Jim, 77, 101
Six of the Best, 37, 44, 145

The Sleeping Beauty, 111
Smith, Gregg, 98
The Sound of Jim, 94
Southdown Hunt, 170
Spotlight On…, 181
Spring Review, 103
Stag Hunting, 171-172
Stage Door Canteen, 49
Standing, Michael, 69
Starr, Freddie, 111
Starr, Roy, 118
Stevens, Ronnie, 139
Stones, David, 125, 126
Strike It Again, 48
Stump the Storyteller, 53
Swan Inn, Fittleworth, 151
Sykes, Eric, 20, 23, 96, 120-124, 140, 141, 144,
    177, 184
Sykes and a Plank, 141

Take It from Here, 18, 22, 55, 57, 63-80, 83, 129,
    159, 164, 176
Take It from Me, 44
Take It from Us, 78, 79
The Talk of the Town, 152
Tate, Harry, 57
Taylor, Edward, 96
Terry-Thomas, 11, 168
Tessie and Jim's London Music Hall, 125-126
Theme Song, 16
These Are the Shows, 92
They're In…They're Out, 63
Thomas, Danny, 102
Three Men in a Boat, 22, 106, 132, 135-137
This Is Your Life, 88, 96
Thomas, Ralph, 132
Tomlinson, David, 106, 132, 135, 136
Took, Barry, 76
Touch and Go, 33-34
The Transit Officers' Mess, 43
Treasure Hunt, 132-133
Treble-4 – the Glider Tug, 44
Treves, Frederick, 96
Trinder, Tommy, 106, 107
Trouble in the Air, 129, 130
"Tubby the Tuba," 117
Turley, Keith, 186
Turner, Joan, 152-153, 184
TV Fun, 16

Van Damm, Betty, 130
Van Damm, Vivian, 49, 50, 51, 53, 100, 130, 131
Variety Bandbox, 53
Vaughan Jones, Ioan, 37
Vaughan Thomas, Wynford, 159
Victoria Palace, 45, 78

Wacko Southsea, 98
Wakefield, Dougie, 11
Waldman, Ronnie, 85
Wall, Max, 12
Warden, May, 130
Warren, Peter, 98
Watson, Ron, 103
Wayne, Naunton, 132
West, Stanley, 52
Whack-O!, 13, 19, 22, 30, 80, 83-98
Wheeler, Jimmy, 14, 19, 106
Whitfield, June 19, 73, 74, 75, 76, 77, 78, 83,
    96, 101, 147, 148, 159
Wife Begins at Forty, 106
Wilkinson, Roly, 112
Willis, Ted, 61, 119
Wimbledon, 28
Windmill Theatre, 15, 49-55, 58, 59, 100
Windsor, Barbara, 147
Winn, Godfrey, 31-32, 149, 151
Woodburn, Eric, 52
Workers' Playtime, 105S
The World of Wodehouse: Blandings Castle, 102,
    104, 184
Worsley, Arthur, 127
Wright, Clarence, 68
Wynter, Mark, 148, 155
You'd Better Go in Disguise, 144

Zahl, Sonny, 103
Zampi, Mario, 98

About the Author

ANTHONY SLIDE is the author or editor of more than 200 books on the history of popular entertainment. He is also a former associate archivist of the American Film Institute and resident film historian of the Academy of Motion Picture Arts and Sciences. In 1990, he was given a Honorary Doctorate of Letters by Bowling Green University, and at that time he was hailed by Lillian Gish as "our preeminent historian of the silent film." Two of his books, *The American Film Industry: A Historical Dictionary* and *The Encyclopedia of Vaudeville,* were named as Best Reference Source of the Year by the American Library Association. Among his more recent volumes are *Inside the Hollywood Fan Magazine: A History of Star Makers, Fabricators, and Gossip Mongers, Hollywood Unknowns: A History of Extras, Bit Players and Stand-Ins, She Could Be Chaplin: The Comedic Brilliance of Alice Howell,* and *It's the Pictures That Got Small: Charles Brackett on Billy Wilder and Hollywood's Golden Age.* The last was named one of the Best Books of the Year by The Guardian newspaper.

Printed in Great Britain
by Amazon

27115132R00116